## *Praise for* Murderi

"Perhaps the most remarkable achievement of this remarkable  
novelist Duff Brenna is its humanity. The characters in this book—hell, it's nonfiction, they're not characters, they're people!—do hateful, hurtful things to one another. They are lost in their needs, their aberrations, their dreams, their longing—too lost to take stock of the effect of their own behavior upon the people with whom they share their lives and who depend upon them, not least the children who are hostages to a kind of madness.

Worst among them is Nick Pappas—tall, dark and handsome as the narrator's mother likes her men, though also the blowhard, bully, boastful, coward, drunken, narcissistic, womanizing, wife-beating, child-beating, child-molesting stepfather of the narrator. Yet despite all there is to despise about the man, the reader is acutely aware of him as a human being. Nick Pappas is human all too human, as is every character peopling these pages. We see their flaws, foibles and failings. We see their humanity in all its fullness—hard working, heartbreaking, sorrowful, tragic, belly-laugh funny at times, pitiful, embarrassing and, yes, occasionally admirable, even loveable, even kind and good-hearted and fun-loving.

This I think, above all, is Brenna's grand achievement here. He is not settling old scores—and god knows there were scores he might well have wanted to settle if he'd a mind to. But no, he is exploring—unsparingly, unflinchingly, but above all fairly, with balance and breathtaking honesty—the humanity of a group of people born into and continually creating a kind of hell in which they thrash around without a clue as to how to get out."
 —Thomas E. Kennedy, author of *In the Company of Angels* and *Falling Sideways*

"Duff Brenna is one of the most talented, brave and daring writers of contemporary American letters. In *Murdering the Mom: A Memoir,* Brenna reaches deep into the darkest recesses of the human psyche. All too often parents treat their children, the very ones they're supposed to love most and protect, with anger and selfishness, violence and neglect, and Brenna, the child, is indeed a victim of circumstance. But Brenna, the man, is not. No one escapes this world unscathed, but in Brenna's case it's something of a miracle, given his upbringing, that this memoir wasn't written from Death Row. With great skill, insight, wisdom, introspection and above all a sense of humanity and forgiveness, a brilliant writer transcends the tragic and turns this powerful, raw, heartfelt story into the finest art."
 – James Brown, author of *This River* and *The Los Angeles Diaries*

"In *Murdering the Mom*, Duff Brenna not only provides a searing memoir of how we try to love in an increasingly heartless America, but invents a savory and snappy idiolect that lets everyday life pass before our eyes all the while reminding us how extraordinary are its traumas and victories"
 —Nicholas Birns, author of *Understanding Anthony Powell*

"Gritty and honest and opening every door to the heart of the telling. It compels right out of the gate and never lets up, the momentum sustained in every sentence."
 — Jack Driscoll, author of *The World of a Few Minutes Ago*

## *Praise for Duff Brenna's Fiction:*

"Crystal-clear writing ... Brenna sees with an unflinching eye, but also with measures of love."
– *Washington Post Book World*

"Brenna is a master at capturing the helplessness of humans, particularly humans with 'tough' written all over them." -- *Los Angeles Times*

"Artfully written, evil and eerie ..." – *Chicago Tribune*

"Master stylist Duff Brenna deftly portrays the comic and sinister consequences of striving to embody the American Dream." – *Star Tribune-Minneapolis*

"Duff Brenna is an American treasure." – *Bloomsbury Review*

[Brenna's prose] is "unfaltering, unflinching, piercing." – *New York Times*

"Duff Brenna displays a spectacular talent for crafting complex, believable characters." – *Wall Street Journal*

"...vivid characters, rich dialogue and spellbinding narrative." – *Publishers Weekly*

"The sheer energy and humanity of [his story] leaves the reader eagerly awaiting Brenna's next act." – *Milwaukee Journal Sentinel*

"...funny, disgusting, poignant,...Duff Brenna has done it again." – *Charleston Post & Courier*

"Finely crafted prose coupled with a powerful story makes this beautiful book a page turner."
– *San Diego Union*

## *Books by Duff Brenna*

Murdering the Mom: A Memoir
Minnesota Memoirs: Stories
Winter Tales: Men Write About Aging
The Law of Falling Bodies
The Willow Man
The Altar of the Body
Too Cool
The Holy Book of the Beard
The Book of Mamie
Waking in Wisconsin (poems)

# DUFF BRENNA

# *murdering* THE MOM
### A MEMOIR

La Grande • 2012

2012 © for Duff Brenna

ISBN: 978-1-877655-74-6
Library of Congress Control Number: 2012930960

First Trade Paperback Edition: June 2012
Cover Design: Kristin Summer (redbat design)
Cover & Family Photos: from Pappas family album
Author Photo: David Memmott
Special Thanks to Robert Mast for his assistance
in preparation of digital conversion of family album photos.

*Except for principle family members, all other
names have been changed to protect everyone's privacy.*

Published by
Wordcraft of Oregon, LLC
PO Box 3235
La Grande, OR 97850
http://www.wordcraftoforegon.com

Wordcraft of Oregon, LLC, is a member
of the Council of Literary Magazines & Presses (CLMP)

Text set in Adobe Garamond Premier Pro

Printed in the U.S.A.

For
Judge Jean Jacobucci, Brighton, Colorado
&
For the mom
Janice E. Miles


*After youth & age, daydream and debris.*
*- Jack Marshall*

> *... remember her ... as she was.*
>
> *- Jack Marshall*

The mom was always looking for love. She had numerous lovers who came and went in her life, one night stands, a few days or weeks, maybe months. Some she even married. She was married six times. The longest marriage was with her fourth husband. They were together thirteen years before he died of cirrhosis in 1975, ten weeks short of his 50th birthday. His name was George Miles. In looks, he resembled her third husband, Nick Pappas—tall, dark, heavily muscled. The two of them might have passed for brothers. Except that George Miles, a retired San Diego police officer, had, for the most part, conquered his dark side. Nick Pappas never conquered his dark side.

George Miles was a decent, supportive, loving husband, a source of strength, guidance and wisdom, which was exactly what the mom needed—someone to be her *keeper*. A rational man, a six-foot-two father figure, a man she couldn't rule or fool. A man she would listen to because she not only loved him, she respected him. Which was something not new, but very rare in her life. Truth is: until George Miles came along, the mom was ambiguous about the male species, dubious, curiously schizophrenic. Cursing them. Adoring them. Cynical about them. Yet time after time *converted*.

She admired manliness, coveted it: Clark Gable/ Charlton Heston types, the Victor Mature of *Demetrius and the Gladiators*, war heroes like John Wayne. She believed he won the battle of Iwo Jima, never knowing her idol had sat out the war "deferred." She wanted men who were broad at the shoulder, narrow at the hip, strong, silent clichés. Admired them, wanted to be *them*, but in her heart of hearts they frightened her. She didn't trust them. She used them, bullied them (if they let her), tried to morph them into the protectorate Daddies that would fill all the needs missing in her life since she was a child. She wanted a man who made her feel safe, secure, loved, cherished—adored. For those thirteen short years, George Miles played the part as if he were born for it. He was five years the mom's junior, but she called him Daddy as she did all her husbands, all of them Daddy-Daddy. Her real daddy abandoned the family when she, little red-haired Janice, was only five. You don't have to be Freud to understand why she needed to be saying Daddy all her life.

I was talking to a friend of hers (this was many years ago; he's dead now (another Alzheimer's victim) who had known her in her late-fifties. His name was Shelly. He told me that men called her The Black Widow. According to him,

Black Widow fit because none of her many husbands (four at that time) had survived her. Shelly also said: Black Widow or not, Janice is riveting. He opined that she was the most charismatic woman he had ever met in his life. He recalled once when they were at a cocktail party, talking quietly in a corner, and for some reason (perhaps to add emphasis to something she was saying) Janice reached out and squeezed his forearm. Her touch was electric! he said. The hairs on my arm and the back of my neck stood up, he said. He was ready to fall on his knees and worship her. Janice still has that effect on men, he said.

Yes, once upon a time Janice had that effect on men. Six husbands came and went, but she was single when she died May 25, 1995, two days short of her 75th birthday.

At least three years prior to her death she had been showing signs of senility: losing her keys, losing her purse, unable to do her own banking or pass her driver's test, dressing oddly (mismatched shoes, pants, skirt, blouses, lipstick askew, eyebrows above eyebrows, hair half-braided, ratty on one side, brushed flat on the other), forgetting where she parked the car when she went to the mall, unable to find her way around Prescott, a town she had lived in for twenty-five years. She couldn't handle her job as head dietician at Yavapai Hospital and was forced to retire. She lived alone with her Shih Tzu (Ho Tep) and her Maltese (Rags) who went blind and pooped and peed all over the house, until he finally died of a heart attack. Janice kept living in her pre-manufactured home with some help from her youngest of two daughters, my half sister Michele Renee, who lived close by and was able to drop in now and then to see how the old girl was managing. Gradually, things got worse and worse and finally at the point where the mom didn't even know how to start her car or where the grocery store was, my sister called me in San Diego and said, You're the son. You have to do something, Duffy.

Something? The last thing I wanted was to do *something*. I hadn't been closely involved in her life since I was fifteen years old and had moved from her home in Colorado to Alaska, and later to Minnesota and ultimately southern California. I definitely didn't want to get intimately involved now, making decisions for her, finding a home for her, taking her to doctors, being responsible for her well being. Just the thought of it raised my blood pressure to dangerous levels (180 over 100) and made me sick to my stomach. Put her in a retirement home, I told my sister. Or let's pay daycare to help out. What do you say? She said it wouldn't work. She said I had to come see for myself. The hell with that, I said. I got my own life to live.

But guilt moves in mysterious ways. Weeks later I found myself renting a U-Haul and moving the mom out of Prescott to Gateway, a retirement home in Poway, California, not far from where I was living at the time. I took Ho Tep home with me. He was the most lovable dog I'd ever had, but he lived only two more years. He had congestive heart failure and the last weeks of his life he could barely breathe. Digitalis didn't do anything for him. When he wasn't sleeping he was leaning against my leg panting as if he had just run a hundred yard dash. Finally, I had a vet put him to sleep. I wish to this day I could have done that for the mom, for my mother, for Janice E. Miles.

For the first month or so at Gateway, she wasn't that bad at all. But her trajectory was still downhill. As she continued to deteriorate she became a sundowner wandering the streets aimlessly, going god knows where, unaware and therefore unable to articulate whatever hunger was driving her. Kindly strangers would bring her back, sometimes the police would find her. She needed far more supervision than Gateway could give her. They refused to be responsible. They told me to move her to a more secure facility, one licensed to deal with dementia. They gave me a month to find her a home. I hired a Mexican caretaker to get her up and showered and dressed and fed, clean her apartment, take her for walks. On Fridays I would take her out for lunch, always a hamburger with fries and salad, Pepsi Cola to wash it down. She would sit picking at her food, usually eat half of it and give the rest to Ho Tep sitting on her lap politely waiting to be fed this or that tidbit. The mom would eat her favorite parts of the salad with her fingers, the firm ends of romaine, picking them up one at a time, showing them to me and saying, These are the best part. These are goooood.

She started forgetting my name and the names of her daughters. Occasionally she wouldn't even know Ho Tep's name. After she lost her false teeth (theory was she flushed them down the toilet) she had to gum pureed meats, pureed vegetables, cream of wheat, Gerber's peaches and apple sauce. She was wasting away, fiddling with her food, a bite or two and she was through. I bought her high potency vitamins and Ginkgo Biloba, putting them in a slotted container marked with each day of the week. I told her to take the pills with breakfast every morning. But of course she couldn't remember to do that. The pill box was always full whenever I checked it.

Once, in a lucid moment, she asked me what was happening to her. What's wrong with me? she said. I lied to her. Lots of people getting old get forgetful, I said. I told her she needed to take her vitamins. She needed to read, needed to work her mind like a muscle. She needed exercise. She needed to watch TV. Keep stimulating your mind, I said. She listened and then, as if realizing what it all meant, said, I wanna die! She moaned it over and over, I wanna die! I wanna die!

Soon enough. We all die soon enough, I told her.

When my sisters and I were growing up, the mom had frequently threatened to shoot herself. Or drive her car off a cliff. Or hang herself in the garage. Or cut her wrists in the bathtub. Or swallow sleeping pills. She said we had no idea what life had done to her, no idea what it was like to live with so much abuse and such black depressions. So when she told me she wanted to die, I wasn't all that upset. Maybe I was seeing a way out for myself. No more being her daddy, her caregiver, her decision-maker. Whatever the reasons, I found myself, for the first time ever, actually agreeing death might be best for her and I said: Well, maybe it is time, Mom. I can probably get you enough pills to do the job.

She stood up, gawking at me, her toothless gums glistening. You want to murder me? I shook my head, told her I didn't want to murder her, but if she really wanted to die, she should do it *herself*. It was her life after all. She cried out as if I had struck her. She yelled. She said, Who the hell are you to tell me to die? God will tell me when … not you! I'm no coward! She started beating my face with her fists. Shouting all the while: I'll show you! I'll show you! I grabbed the wrists of what had become an alien woman. Sat her down. Walked out. Unable to feel anything but bitterness, anger, revulsion. Did I ever love her? Did I ever love the mom? I mean *purely*? I must have. All little boys love their mothers, don't they? Yes, but love changes—it evolves, the purity of it becoming perverse mixtures of love and adoration, hatred and jealousy, tenderness, passion, devotion, loathing. What was left of those tumultuous emotions? I couldn't sort it out. I *still* can't sort it out.

But what a complicated creature she was! And how strange she had become spiraling downward—down toward the decisive darkness. Fierce yet feeble, bent yet proud, emaciated, withered, yet mysteriously vital. What was going on in her mind? Was it mostly static, a television tuned to a dead channel, until something or someone pressed the on/off switch deep inside her?

Confronting me was definitely not the mom I had known for more than fifty years. This was a woman wounded by the life she had lived, a woman lugging her carcass through bewildering days and nomadic nights. A brittle-boned woman, sharp shoulders and elbows. Hammer-head knees. Eyes cataract filmy. In her youth those eyes had been alluring—luminous then, full of longing and expectation and a need to live life to its fullest. This once petite beauty, this magnet to men. Men she brought home, men she drank with, whored with, cast off. Found others. Which of them knew her or wanted her now, so far from the lovely thing she once was?

It's brief, isn't it, Janice? Poor wretch caught in the talons that catch all of us … if we live long enough. What's it all about was a question she repeated over and over for as long as I had known her. Why am I here? What does God want me to do?

A month after Gateway gave me notice I took her to a place that had been recommended. It was a facility specializing in caring for women with dementia.

The patients were housed in a four-bedroom, ranch-style house run by a woman who said she was a registered geriatric nurse. I didn't check her credentials. Maybe I should have, but all I wanted at that point was to be rid of the mom. I needed someone to take charge and leave me out of it.

The place was nicer than I had expected. I had expected to see old people in hospital gowns roaming the halls with their backsides and age spots showing, metal walkers clumping. Here and there a creature mummified in bed. I expected to hear moans, groans, reedy voices crying out like frightened cats. But there was none of that. The patients were quiet. Everything was clean and bright.

And white. White furniture, white walls, white rug.

In the living room were a TV and a CD system. Three ghostly old ladies with white hair and wearing white terrycloth robes were sitting on a huge white sofa watching an episode of *The Muppet Show*. The TV was loud. It overwhelmed the classical music trickling from speakers in the ceiling. The old ladies were like lumps of white mold sinking into the white cushions. The mom was nervous that day, as if she knew I was more or less deserting her. I imagined her as a puff of white cotton vegetating with the others staring at the television, and I almost changed my mind.

But I had nowhere to take her. So I left her in the care of a stranger, I ran away.

I was working on the proofs of my second novel at that time. I was teaching classes at Cal-State San Marcos, where I was an associate professor. I was trying to keep up my routine of writing and reading, reading and writing, lecturing and grading, committee work, endless meetings that more often than not were senseless and time-consuming exercises in a common academic affliction—too many jabbering voices, too much logorrhea. The mom had always told me that a fool is known when he opens his mouth. She was generally referring to me, something stupid I had said. And she was almost always right: I was a fool for most of my early life. I'm still a fool probably. Writing this memoir may be foolish. But I'll do it anyway. Follow it to wherever it goes.

It wants to go to the mom in the dementia home, the image of her unwashed hands and face, her sour smell, her slovenly pants and sweatshirt full of food stains, this once vain, immaculate woman who could no longer keep up appearances. I didn't complain to the caretaker. She had her hands full with the others. I went once a week and gave the mom a bath, washed her hair, trimmed her filthy nails, scrubbed the often feces-grained rims of them. Dressed her in fresh clothes, always baggy pants held up by an elastic band, a sweatshirt that said JESUS IS COMING AND BOY IS HE PISSED or (my favorite) MARRY MONEY. She wore tennis shoes, the Velcro kind because she had forgotten how to tie laces, how to make bows. Actually, it wasn't long before she couldn't figure out the Velcro either. Maddening to see how something as simple as that baffled her.

After I had her cleaned up, I would take her to the mall, to Rocky Mountain Chocolate, where I bought her chocolate-covered cherries and Pepsi Cola. We would sit on the bench in front of a fountain. The water splashing. People passing. Mild Musak riding the air. Multifarious voices. Rustling clothes. The clicking of women in high heels. Giggling children. All so ordinary! So *normal*. But I knew they all had stories. I knew they could tell me a thing or two about sorrow about heartache about anger about hate. About love. About stepping up and doing what needs to be done when you're called upon.

That's what I wasn't good at.

But if I could do it over, would I do it better? Probably not.

When she finished her treats, her mouth and fingers stained with chocolate and sticky Pepsi, I would wash her with Clean Wipes. And then take her back to the home. Get rid of her for a week. Sometimes two.

During one of our mall episodes, she wandered off while I was at the counter buying what she called, Yummies! When I returned to the bench, she was nowhere in sight. I looked left, I looked right, I panicked. Hundreds of people were there that day. I rushed from one face to another asking if they had seen a little old redhaired lady, about so high, wearing blue pants and a pink sweatshirt that said MARRY MONEY. An older man wearing a black beret and sporting a goatee said he would help me search. He said, Don't worry, we'll find her. He went one way, I went the other. Have you seen a little old redhaired lady? I kept asking, my voice rising with every encounter, until I was nearly shouting, Anyone seen a little old redhaired lady? Shoppers stopping. Turning away from the glittering windows. Staring at me as if I were an embarrassment, or possibly a threat. Some of them shrugging. Some of them shaking their heads. I went all the way to the last store, a Penny's, rushing through it and turning back towards the Sear's at the other end of the mall.

I was looking for someone from security when I finally saw the mom. The man helping me search had found her. He was leading her by the hand, she following docilely, like a child, a toddler. A look of pleasure, pure bliss on her face. Your mother? he asked me. I nodded my head and said, Can't thank you enough, sir. He said he was glad to help. He said, We all need help sooner or later. She thought I was her husband. She called me Hud. And she asked where I've been. She said she wanted to go home now.

Hud was my father. Hud had been dead for fifty-one years at that time.

Home. I wanna go home, she would say whenever I came to visit. Home: the word a mantra, a meditation, a holy word. Home. I wanna go home. I always lied to her, told her she was home, that this was her home. Mine? she would say, looking at the walls the ceiling the furniture. Yes, yours, Mom. You own it. This is your place, this is where you live now. It puzzled her. Her eyes would narrow, her head twisting side to side while she tried to process what I was saying. Even in the depths of her tangled mind I doubt she ever really believed me. In any case, it didn't much matter. Within a minute or two she would forget what I had said.

After the wandering episode, I never took the mom to the mall again. And, coldheartedly, saying I was preserving myself, I started visiting her less and less.

After that day of her disappearance and her latching on to a surrogate husband, calling him Hud, I began seriously worrying about losing my own mind. Is it genetic? Will I have it? Am I doomed? Someday will I no longer be me? Just a husk of what was Duff Brenna, a man who had once taught Shakespeare and could quote dozens of lines from his sonnets and plays, but now no longer able to do so. Perhaps no longer even knowing the great bard's name, not him nor Tolstoy nor Dostoevsky nor Faulkner nor James Joyce nor …

The mom would look in the mirror and not know who that person was. Seems impossible. But it's true.

If it could happen to her, it could happen to me.

In dread and defiance I typed out and memorized the first page of Joyce's *Finnegans Wake*. I quoted it to myself as a kind of prayer before I fell asleep each night. It was (and is) my mental insurance. The way I see it, no one could quote: *riverrun past Eve and Adam's from swerve of shore to bend of bay, brings us by a commodious vicus of recirculation back to Howth Castle and environs*, etc. etc. if he or she had dementia or Alzheimer's. Right?

She lasted only another nine weeks in the crazy lady place before she had a stroke. The caretaker called and said I should call hospice. I drove to the home and found a hardly recognizable Janice curled on her bed. I tried to get her to respond to me, but all she would murmur was:

Home.

Home.

Home.

I sat by her all morning dripping water into her mouth through a straw and doing my best to comfort her, stroking her, telling her that everything was all right. She needed to rest. She needed to sleep.

Later, I called Carol Marie, my older sister living in Point Loma, and asked her if I could bring the mom to her house. She didn't want that. I bullied her into it. I bathed the mom first, clipped her impossibly long toenails, put a fresh nightgown on her, wrapped her in a robe, carried her like a baby to my car. And drove her to Carol Marie's, where I put her to bed in the guest room. By now she wasn't moaning or mumbling or saying Home or anything.

Carol Marie and I fought about her that day, Carol Marie wanting to take her to hospice; I wanting to let her die in a home, even if it wasn't *her* home. Carol Marie believed the mom could last for days, even weeks. I said she would be dead by tonight or tomorrow. My sister and I were mean to each other. The mom's pitiful condition made both of us overly sensitive, frightened and, frankly, cowardly crazy. We yelled at each other. She pushed me. I pushed her. Backed her up until she fell on her rump. Terrible thing it can be, the family.

And there's this about the decaying process of a loved one, where the brain implodes and all you've got to work with is a detached body scarcely familiar: it often brings out the worst in people. Caregivers, relatives, friends.

I told my sister that the mom was her problem now. Hurriedly, I drove back to my own house, stopping only to buy a bottle of vodka.

My sister called me the next morning and said the mom would be dead soon and I should come say goodbye to her. Her kidneys had shut down. She was barely breathing, making no other sound but the air going in and out through her mouth. You were right, Duffy, she said. Mom really is dying. Are you coming?

That afternoon around 12:30 I crawled onto the bed holding what was left of Janice E. Miles. Wrapping an arm around her neck, I held her close and placed my hand over her heart, catching its last feeble beat seconds after I told her not to be afraid, it was okay to go.

But the child inside me who was still her child didn't wholly agree it was okay to go. With the last handful of breath expelled, the last light fading from her gray-green eyes, I broke down totally.

By the age of twelve or thirteen, I had trained myself never to cry. For decades I had not shed tears if I didn't want to shed tears. I would shut down if anything emotional threatened my stoic facade. At the age of thirty, when I took a psychology course in college, I learned the term for what I had taught myself to do—disassociation: distancing the self. I was good at it and I know now that it helped me to survive what was to come as I grew from adolescence into manhood. I'm sure there were times I came across as a person who had little or no compassion for others. Cold, uncaring, certainly selfish. I wanted to be durable, tough, unemotional, fearless. I wanted to drown the hedonism trying to rise and rule me. Partly I was able, partly I was not. The mom's death was one of those moments when I was unable to hold back my feelings. The tears rushed out of me as if from a ruptured pipe. Those tears caught me off guard. It was a torrent I couldn't stop.

Looking backwards, I think those were the sobs of a bitter heart, a heart understanding that whatever connection we once had, however badly broken, this instant of the mom's death would not mend us. Not mend anything. The split was infinite now.

I know, or think I know, what hardened me all those years ago, but I will never know what hardened her so much. I do believe it wasn't really her fault. I'd tell her that if I could. I'd say, It wasn't your fault, Mom. Really, I understand.

Fault or no fault, nothing will ever be made right between us. There will be no breakthrough, no meeting of the minds—never-never—no talk of love or forgiveness, no reconciliation of any sort. Gone. Too late now. All debts canceled between the mom and her children forever, their splintered, used up, worn out, mystifying mother who never knew them, or knew how to love them. The woman they are still trying to fathom twenty-five years after witnessing her death. Her *nada, nada*. No more memories. No more suffering. No regrets. No longing. No passions. No fears. No more obsessive fevers of life controlling her. No more yearning for *Daddy*.

> *They fuck you up, your mum and dad.*
>
> *- Philip Larkin*

The past: a fathomless mystery.

Memories: distortions, deceptions, lines of reasoning that reason knows nothing of.

Early years filled with vignettes, timelines variable: the mom leaves her husband, moves you and your sister from the Midwest to Alameda, California, gets a job at a navy post exchange. The mom takes a picture, sends it to Grandma Inez in Minneapolis: Duffy and Carol Marie standing against a wall, beneath a window. You are wearing a dark wool skullcap with earflaps. Sis towers over you. She is a tousled blond, pouty, wary. You both smile cautiously. Wearing winter coats, you are squinting in the California sun as if you're not used to it. As if you are out of your element.

Within sight of the naval base and parked planes on the tarmac (wings folded upwards, like hands praying to a huge-domed hanger in front of them) is off-base housing sold for civilian use. Yours is an upstairs apartment 104-C Gibbs Avenue. You and your sister share a room, beds angling 90 degrees. Over your bed: a window where you can look upon a vast courtyard surrounded by fading olive-green apartments on all sides. Children play there, play stickball, football, tag and wrestling, fist-fighting, shoot'em-up Cowboys & Indians, war games, hide and seek, kick the can, mumbly peg, make the sissy eat dirt.

Carol Marie leads you by the hand to kindergarten. She leaves you and goes off to grade school. You have a towel for naptime. The teacher gives everyone a spoonful of cod liver oil each morning. Terrible stuff. Fishy. But after you swallow it, you are given a sip of grape juice, so maybe yuck followed by yum makes the ordeal worthwhile? Reading-time is best, when teacher reads stories aloud; naptime is next best; playing outside in the sandbox is good. The sides of the sandbox are carved to resemble the sides of a World War Two Jeep. Kids sit inside making engine noises, tire screeching noises, machinegun noises, wounded noises, dying noises.

When the day is over you sit on the front steps to wait for your sister. You probably won't have to wait long, but some days it seems forever. The sun going down. No one around. A maniac might grab you. Take you home. Cook you. Carve you. Serve you on a platter like a modest proposal. Waiting for the sis makes you terribly anxious. The isolation. The sense of abandonment.

~~

How George Allison comes into your lives remains a mystery. Where did the mom find him? When did she marry him? DID she marry him? There is a Sunday Missal with an inscription inside that says: Carol Marie Allison. So maybe Allison and the mom were married. She claims they were married, but the mom is at best an unreliable narrator. In any case, let's call Allison number two—pun intended.

This Daddy Allison has a skunk streak of white hair running backwards from a pumped up widow's peak, a condition called poliosis. The rest of his hair is black and wavy. You imagine Daddy Allison is handsome (the mom is a magnet for handsome men), but all you see currently are emotional shadows. The man's anger. His spankings. His putting you in the closet with your sailor doll.

Punctuated points: He pulls the string, the light comes on, Play quiet, he says as he closes the door. You haven't a clue why he makes the closet a playroom, other than perhaps you get in his way when it comes to having exclusive access to the mom and the sis. You don't cry in the closet. Really, you don't mind it much at all. It's a safe, quiet place. Peaceful.

Soon after Daddy Allison moves in, you start wetting the bed. Out comes the hairbrush, a wet bottom making it sting all the more as you hop around shrieking. If you try to cover your behind with your hands your knuckles get rapped. The mom generally gives you three or four smacks, but when Daddy Allison does it, you never know when the spanking will stop. One time Daddy Allison hits you so hard the handle breaks. He isn't about to get pee on his palm, so he lets you go. The next day there is a new hairbrush. You keep wetting the bed, Duffy. You don't know until you wake up that you've done it again. I mean, come on what's your problem?

Some mornings the mom and Daddy Allison are in too much of a hurry to check you. They rush out the door leaving you to your sister's care. She pulls back the covers, opens the window. Lets the air dry the sheets. She never asks why you wet. It seems like she knows. If so, she knows more than you do. She drapes your pajamas over the windowsill and gets you washed and dressed, feeds you cereal, takes you to kindergarten, leaves you there for another round of cod liver oil, stories, naps, sandbox, etcetera et-sis.

This Daddy Allison comes as a ghost and floats through chambers not quite buried, not totally dark. Faint gray light brings him into the bedroom, brings him on his knees beside Carol Marie, brings her blanket down, brings his head between her legs, brings his gorged cock into his hand as his head moves up and down, nodding head saying yes, yes, brings the slick sound of his tongue lapping, brings her awake, brings her to say: Daddy, I have to go pee-pee. When he's finished he wipes himself with a hanky, wads it, walks away, leaves her sprawled, her arms over her eyes as he goes back to the other bedroom. Where the mom is sound asleep and never knows a thing. A common theme.

Comes a night when her piercing wails wake you. Mama crying? You toddle down the hall. Open the door to her room. She is naked and hanging over Daddy Allison's lap and he is spanking her. With every slap of his bare hand she cries out pitifully. You're in shock. A grownup spanking a grownup? Unheard of. Impossible. But there it is. Whap! Ahhh! Smack! Ahhh!

You stand in the doorway for a long time before Daddy Allison notices. He smiles kindly and says, Mommy's been bad. You know what happens when you're bad, Duffy? You nod and reply, Spanking. Daddy Allison says, Good boy. Go back to bed now. Mommy will be all right.

~~

There is an old woman whose name you'll never know. This old woman has a house, a fenced yard, a garden. Plants in pots galore, which she tends with loving care. The mom takes the two of you there, gives you to the old woman. Leaves you with her so long you start calling her Mama. She encourages it. She tries to get Carol Marie to call her Mama, but Carol Marie won't. The old woman warns both of you to stay away from her plants. She screams if you so much as bend down to smell a pot full of flowers. Don't touch that! she will say. Get away from that! she will say. Stay away from that, you brat!

You sleep in bunk beds, Carol Marie on top. The woman comes in every morning to check to see if you've wet the bed again. The nights when you don't are very rare. This woman's punishment for such a dirty habit is unique. She rubs your face in the wet sheet and tells you you're a very bad dog. Bad dog, bad dog, she will say. The pee stings, makes your eyes watery. You reek. You stink. But you would rather smell like urine than take a bath. You really, really hate baths and avoid them if you can. You especially hate soap. You were born with ichthyosis (fish-skin), a disease that causes your skin to be rough dry scaly. Often the skin will crack in certain places, especially the knuckles, which will split open in winter and bleed. Blanket fuzz will get in the cracks and stick to the blood. Tugging the bloody fuzz out is as fun as picking a scab. Your body is always flaky, flakes of skin raining like dandruff. Soapy baths making the skin itch as if you've played in poison ivy. You scratch yourself so much you leave lesions, lacerations all over your scrawny body. Bed-wetting continues boiling the skin around your thighs and buttocks. All of it lobster red. All of it raw.

The mom is gone for what seems months. The time moves slowly. It must be summer because you don't go to school. Daily life becomes a blur, but one day the mom is there telling you to pack your things. She gets in an argument with the old woman. It's about money. The expense of keeping the children was far more than the woman anticipated. While the grownups are working it out,

Carol Marie comes in from the back yard and tells you to come see what she's done. You go with her and there in a prized pot she shows you a turd. It is folded like a fat brown snake in the middle of a plant whose tiny leaves spread out like a nest. There is a gleefully sinister look on sister's face. Got her! she says vengefully.

~~

Where did George Allison go? Why did the mom replace him with Nick Pappas? In your mind they are as alike as kidney beans. Daddy Allison blends into Pappas and nothing really changes. But it doesn't seem like it is going to be that way, not at first, not when she first brings Pappas home in his heroic sailor suit. He takes his cap off and puts it on your head, hoists you to the ceiling and says now Duffy is a sailor boy too. Pappas carries you around the room, the mom's joyful eyes following, her lovely mouth beaming. You are told to call him Pappy. Later, Pappy changes to Daddy or Sir. Even though he is three years younger than the mom she calls him Daddy too.

From him you learn: the Greeks are the chosen people, the smartest, most inventive, most advanced race of white men on this earth, the Greeks invented everything, including books and writing and poetry and plays, the Greeks are the best warriors for war, in the ancient world no one could conquer a Greek, especially if he was Spartan Greek. For years you will find yourself wishing you could be Greek too.

(Duffy will lie and tell people he is Greek and Nick Pappas is his real daddy. He doubts that many are fooled looking at this towheaded emaciated stick figure with skin so pale and translucent anyone can see veins running like blue tentacles over his chest and arms. Easy to count his ribs. His spindly legs are hollow things with knobby knees and blades for ankles. His blue eyes, blond hair, high forehead, little round chin make him look Scandinavian. Half of him is. The other half Irish.)

Pappas is six foot two, 200-plus pounds. Size 13 shoes that boom like bass drums when he walks across the floor. He has black wavy hair, bulbous lips that can thin into a line that looks chillingly grim. He has a large nose with a hump in it. His teeth, though very even and very white, are surprisingly small. His irises are so intensely brown they're almost black. The eyes are mildly hooded. The black brows arching and well-defined, the forehead smoothly broad. The mom says he looks like Victor Mature and John Wayne rolled into one.

So this Pappas is the new daddy. The mom loves him like a god. She says he is gorgeous. She keeps saying he is a veteran of the war, a hero six-footer real man, a man from head to toe. They marry quickly. You have seen the wedding picture, so you know it's true. It is a disappointing picture because Pappas is wearing a suit and tie. Without his sailor suit the shine is off him.

~~

Turn the page to an early evening, one of the first with Pappas as Daddy. A man leads a pinto pony around the courtyard. The man has a camera. For a fee kids get to sit on the pony and wear a cowboy hat and chaps and have their picture taken. The Pappas family is at the table eating dinner when the pony man comes by. You can see him out the window. Kids are climbing in and out of the saddle. It looks thrilling. Carol Marie bolts her dinner and gets permission to go downstairs and get a cowgirl picture taken. You can go too if you finish your liver and onions.

You eat the liver but push the greasy onions aside. The mom has never made you eat fried onions before, but those mollycoddling days are over. Pappas insists you eat the onions. No pony picture for boys who won't eat fried onions. This is the first time Pappas asserts his new daddy-authority with the mom present. You try to eat the onions. But by the time you put the first forkful in your mouth the onions are cold. Cold and slimy. Repulsive. You choke on them. Spit them back on your plate coughing and retching. You little bastard! Pappas roars. He slaps your face. Of course, sniveling little snot you always are, you immediately start wailing. Pappas slaps you again. Startles you even more. Stop that goddamn crying! he orders jabbing his finger into your chest.

Pappas's anger is terrifying. Stinging cheek and shock notwithstanding, you stifle your sobs, control that heaving chest, wipe those eyes, and make the tears stop rolling. You try again to eat the onions. But no matter what, you just can't do it. Go ahead, kill me, you're thinking. You'd rather die than eat poisonous onions. Pappas rages, threatens, says he is going to whip you with the belt. He slides it out of his trouser loops. Stands there like Lash La Rue, the whip snaking beside his leg.

The mom is watching, tears brimming in her eyes. In a pleading voice she begs, Oh, Duffy, won't you please eat your onions for Mommy? Don't make Daddy mad. One of the worst sins in the world is to waste food. People in China are starving. Be a good boy. Eat your onions. Swallow them with your milk.

Swallow them with your milk! Why hadn't you thought of that, dumbbell? Bravely, desperately, you fork oily onions into your mouth. Drown them in great gulps of milk, feel them burning your belly, the nausea simmering. But at last the trauma is over. Carol Marie is back by then. The pony-picture man is gone. It's getting dark. And the world turns. And turning with it is the frightening fact that you are in for it. In for the battle of your life. Some intuitive part of your brain already knows it.

~~

The year of the onions continues: Pappas gathers neighbor boys in the living room. He has boxing gloves. He is going to give everyone lessons in what he calls the sweet science. He ties the gloves on you. Puts a pair on another kid.

Who gives you a pounding. You try ducking and covering, turning your back, crouching. But all these maneuvers do little good. Until you stand your ground you are not permitted to take the gloves off. Boys punch you. Punch you and punch you. When they get tired they hand the gloves off to the next boy in line.

Eventually, you start fighting back. Your arms so heavy you can barely raise them. Nose bleeding, blood running down your skeletal chest. Blood smearing your arm when you wipe your nose. Mouth wide open and gasping. The air burning your throat and lungs. You know you are being murdered, but there's nothing you can do about it. How humiliating to be so weak and brittle. Duffy, you pitiable worm! Not a tough bone in his body this boy. In the end you curl on the floor and refuse to rise no matter how much Pappas berates you, no matter what he says: Stand up and fight, you yellow-bellied coward, little bedwetter! It is the first time he says bedwetter, but it is far from the last. The other boys giggling. The word bedwetter whispering around the room. Some kid saying, What a sissy! Geez, my pa would kill him. Pappas picks you up by your neck and one leg, carries you to the bedroom, tosses you inside. You still have the gloves on. There will be many more bouts in the living room. You're a sissy and a slow learner, but eventually the years will go by and you'll be able to hold your own and pacify Pappas... well, sort of.

~~

Sideshow: The parents leave Duffy and Carol Marie with a man who has a cabin in the mountains. Maybe the parents just need to get away. Maybe it's their honeymoon. In any case, this man, whose name now floats in the Lethe River, takes Carol Marie and Duffy target shooting. Duffy shoots at a tree with a bull's-eye nailed to it. The man has put the barrel of the rifle on a log and shaped the boy's body to lie behind it. The butt of the rifle is under his armpit. His head leaning at an angle, so he can line up the sights. There, now squeeze the trigger, the man says, don't pull hard. Ease it like you're fingering a virgin.

Fingering what?

Go ahead, the man says.

You definitely like squeezing the trigger, hearing the bang and seeing the target ripple. You load up and fire bullet after bullet. The rifle has very little kick to it. The target is shattering, coming apart, chips of paper falling, whirling like snowflakes. At one point you look behind to see if the man is admiring what a sharpshooter you are. What you see is Carol Marie sitting on the man's lap, his hand rubbing her hip as she stares god knows where. Her round eyes wide. Her round eyes fearful.

That night when everyone is in bed the man comes in. Sits on the edge of the mattress and plays with Carol Marie's privates. She pretends to sleep. When it is over and the man is gone, she looks at you, her eyes a pair of question marks.

I knew he would come, she says.

~~

Following shooting the target and Carol Marie molested again comes Halloween. You are carrying a paper bag, wearing a white sailor suit and yelling Trick or treat! You climb some apartment stairs. Knock on a door. The door opens. A man in a Robin Hood outfit lifts you up, turns and says, Look what I found! There is a party going on. The apartment is brimming with men. They are dancing with each other. They are shouting. Laughing. The man passes you around. Men carry you swaying to the music. Men kissing you, patting your butt, loving you up. It's wonderful. It's heaven. When you're finally put down by the door and given a big bottle of Seven-Up you don't want to leave. Go home, sweetie, you're told. The door closes. Bereft Duffy doesn't like Halloween anymore. Back in the apartment Carol Marie and you open the Seven-Up bottle and take turns drinking it. Like out of control alcoholics the two of you drink the whole thing. In the morning you take the bottle to the store and redeem it for a nickel with which to buy penny candy, licorice, maltballs, wax lips, chick-o-sticks.

~~

The parents decide to move to Colorado and live on a farm with Pappas's father and look for jobs. The family drives to the airport with a chain-smoking old man who often came over and drank beer with Pappas, the two of them talking about the wars, the old man a hero of the first, Pappas a hero of the second. They have medals to prove it. Campaign and Good Conduct Medals. Old man has a Bronze Star. Pappas claims a Silver Star for Conspicuous Bravery Above and Beyond the Call of Duty at the Battle of Pearl Harbor. The medal was stolen by a shipmate. He doesn't know who. What matters is the award and the description of his heroism constitutes a whole page of his service records. The mom says she's seen it, she knows it's true. Sometimes the two men got so drunk and spoke so much about the horrors, they choked up. They leaned on each other's shoulders and claimed to be brothers of the blood, brothers to the end. The night before the move to Colorado, they both got slurry and Pappas promised to send for his blood brother once the family is settled. You always got a home with us, Pappas told him.

The old man's rattling Plymouth has a governor that won't it let go over 35 miles an hour. Cars piling up, horns honking. The mom rubs her temples and complains of a migraine. The old man keeps talking about the governor and how everyone should have one. If everyone had a governor the roads would be a lot safer. At one point he yells out the window, Honk your fool heads off! I ain't goin no faster! And he doesn't. In fact, it seems he goes slower. He's so ornery, the mom whispers. Pappas in front has an elbow out the window, a cigarette in his mouth. He has a headache. Acid is eating his stomach. His lips are chalky with TUMS FOR THE TUMMY.

Just moments before the plane is ready to fly away, the family arrives. They rush through the airport. Enter the monstrous plane and take their seats. The props whirl, the engines roar. The plane picks up speed and climbs as if Superman is underneath lifting it.

Before long you are above the clouds. You're looking *down* on them, the top sides which you've never seen. So this is heaven! *THE* Heaven. A Heaven looking like what? No Golden Gates, no Saint Peter, no angels with wings. Rumpled sheets is what you see. Very disappointed, but your eyes still as wide as they'll go waiting to capture the instant God shows.

But He doesn't come. Where is He? What's the deal? C'mon God.

Standing on the seat, you look over the back at the mom and say, Mom, where's God?

People tittering, grownups grinning, mom smiling sweetly. Pappas chuckling. He looks as if he actually likes you. You've made a funny. You've been cute. A cute kid. You like everyone liking you. So you say it again. Where's God, Mom? She says, God is in another part of Heaven. But if you keep your eyes peeled, maybe you'll see an angel or two. So for a while that's what you do, keep your nose to the cold glass, eyes peeled. At some point, though, you curl on the seat and fall asleep. The plane flies on. No god comes.

~~

After the plane lands in Denver, a bald man with a bushy mustache picks the family up. He limps. He uses a cane. He's a war vet. He was in the Navy same as Pappas. They talk war talk, while the man drives to Grandpa Mike's farm in Frederick, a little farm, only five acres, with a small barn, a goat pen, rabbit pens, a chicken coop, an outhouse two-seater with a Sears & Roebuck catalog for toilet paper. Next to the outhouse is an adobe hut where Grandpa Mike keeps his tools and where he slaughters a goat or a sheep when he needs to. The main house is white with a green asphalt roof. There are lots of trees and lots of shade. A great elm spreads its arms at the back end of the barnyard, the tree so huge it's like a canopy covering everything out there. Pappas claims it's the tallest tree in town.

Frederick is not a big town, two hundred people, maybe. It has one main street with a Red & White Grocery, a feed store, a barber shop, a general store, a movie house called the REO, a bar that plays Mexican music, a city hall, a volunteer firefighter's station, a great silver water tower with a row of fire hoses hanging from it. You'll learn later that you can swing on those hoses until a firefighter comes out and yells at you. Most of the men in town work at the Colorado coalmines. Grandpa Mike is a driller, a dynamiter. He raised two sons by himself in Frederick, Nick and George. George lives in Chicago. It's in

Chicago where George will get gunned down by the cops. You'll never know exactly why, only that he was Mafioso and Mafioso means bad news.

Grandpa Mike is a Greek from the island of Crete. He is shaped like a wine barrel. He barely speaks English. But he speaks Greek and Spanish and Italian easily. He lives alone because his wife left him. She ran off with another man and lives in Utah and runs a trucking company. Pappas hasn't seen her since he was five or six years old. There are three chow chows chained to their doghouses in the yard and one running free, an old gray-muzzle named Husky, who roams the fence and barks whenever he sees anyone walking along the dirt road. In the little field behind the barn are rows of sweet corn sprouting. Closer to the house is a garden. Grandpa Mike has a green thumb. The mom has a green thumb too. She thinks people who have green thumbs are blessed. They are special. God loves them.

~~

On the patio up against the house is a huge galvanized tub filled with clear water. Floating inside, looking helpless as infants, are rabbits, four of them, their fur coats off, their pink skin glistening. They're fresh killed for dinner, where you'll find out that rabbit tastes a lot like chicken. In the back of the barn is a Holstein named Irini lying on a hill of old manure chewing her cud. Near her is a steer, her son Plato. When he gets older Grandpa Mike will ship him to packerland for slaughter. According to Pappas, Irini was named after Irini Papas, the Greek film star, who is Pappas's cousin, he says. She dropped the second P from her name to make it more distinctive, he claims.

Grandpa Mike sits you on his knee and starts talking in what is meant to be English. The old man's accent is so thick you can't understand very much of what he's saying. You wait for him to ask, You savvy, kiddy, you savvy? (The cue to nod and say uh-huh.) The parents are smiling, wanting the old man to like the Duffer. After Grandpa Mike puts him down, Carol Marie is told to sit on the old man's lap, but she is hanging back. The mom coaxing her, but Carol Marie keeps shaking her head and whining, I don't want to, I don't want to. The mom gets exasperated. She grabs Carol Marie's arm. Leads her, lifts her into Grandpa Mike's waiting arms. He talks to her. Jabbering God knows what.

~~

Every morning before sunrise, Grandpa Mike gets you out of bed, takes you to the barn to do chores and milk Irini. He fills a glass straight from the teat for you. The milk is warm and creamy. He wants to fatten you up. You too skeenee, kiddy, he says. Together you and the old man clean the barn. Go to the coop and gather eggs. Grandma Mike taps a hole in the crown of an egg and tells you to suck out the contents. After you swallow the raw egg he gives you a dime to buy candy at the Red & White. The two of you head back to the house for breakfast.

When Grandpa Mike has eaten, he takes his lunch pail, walks out to the road to catch his ride to work. The parents leave in their newly purchased '48 Dodge for their jobs at Lowry Air Force Base in Denver. Pappas has enlisted in the Air Force as a flight engineer, given the rank of sergeant E-5. The mom works as a waitress at one of the base cafeterias.

~~

On Sunday there is usually a fried chicken dinner, with mash potatoes and milk gravy and peas. Or maybe carrots. Or both. Grandpa Mike teaches you how to corner a chicken, catch it by throwing a gunny sack over it, reach under and grab the legs, lay it on the chopping block, take the hatchet and chop its head off, throw the body into the air, watching the wings flap, legs churning, blood spouting. Until the chicken is still. Sundays you always kill two. The mom guts them. Carol Marie and you pull the feathers after they've been loosened in hot water. You don't like any part of this stinky job, but no grownup seems bothered by it. They chatter and laugh. They give you laughing advice as you run the doomed chickens into corners and toss burlap over them. Swing the axe as if beheading them means nothing at all to you.

~~

One bright blue afternoon, Husky is sitting on a stack of wooden crates that were full of grapes Grandpa Mike and Pappas pressed to make wine. Husky is watching you take the empty crates out to the road, where someone will come by with a truck and pick them up. By now, two months into living on the farm, you have played with Husky a lot and believe he likes you as much as you like him. When you throw sticks the dog will fetch them. He likes to play tug of war with a piece of rope or a rag. He likes to have his lower back scratched with the heel of your boot. You think he is a great dog. You love hugging him and burying your face in his reddish fur.

Which is what you do this particular day, Duffy. You tell him he has to get off the crates, so you can take the rest of them to the road. Then you hug him and Husky goes crazy. He rips your lower lip and leaves a corner of it flapping on your chin. He bites into the arm you have thrown up as an offering. Whirling, you run for the house. Husky goes for your left leg, tries to hamstring you, bring you down. But you know if you go down the dog will go for your throat. Your only chance is to stay upright and get to the door. The dog jerks and jerks on your leg. You slip on blood and nearly fall, using your bloody hands to bounce back to your feet again. Husky lets go of the leg. Sinking his fangs into your right arm, he yanks on it as if it's a rag or a rope and the two of you are playing a tug of war game. All the while this is happening Duffy is shrieking. What did the shrieks sound like? The mom said it sounded like you were playing Cowboys & Indians. It took awhile for those inside to realize you weren't doing war whoops.

Finally they get the message. The door opens, Pappas leading the charge. The mom has a broom in her hand. Grandpa Mike and Pappas start kicking the dog. The mom is beating Husky with the broom. He lets go of you and tries to bite them, the men stomping him. They stomp him and stomp him, until he is on his side quivering, a hind leg pawing the air. By then you are cradled in the mom's arms. You don't feel any pain, not really. You don't cry. But you do gawk at quivering, bloody-muzzled Husky. What happened, you want to ask him.

~~

At the hospital Duffy is allowed to go past all the other patients waiting for treatment. Rushed into a room and laid on a table. Look at Pappas and be astonished to see how shaken he is, how pale and how his fat lips are trembling. The mom's clothes are streaked with blood that looks like finger paintings. She is shaking. Shaking and weeping as you say to Pappas: Husky didn't make me cry, sir. Pappas nods and says, You're a brave boy, Duffy. I'm proud of you. When he pats your head and caresses your cheek, it seems as if the wounds are worth it. A nurse holds a hanky to your face and tells you to smell her perfume. You hate the smell and try to push it away, but Pappas holds your arms down and you breathe in-and-out-in-and-out-

~~

When you wake, you're home in bed and in pain. You hear the mom telling someone, My baby nearly died he lost so much blood. You smell iodine, a disgusting cloud of it. When you groan, the mom comes in and gives you a pill. The pain becomes an all body ache as if you have a fever. But in minutes your mind grows drowsy and sleep rescues you.

Days and nights, the same routine of the mom removing the bandages, cleaning the wounds, giving you pain pills. Sleep. Lots and lots of sleep. Husky did a good job. Two deep punctures on your right arm, two on the left, a gouge in your right side looking like a bullet went after the third rib, three stabs on the left thigh. And there is the tear on your lip, the lower right corner. Your body is full of itchy stitches.

Weeks later the mom drives you back to the doctor. Who takes out the stitches and says you may always have a limp now. Your left leg was badly mauled.

Imagine the future: poor Duffy a pitiful thing forever limping like the war vet who picked the family up at the airport. Will people feel sorry for you the way you felt sorry for him? There goes the poor little crippled boy. His father said he was very brave when the chow chow tried to kill him. Maybe you'll need a cane, Duffy!

On the drive home you ask the mom about it. Her eyes flash with gray-green fire. You won't need a cane, she says. You won't have a limp. You're going to be fine, Duffy! Just fine! And she's right. By the time you go back to school you have almost no limp at all. Just a tiny one no one seems to notice, even when you exaggerate it. You'd rather need a cane and see looks of pity in everyone's eyes.

~~

Walking home from school one winter day you argue with Danny Sanchez. It will be Christmas soon and you still believe in Santa. Danny is older and says, You're really a dumb kid, there's no goddamn Santa. By the time you're six or seven you shouldn't believe that crap, kid. You tell him knowingly that not believing in Santa is the same as not believing in God. Those who don't believe will go to hell, Danny. When he laughs in your face, you punch him in the stomach. Heroically, you fight for Santa. You go at Danny head down, arms whirling. Danny keeps uppercutting you and telling you how stupid you are to fight with your head down like that. Of course he's right. You're not fighting at all like Pappas taught you. You warn Danny he better take it back about Santa. Danny spins away laughing. Leaves you with a split lip and achy teeth and a stinking hunch he's right about Santa. Have you been duped all these years?

That evening you ask the mom. Mom, is Santa Claus real? She pauses. Her fingers pressing her temples, her eyes shifting back and forth as if she's looking for a way out. Nope, there's no Santa, she says. Santa is a story for little kids, so they can be happy at Christmas. Santa is the spirit of Christmas, the spirit of giving. Strange to say, you're not all that upset. Feel like a dope, though, and blurt out what comes next: Okay, if there's no Santa does that mean there's no God? The mom comes unglued. She shakes her finger and shouts, You must never say such a thing ever! Of course there's a God! Who do you think made life? Who do you think made you?

Considering what she says, you conclude she must be right. Where did everything come from? Who made the world and the animals on it? Who made the sun and the moon and the Milky Way? Okay, so God is real, but not Santa. Angels are real, but not Santa. Heaven is real, but not Santa. Presents come from parents not Santa.

~~

Not long after Christmas, Pappas has an accident. He is driving the Dodge and spins out on an icy road, rolls over in a ditch, breaks his arm, separates his shoulder, which they have to pin back together. When you see him he is wrapped up and has a sling like the one you wore for a while.

At home the first day Pappas is in lots of pain. He drinks wine rather than take the pain pills. At some point in the evening, when you and your sister are in your bunk beds, Pappas is in the kitchen moaning and groaning. He says the pain is excruciating. He breaks down in tears. The mom comforts him. She says, My poor baby, my poor baby. The sound of him crying is dumbfounding. Never would the Duffer have believed such a thing could happen. Pappas crying because of pain? No way. You start to say something to Carol Marie about it, but she leans over her bunk, puts her finger to her lips and says, Shh! Go to sleep. Don't make trouble.

~~

Each night Grandpa Mike wakes you, hands you the empty coffee can and says to pee in it. This routine works. The winter passes without once wetting the bed. No spankings, no threats, nothing but praises from the mom. Life is calm. Life is peaceful. Life is spoiling the Duffer. He's letting his guard down.

~~

Winter becomes spring and the old man, who occasionally got chased down the road by his wife hitting him with a broom, suddenly dies. The family is Italian, thirteen of them. At the old man's funeral, the priest talks Latin and walks around the coffin shaking a smoking brass bowl and chanting. The old lady weeps throughout the Mass. Now and then she cries out, *Mi senti, oh Dio? Mi senti?* Which means can you hear me, oh God? This is followed by breast-beating and loud wails.

Finally everyone goes outside and the coffin is loaded into the bed of a pickup. Mourners walk behind it to the cemetery. Where it is laid beside a narrow hole in the ground. The priest speaks more Latin. The old woman wails *Mi senti, oh Dio!* She tears at her clothes and hair. After the coffin is lowered, the old lady throws herself into the grave and has to be hauled out by her sons, all of them weeping, all of them wailing Mam*ma!* Mam*ma!*

So this is death, this is what happens. It's awful to see big people crying so much. Death is more than sad, it's terrifying. But when you get back home, the mom says the old lady made a spectacle of herself. It was disgusting. And this is the old bitch who chased that poor man down the street hitting him over the head with a broom!

Death is huge in your head now, very, very scary. Also thinking: Does everyone die? Will the mom? Will Pappas and Grandpa Mike and Carol Marie? Will Duffy die? He can't die, can he? And yet he nearly did. The dog. Always remember the dog. Born to die too, that dog. But not before he got you good. Scars stopping time for the rest of your life every time you look at them, taking you backwards—just like the sparrow falling, you are a prisoner of God's will. When he sends Death, you'll have nothing to say about it. This thought makes you pray very hard every night at your bedside. Now I lay me down to sleep, pray the Lord my soul to keep. If I should *die* before I wake …

~~

The following summer the family (minus Grandpa Mike) moves to Aurora, to a new house at 1648 Ironton Street. Carol Marie and you have your very own rooms! The living room furniture includes a pale green love seat and couch sitting at an L angle, a glass-topped corner table connecting the two. The love seat jutting like a pier into the living room. A person has to walk around it to go into the kitchen. On the table is a tall lamp in the shape of a naked woman. She is jade green. She is curvy. According to the mom, the lady of the lamp is *art*.

Hanging on the wall behind the couch is a rectangular mirror, where Pappas will pose with his shirt off, his muscles bulging, his proud voice saying, What a man! What a man! On the opposite wall is a big picture window facing west. Beneath it is a stuffed chair, an end table, a rhododendron in a pot. Looking out the picture window you can see the snowcapped Rockies. They look so close it's as if you could walk there in no time. There are lots of plants flourishing in the living room, hanging from the ceiling and sitting on the little tables. There is also a big Packard Bell radio record player combo. At night everyone gathers around the radio and listens to *Amos & Andy, Inner Sanctum, Hopalong Cassidy, Sam Spade, You Bet Your Life*.

This then is another new world: up and coming family of four. The future secure. But unfortunately the move to Aurora, the removal of Grandpa Mike's influence from your lives, brings the old, irritable Pappas back and stupid Duffy starts wetting the bed again. Pappas says you do it to spite him. The parents decide that if the kid is going to act like a baby, they are going to treat him like a baby. The mom buys a bunch of diapers and every night she pins one on you, looking really silly, eight years old, a beanpole with rippling ribs and bony legs wearing a white diaper that will fall off if you don't clutch it when you stand up.

Diapers do no good, you wet them too. Pappas gets ferocious about it and starts beating you with a thick belt that has a steel washer embedded in it for attaching a set of keys if you have them. One whack produces a hollow-centered welt that turns red to purple to yellow. The beatings come and go, one day yes, one day no, depending on if you wet the bed and also on Pappas's mood. Which is always unpredictable. Extremely so.

Early evening in the glow of the cocktail hour, he might sit you on his lap, caress you, give you kisses and tell you stories about the war, being at Pearl Harbor manning a machinegun, bombs going off, Jap Zeros sinking ships, sailors diving over the sides into flaming water. Never trust a Jap, he says. Those slanty eyes, he says. Those slanty eyes hiding their slanty thoughts. I'm glad we dropped the bomb on those bastards. The goddamn Russians are next.

~~

At noon one day you come home from school to make lunch. When you round the corner into the kitchen, Pappas is sitting at the table in his blue uniform. When he shifts in his chair, you see that familiar rage contorting his face. You don't have a chance to backpedal before his fist catches you flush on your left eye. Down but not knocked out, just dazed just dazzled. And not having the faintest idea why Pappas has punched you this time. Usually, you can figure it out: Pappas found dust on the radio; he found mud on your shoes and mud on the rug; he's sick of how disgusting you smell; he's not going to tell you again to bathe; he's not going to tell you again to take out the trash; he's not going to tell you again to burn it in the incinerator and sift the ashes for cans. Yes, generally you have an inkling of what you've done to piss off Pappas, but this time not a clue. Maybe his superior officer chewed him out. Maybe he's nursing a hangover. Maybe he needs a drink or a piece of ass. Maybe Duffy looks like a Jap. It's impossible to say. All you know is—Pappas slugs you. Then goes into the bedroom and gets your hat, the felt fedora you wear when the mom occasionally takes you and Carol Marie to Mass. Pappas cocks the hat on your head, the brim partially covering the rapid swelling.

You go back to school. Swing on the swings. Feel the air cooling the throbbing eye every time you swing forward. Teacher doesn't ask what happened, but if she had you would have told her what you told the mom when she asked what happened. I tripped and fell was the answer. It's what Pappas told you to say.

~~

You start having lots of tummy trouble. Colic, says the mom. Maybe you're allergic to milk, she says. While lounging on the couch, listening to the radio at night, she has you lie with your head in her lap, while she rubs your belly nicely. Her soft palm soothing, calming puts you to sleep. She calls you her crocodile. Crocodile Duffer, she says.

One night she tells Pappas and Carol Marie, Watch this, watch me put my crocodile to sleep. She rubs your tummy round and round. You close your eyes. Now that she expects you to fall asleep, you can't. So you fake it. After a minute or two you snore lightly through your nose, hearing her whisper, See? He can't help himself. It's magic.

But the stomachaches continue, so finally she takes you to the doctor. He examines you. Very thin, he says. Underweight. Maybe he has worms. Maybe a tapeworm. I'll need a stool sample. His pulse is rapid. Blood pressure somewhat high for a boy his age. Reflexes good, but look how his fingers tremble when he holds them out. In my judgment this boy is full of nervous tension. Anxiety. He has a high-strung nature. It affects his stomach and is probably why he can't gain weight. It's possible the boy has an ulcer, but that's very rare in a child this age. Give him antacids morning, noon and night. Sometimes an ice pack helps. Could be his appendix flaring up. Ice can help that too. If he doesn't get better I can prescribe a bromide.

The mom is staring at the doctor as if he is God. When she asks about the bedwetting he says: Immature bladder. She tells him her son stopped peeing the bed by the time he was three, before starting again around the age of four. The doctor nods wisely. It sometimes happens. Not to worry, Mrs. Pappas. As his bladder grows he'll be able to hold more urine and the bedwetting will stop. Make sure he goes to the bathroom before going to bed at night. He always does, she tells him. Don't you, Duffy. Yes ma'am. Uh-huh. What's a stool sample? Both she and the doctor laugh at the question.

Turns out later you don't have worms. *Highly strung, highly sensitive, easily agitated* is the final verdict. He'll grow out of it.

Now Pappas and you have something in common: You both consume Tums by the handful.

~~

Some boys from The Highlanders ask if you want to join their organization. Absolutely! Get to wear a uniform and go camping, earn badges that look like war medals. Two of the bigger boys come to the house in their manly outfits and ask the mom to sign a paper saying you have her permission. She tells them she is sorry but no: It wouldn't work for him. He still wets the bed. He couldn't go on camping trips. The boys are embarrassed. One boy looks at you as if he can't believe what the mom just said. What could you have told him? What does Duffy know? Duffy's a dope. He knows almost nothing, and what he does know he would rather not know.

~~

Winter day: it is snowing and you're hoping it will snow enough to shut down school. You leave the house willing the snow to fall faster. You walk to the drainage ditch to see if there is scary ice to walk on. The ditch is a large, watery depression ringed in trees and dead yellow rushes. Drainage pours into the ditch from the streets and from a pipe big enough to walk through all the way to East Colfax Avenue, where you can watch traffic from a rat's eye view.

When you get to the ditch, the water is frozen. You slide onto it, onto the ice, where, face down, you lick it, feel it tugging your tongue. Rub the ice smooth with the sleeve of your jacket to see what is hiding below: dead vegetation and chunks of cement, lots more things, some of which you put there yourself, a tire, a bicycle chain, an assortment of spokes forming a spiny star, the head of a smirky doll, the dome of a buried golf ball looking like a little white moon down there. You also see something green. It's a green snake, a fat one. A python. You scurry on hands and knees to the edge of the ditch. Where you stop and look back. The ice isn't moving, no python breaking through to chase you. Pythons eat people all the time in the Congo. Pappas has said so. One of them ate a pregnant woman and when they cut it open the woman was crushed inside; but when they cut her open, the baby was still alive. It's one of the neatest stories you've ever heard. Telling it to some girls at school, you made them scream. The woman was bleached white by the snake sucking out her blood, you added.

When the python doesn't appear, you search the snow where there are concrete chunks someone dumped. Tossing a big piece at the spot where the python lives, the cement breaks a hole in the ice and the green thing bobs up, floats on the water. It isn't a python at all. It's something rubbery. Round as lifesaver. With a stick you pull it across the ice and find out it's some kind of wreath. You dry it on your jacket. In your pocket is a black crayon. With the crayon you draw a snakehead, slit of an eye, dots for nostrils, mouth open, tip of its tail going into the mouth, huge fangs dripping venom. Carrying it looped over your shoulder, you head to school, where kids are outside waiting for the bell.

Sarah Gramm is there. Her father owns Gramm's Grocery on East Colfax Avenue. You love her. You want to show your snake to her. The first time she smiled at you your heart was hers. Once while she was watching, you piled a handful of dirt and ate it. Another time you dove headfirst down the slide and skinned your palms so bad they bled. These are small sacrifices you're willing to make to show Sarah Gramm your love for her. You have a plan that one day, when some stupid boy flicks her suspenders, Duffy the hero will fly to her rescue and sock that boy in the jaw.

Today Sarah is in her red coat and red stocking cap, blond hair falling over her shoulders. She is wearing white boots that blend with the snow. Carol Marie is standing next to her. Where you been? Carol Marie says. What's that thing on your shoulder? You answer, It's a roundsnake. I caught it frozed at the ditch and brought it back to life. He's my friend. Carol Marie says: It's no snake, stupid. It's something made of rubber. You hold it out like a loop of rope. And say: If I tell it to, it'll let go of its tail and bite your ass and you'll die. She inspects the roundsnake, her eyes inches from it. And she says: You know what this is? This is what they use to hold flowers and ferns to make funeral wreaths. Grow up, Duffy. You tell her to feel it. She feels it and says it sure feels nasty.

It does look like a snake, says Sarah. You ask her if she wants to pet the roundsnake. She touches it. She says, Feels funny. Feels like cold skin. Watching her hand caress the roundsnake makes you want to kiss her fingers. And so you tell her she can have the roundsnake for a kiss. I can't kiss you, she says, blushing. You say you'll give her a nickel. Her left hand keeps rubbing circles on the slick skin. And she says, But if you want me to, I can spit on him. More than anything you want to see her spit! Go on, you tell her. Do it. She bends over the roundsnake and spits. Her face flushing all over. Spit bubbling like airplane glue on the surface of the roundsnake. You stick a finger in it, smearing it round and round, making the surface slicker. Raising the roundsnake close, you sniff then lick Sarah's sweet spit. Reaching in your pocket, you pull out a nickel and give it to her.

~~

At home you start stealing nickels from the change Pappas leaves in the ashtray on top of the radio. One nickel a week and Pappas never finds out. Each nickel gets you a kiss from Sarah. The two of you hide behind the trees and bushes outside her place and hold your breaths while you peck away at each other. Lips closed. Lips flat and dry. Kissing her always gets you a boner, which you rub against Sarah. She lets you do that, but she won't allow any touches beneath her shoulders. No rubbing or patting her bottom.

Summer comes, school is out and you keep going to Sarah's house every week and kissing her. Sometimes she spits on a tree leaf and lets your smear it with your finger and kiss it and then kiss her. One day after doing this, you blurt it out, blurt out what you really want. I want to see your tee-tee, you say. I can give you two nickels for that. Her mouth drops open. She is shocked. Shame on you! she says. What do you think I am? She hurries back to her house and that is the last time she trades nickels for kisses.

~~

After dinner one night the mom says she has something important to say. She announces she's going to have a baby. A lousy idea as far as you're concerned. A baby! Grandma Inez has come from Minnesota and moved in. She says a baby is just what this family needs. It will bind the marriage, she says. Babies can do that. Her breathy laugh smells like gin. She winks at you like it's all a joke as she places her forefinger like the barrel of a gun aiming at her forehead. You have no idea what she means by this gesture.

The mom says, What are you thinking, Duffy?

Straight out you tell her you do not want no baby. She giggles. But you're not being funny. What are we going to do with a baby? She frowns. She shakes her head. She says, You are being selfish again. You want to stay the baby of the family. Like hell I do, you tell her. And she says, You better watch that mouth, young man. Pappas tells you not to talk with your mouth full. Close your goddamn mouth when you chew. I hope it's a boy, says the mom. You choke on her words, you cough. You're really going to be sick thinking about what she just said. Another boy in the house? Jesus, the poor bastard has no idea what he is in for. You want to put your mouth on the mom's belly and yell, Do not come out of there, little guy! You will be sorry if you do.

~~

You sort of like Grandma Inez sometimes because she takes you on the bus to the sports arena, takes you inside to watch professional wrestlers beat the shit out of each other. Root for the good guy who always wears brighter, more colorful trunks than the bad guy. Boo the bad guy. Grandma Inez yells, Kill him! Kill him! She stands up shaking her fist. Very exciting to watch the wrestlers throw each other all over the ring. Grandma Inez instructs you in the finer points: That's a crossbody block! That's a stinger! Oh look at that dirty bastard giving him the bell clap, that'll just kill your ears! There, you see that! That's the Lou Thez press, he'll pin him with that, the body scissors! Get him in the body scissors, you idiot! Her favorite wrestler is Lou Thez. She calls him The Great One and says he is Heavyweight Champion of the World. She loves him.

One day you come home from school and hear a noise in Carol Marie's bedroom, open the door and see Grandma Inez naked with a naked man on top of her. She throws him off, jumps up and puts on a robe. Takes you by the hand. Walks you to the door. Tells you not to tell anyone what you saw. She gives you a quarter and says, Go buy some candy. Then she locks you out of the house. Later, you see the man and Grandma Inez walking down Ironton smoking cigarettes and talking. You follow them to the Zanzibar around the corner on East Colfax. The Zanzibar becomes Grandma Inez's favorite hangout from then on.

She knows Chippewa and how to dance Indian style. Sometimes she comes home happy from the Zanzibar and dances, going in circles and chanting Hiya! Hiya! She'll grab you, swing you round and round. Both of you singing, Hiya! Hiya! She'll talk Chippewa, but no one knows what she's saying. Now and then she translates. A plane will fly over and she'll point to the sky and say, *Bemi-se-gak*: thing that flies! She'll pour coffee and say *Maka-de-mash-kiki-waa-boo*. The chair she sits on is *desabi-win*. She'll rattle off sentences that make no sense at all and then laugh at your baffled faces. She says the name of God is Gichi Manidoo, that's who she prays to every morning every night. She says, When we pray we should wear bright clothes, so Gichi Manidoo can spot us. It's important to smoke when we pray. Smoke carries prayers up to Gichi Manidoo. It's true! Listen, why do you think the land of India burns their dead? They send em up in smoke. *Booz-hoo ahnee*, she says. It means Greetings, or Hello, or something like that. Or maybe it means nothing. She rattles off strings of Indian words that sound like twisted forms of pig Latin. She swears they are potent prayers to Giche Manidoo. Holy Rollers might say she is talking in tongues.

~~

April 12, 1951, Michele Renee Pappas is born at Fitzsimmons Army Hospital in Aurora. When the mom brings her home, she wants the kids to sit nice and hold the tiny inert lump. Carol Marie jumps right in, a natural mother. You stare at Michele Renee's face and are definitely not impressed. She is ugly, a squinty puss poking out looking like a pissed off Apache, like Geronimo in that picture where he is squatting with a rifle hating the world. His face saying he would kill all whites if he could.

Pappas doesn't care much for his daughter. Not once do you ever see him hold her. Not once do you see him feed her or even chuck her chin or test her hand to see how well it can grip his finger. You're not that standoffish. Eventually you do hold her on your lap, feed her a bottle and play with her toes. As the months go by she morphs into an acceptable specimen of her species. You get a kick tickling her, making her giggle and coo. You let her suck your finger. You dance with her. Carol Marie dances with her too. The mom says that if you dance with the baby now it will instill rhythm in her bones and she'll be a good dancer when she grows up. The mom is a fabulous dancer. Could have been professional, she says over and over.

~~

Grandma Inez is a tough, hard drinking, chain-smoker who has had two husbands and will never have another. She doesn't trust men as far as she can throw them. In her cups she will tell how her first husband abandoned her and their two kids, Janice and Dean, in Pierre, South Dakota. Their father drove off like he was going to work one morning and never returned. The mom remembers it, remembers standing on the porch at the end of the day and for many days after, waiting for her daddy and saying, When's my daddy coming home? He disappeared into the unknown and Janice never got over it. A drink or two and she will tell the story again. Standing on the porch, searching the road, waiting, saying, When's my daddy coming *home*?

Grandma Inez divorced her first husband on grounds of abandonment and married a man named Ed Nielson who was wild and crazy. Both of them loved to party. Nielson turned out to be a wife-beater. After one of the beatings, in which Janice, not more than twelve years old, hit Nielson over the head with a vase and floored him, Grandma Inez packed up her brood and moved to her relatives in Foreston, Minnesota. She placed her children with her sister Eunice and brother-in-law Jack Strumwall. They lived on the land that used to be the site of what was called the Deans House, after George Deans, a Minnesota state senator, Inez and Eunice's father. That house burned down and burned up Inez's new shoes. She obsesses on those shoes the way Janice obsesses on her missing daddy. The fire also destroyed the trunk in the attic where it is said George Deans kept most of his money. We were rich and then we weren't, Grandma Inez claims. Damn it all, damn it to hell! My shoes burned to ashes. I used to wear diamonds and rubies. Look at me now! Shitfire and damnation! Her father rebuilt, but the new house was more modest than the old one. A common little cottage she calls it.

Her story gets fuzzy after she leaves Janice and Dean with Eunice and Jack. She won't talk about it except to say she worked hard scrubbing floors on her hands and knees, which is why she has such big ugly knots on her shinbones. She also worked as a short-order cook and sent money to her sister for keeping Janice and Dean. A peaceful time in Janice's life as she tells it. The farm was kid-paradise. She adored her aunt, whom she called Sister.

Dean and Janice stayed there for five or six years. But then Sister was diagnosed with breast cancer and didn't last long. Janice recalls how horrible it was hearing her aunt screaming in pain upstairs in her bedroom. The word cancer always widens Janice's eyes with fear and worry. All her life she will expect the same thing to happen to her. Every pain, every lump, every unexplained stirring will have her running to doctors, telling them to operate, cut it out of her. She will have many operations in her life, an appendix removed, a hysterectomy, exploratory surgery because of a chronic pain in her side, another surgery to remove adhesions, another to remove hemorrhoids. None of the operations will find the cancer she was always sure would take her.

~~

In early fall 1951 Pappas gets transferred to Chanute Air Force Base in Illinois. In October Grandma Inez moves back to Minnesota. The mom rents out the Aurora house and drives her brood cross-country to Champaign-Urbana bordering Indiana. The family moves into an ugly two-bedroom house on a corner lot, not far from the municipal swimming pool and park and Washington grade school. The house is covered in dark brown wooden shingles. It has yellowy trim round the windows, a large front porch and an elm in the front yard. In the shadowy basement is a coal-fired furnace.

The loft where you sleep has no windows and is very scary at night. So black a space you can't see your hand in front of your face after you pull the chain at the head of the stairs to turn out the light. At that point, you get down on your hands and knees and crawl to the bed. There are no guardrails, so you're always afraid of falling down the stairwell and breaking your legs or killing yourself. You keep a coffee can under the bed because you don't want to grope your way to the light in order to go down to the bathroom when you need to pee at two in the morning.

~~

You go to school and fall madly in love with your teacher, Miss Cima, who is younger and every bit as pretty as the mom. Maybe even prettier. You've never had a nicer, kinder teacher. You love her so much that for the first time in your life you actually work to get good grades and earn her approval. From her you get your first (and last) A's in Spelling and Reading, Grammar and Punctuation. For every A you get, she sticks a gold star on your forehead, which you proudly wear round the house. When the mom sees the first star on your forehead, she asks about it. Spelling, you tell her. A hundred percent on the test today. Ah-ha, she says, You see what you can do when you put your mind to it? That's my boy, that's my Duffer! And she adds that she was a good speller too. She got straight A's in everything. You're a chip off the old block, she tells you. You're going to be a doctor. I should have been a doctor, she adds.

For the rest of the year you're in heaven whenever you behold Miss Cima in the classroom. You want to grow up and marry her. When you tell Carol Marie how you feel about Miss Cima and add that you will marry her as soon as you're old enough, she, Carol Marie, says, Don't be stupid, Duffy. By the time you grow up, she'll be an old lady. But you insist you'll get older than Miss Cima. And I'll get older than you too, Carol Marie! She shakes her head, rolls her eyes, says, It's not possible, you dumbbell. How you think you'll do that? Musing on what she's saying, it suddenly strikes you that she's horribly right. You might get taller and older and big in the shoulders like Pappas, but Miss Cima and you will never be man and wife. This knowledge is a gasping blow to your view of being alive—how it's a day-to-day thing always moving in one unavoidable direction. Time has more power than anything or anyone. You start fearing clocks, obsessing on them, especially clocks that have a needle going round and round ticking off seconds of your life. Every minute moving toward death waiting for you like a spider waiting for a fly. What will it be? An accident? Some nasty disease? Cancer? One of Pappas's beatings? That old man in Frederick who got chased by his wife, he was a boy your age once. Then he got gray hair and a wrinkly face and his heart stopped. When you asked what he died of, the mom said he died of old age. You said you never want to get that old. And the mom said: A fool is known when he opens his mouth. Who do you think you are? You think you're Joshua? He might have made the sun standstill, but even that didn't stop him getting old and dying.

~~

Pappas stays up late at the table in the kitchen listening to the Gillette Friday Night Fights. One night it is Rocky Marciano versus Joe Louis. The date is October 26, 1951. Pappas fights the fight along with what he hears on the radio, Marciano taking it to Louis, knocking him all over the ring. Louis is getting what the announcer calls, A terrific beating! Pappas is saying, Get him! Get that nigger! In the eighth round Louis is knocked through the ropes and the fight is over. Pappas is beaming. He punches your shoulder and growls, What did I tell you? I told you he was going to kick that nigger's ass!

The one thing Pappas and you will have in common from that point on is that you both like listening to the fights and discussing the pros and cons of the fighters you follow. Stepfather and stepson will box with the gloves and you will get stronger and better. Pappas will let you hit him a few times before he invariably knocks you down. He will tell you numerous times that you're lucky to have him for a father because he is making a man out of a sissy. Maybe there is some truth in that?

~~

Just before school lets out for Christmas, someone hangs mistletoe over the door in the classroom. When Miss Cima enters, the girls and boys stop her under the mistletoe. One at a time the boys climb on a chair and kiss their teacher on the cheek. So excited you are practically panting, you line up for your turn too, but after a few more kisses, she says, Okay, that's enough, you kids. Take your seats. Your heart falls. No kiss ever from the love of your life. So dejected you feel like crying, you go back to your desk and somehow hold your heartbroken self together through the rest of the day. When the bell rings, you don't realize it is tolling the end of any chance to ever see Miss Cima again. She will get married over the holidays, change her last name and move you'll never know where.

~~

For Christmas you get a Red Ryder Air Rifle and a cylinder of BBs. Pappas tells you not to use your mouth to spit the BBs into the magazine. To illustrate what could happen, he sticks out his tongue and tells you to feel it top and bottom. He guides your fingers to his tongue, where you feel something hard and round inside. Pappas claims it is a BB he shot into his own tongue by accident when he was a boy your age. He was loading the chamber, spitting a mouthful of BBs into it, when the gun went off. He wasn't able to get the BB out. After the first day the wound didn't hurt anymore. He says the BB in his tongue is a button pusher. He says, Someday you'll know what that means. He grins. He laughs. He messes your hair, puts you in a headlock and gives you an Indian rug-burn, just enough to make you say, Ow, Daddy, uncle! uncle!

~~

After the Christmas break you have a new fifth grade teacher, Mrs. Stern. She very much lives up to her name. Mrs. Stern doesn't care much for kids, especially ten-year-old boys. She has a peachwood paddle drilled with holes to make it smart. Any kid acting up will get spanked hard. It happens once to you for turning round in your seat and talking to notorious Raymond Hedreth, bicycle thief and tough guy, but not as tough as his cousin Bucky Hedreth whom you adore. The teacher pulls you out on the floor and tells you, No talking in class! Her hand pulling your arm makes you instantly angry. You twist away ordering, Lemme alone, goddammit! She swats your backside with the paddle and Christ almighty the thing stings! She orders you back to your desk and tells you to keep your mouth shut from now on. You glower but don't argue. Raymond pats you on the shoulder and whispers, Fuck her.

A few days later Raymond is getting paddled and as the teacher swings, Raymond cocks his foot backwards, the paddle hitting the heel of his shoe and shattering. Don't worry, says Mrs. Stern, my husband will make me another. Your grades drop. You get C's and D's from her, an F in math. In the comments section of your report card, she writes: *Duffy is lacking in all areas. He seems to have been born without any motivation to learn. If he doesn't try harder, his only future employment will be that of the village idiot.*

You have Carol Marie sign the card. When you give it back to Mrs. Stern, she looks it over and says, No reply? You shake your head and she says, Well, no wonder.

What does she mean by no wonder, you wonder. Wonder what? That you're so stupid?

~~

The winter gym class for boys is wrestling. The wrestling coach teaches the basic stuff, headlocks, cradles, body scissors, hip throws, takedowns, escapes, reversals. For the first week the class practices these moves. The second week the boys are paired by size and urged to have at it. To Duffy's amazement he turns out to be a good wrestler and wins his first matches easily. You are lightning fast and strong for your size. You always considered yourself puny, but maybe you're not. Could it be the wrestling prowess comes from boxing so much with Pappas? Or maybe from shoveling heavy coal into the basement furnace twice a day? Coach calls you wiry, a term you've never heard before. But you know wiry is a compliment, so you like Coach and wrestling a lot.

Every day that you compete you win. No one can beat you, not even the heavier boys, none of them as fast as you are. You've never been able to beat anyone at anything. But in wrestling you've found your calling. Boys like Bucky Hedreth and his cousin Raymond start hanging around with you. Bucky is the best wrestler in fifth grade. He has also won all his matches. He is slightly taller than you and six pounds heavier. Coach says the two of you are well-enough matched and he wants to see you on the mat.

You do and don't want to wrestle Bucky. You look up to him. He's your hero. You think he's handsome and you like the way his hair curls behind his ears. You try to train your hair to do the same thing, but it always wants to curl out rather than in.

The day the two of you meet for a match, the boys shouting your names is the coolest thing that's ever happened to you. Bucky and Duffy. Duffy and Bucky: the center of the ring, the center of everything, fifth grade's brightest stars. Get him, Bucky! Throw him, Duffy!

You throw each other and gather points, do headlocks, hip throws, side mounts and escapes. Nearing the end, the match is even. In the midst of it, you have the sense that you can beat Bucky if you really want to. You can tell his lungs are burning. He's panting and his cheeks are as red as cherries. You're not very tired at all. You have enough wind to go on a lot longer. But you don't really want to. What you want is for Bucky to like you. Want to keep him as a friend, and if you beat him in front of God and everybody he might hate you. And so in the end, you fake it, you stop trying and Bucky wins on points. He might have beaten you anyway, who can say? When the match is over he hugs you, and you wish with all your heart Bucky was your brother. Later, he talks about the fall season, sixth grade flag football. He will be the quarterback and captain and he wants you on his team. You know next to nothing about football.

~~

There is a chubby girl who lives four houses down the street. Her name is Karen Fielding. Next door to her lives Bart Moore and his little sister Bonnie. Karen and Bart are eleven and one grade in front of you. Bonnie is nine and a grade behind. That summer you play baseball with other kids in the park. Karen is better than everyone. She's a natural, the Babe Ruth of girls with the bat, and, living up to her last name, she can field. She's not as fast a runner as Bart, but she can beat you, unless the race is for distance. When it comes to long distance, the 440 the 880, you can beat almost anyone. Philip of the green buckteeth is pretty good at baseball. You might like him if his teeth weren't so ugly. He's also good at football. But so is Karen. She's always saying she should have been born a boy.

Bart becomes your best friend. You go hunting with him, shooting at anything that moves. One day you shoot a starling sitting on a branch. It falls to the ground but isn't dead. Its yellow eye is wide with wonder. What have you done to me the eye says. You're feeling really bad. Warm in your palm, a living thing. You pet its silky feathers. Bart pets it too. You decide to name it Bird. The wound is on the right side of its stomach. You take it to your house and operate. Bart holds its wing out while you use the tip of a straight pin to pick the copper BB out. You clean the tiny hole with Mercurochrome, wrap the wound in gauze and tape it. You dip Bird's beak in a cup of water but can't tell if it drinks. Make crumbs from a slice of bread, but Bird won't eat any. Using one of the mom's old cooking pots, you gather grass and make a nest. Bird's new home until it heals and flies away. The nest goes under the steps of the porch, where you can easily reach it and nurse Bird back to health.

Bart and you take up your rifles and go hunting again. You tell Bart that the mom will cook pigeon pot pie if either of you can shoot some pigeons. The mom hasn't actually said she would cook pigeon pot pie, but you like the sound of saying pigeon pot pie, especially the pie part, so you make up the mom's place in your plan. There is an old house not far away, where pigeons roam the peak of the poop-smeared roof. You shoot BBs at them, but don't hit any and finally give up and start discussing sex. Bart asks if you've ever done IT. You tell him no! You're an expert on the subject of sex, so you tell him only married people are supposed to IT. In your mind you're picturing Grandma Inez and that strange man in Carol Marie's bedroom. The people who aren't married go to hell if they do IT, you say. And Bart says, Yeah, but what a way to go.

You're not sure what to make of him. How do you know? you ask. Bart says he's fucked Karen lots of times and also Bonnie his sister. Karen's older brother fucks her too. In fact, he showed her how and she showed Bart.

You're dumbfounded, speechless.

When you go to bed that night the idea haunts you. You think of George Allison licking Carol Marie and spanking the mom. You think of the man who taught you to shoot a .22 and how he played with Carol Marie's privates. You think about rubbing up against Sarah and how good that felt. You think about how your privates brought mostly nothing but grief every morning when you woke up wet. You think of Karen and Bart and Bonnie living right next door to each other and doing IT.

In the morning, you rush downstairs and out the door to see how Bird is doing. Bird is gone. A few feathers scattered around. A wad of filthy gauze. Cat paw prints in the dirt. You spend the morning hunting cats with your air rifle, heart full of hatred full of revenge, but it's as if they know you're after them. The streets of Urbana stay cat free and your hatred turns to boredom. You go home and sit on the steps in the shade of the elm, where birds are calling. You stare at Karen's house and think of her. Her and Bart. Her and her brother and Bart and Bonnie.

IT.

~~

Karen has a plain round face, sandy-colored hair, blue eyes and freckles. She is gat-toothed and has a smile that reminds you of a Halloween pumpkin. She's both chubby and muscular. Bart is lean. His complexion is much darker than yours. You look like an albino standing next to him. He says he is black Irish. The two of you spend the rest of the summer fucking Karen.

The first time is in Bart's basement. It starts with an argument, Bart and Karen trying to talk you into doing it, but you're scared and resisting. What seals the deal is Karen saying, I bet you don't even know how! You tell her you know all about it. Prove it, she says.

In Bart's basement there's a little room loaded with cardboard boxes full of junk surrounding a rolled out sleeping bag, where Karen lies down. She shuffles her jeans and underpants off. Bart drops his drawers and climbs onto her. You put it right here, he says, plunging in and moving up and down. You're very nervous wondering if Bart's mother might come to the basement to get something. Maybe she'll hear what's going on. The vacuum is roaring upstairs. After a minute or two Bart says, Your turn. You hesitate. You'll go to hell if you do this, Duffy. God will hate you. Come on, Duffy, says Karen. We ain't got all day. Okay, so you drop your pants and skivvies and lay on Karen. She reaches down, grabs you, puts you in her. What a sensation! Nothing has ever felt so thrilling, not even rubbing against Sarah. Karen's gat-tooth smile is right in your face taunting. See? she says.

You can only nod in agreement. She pulls your mouth to her mouth, gives you a wet kiss, sticks her tongue in your mouth, which doesn't add anything to the act as far as you're concerned. Then she says, Okay, that's enough for now. Get off. Let's get outta here. Let's play football. You guys try to tackle me. See if you can bring me down.

~~

In Bart's backyard there is a mound, a sort of fort behind which kids shoot BB guns at Indians or attacking Japs. Sometimes Bart's sister Bonnie plays too. One day after a battle, you watch Bart lie down on his back with his penis out. He has Bonnie sit on him and go up and down. You don't take part in it other than to watch.

Karen isn't there that day. But later when you tell her what Bart and Bonnie did she says she and her brother do the same thing all the time. She asks if you've ever fucked Carol Marie. No! I'd never do that, you tell her. But then you wonder if Carol Marie is doing it with someone. Would she do such a thing? Karen says, Ask her to come over and do it with my brother. You go home and tell Carol Marie about Karen's offer. Carol Marie eyes get big as silver dollars. You see shock and worry in them. No, no, no! she says, don't be talking like that, Duffy. You want me to have a baby?

~~

Pappas has noticed how much Karen and you hang together in the street throwing footballs and baseballs. If he's there on the porch smoking a cigarette, his eyes watch Karen hustling. When you are through playing and go inside, he always says: You getting any of that? You know that Pappas somehow knows what's going on with Karen, knows it like a mind reader, a sex sniffer. When he asks if you're getting any, you play dumb, always pretending you don't know what the man is talking about. Any what? It makes Pappas smile. It makes him wink. It makes him give a look that says, You ain't fooling me, pal.

~~

Playing tackle football at the park in the fall of 1952, Karen and Philip of the green buckteeth get into an argument and start fighting. They slug each other. They pull each other's hair and wrestle. The rest of the players surround them and yell: Get him, Karen! Get her, Phil! For a minute the fight is even, but then Karen starts to lose. She goes down and Philip jumps on top of her.

You're torn about what to do. It's a fair fight, but Karen is your girlfriend. Sort of. Shouldn't you help her, Duffy? But if you help her the other boys might beat you up. Most of them are Philip's friends and they all look older and tougher than you. So it's a moment of truth and you don't do anything except stand there and yell Karen's name. When she starts crying, Philip gets off and says he won. He and the other boys walk away talking about how he kicked Fielding's fat ass.

Only Bart and you are still on Karen's side. Together you help her up. Her nose is bleeding. You grab a leaf off a tree and she holds it to her nose, bleeds all over it and down the front of her sweat shirt as she walks home, you and Bart following, your heads hanging in shame.

Her mother is very upset. You should have stuck up for her, she says. She washes the blood off Karen and puts her to bed. You and Bart are allowed to see her and say sorry. You tell her, We couldn't do nothing. The other boys wouldn't let us. She says, Okay, I know you tried.

It's a long time before you see Karen again. She starts playing with some girls from school. You see her with Shirley her fat cousin who puts out too, and you're jealous. When you try to get Karen to play, she always finds excuses not to.

~~

At school in the fall, you go out for flag football and make the team as a receiver and defensive back. Truth is: you're not very good at receiving. You drop as many passes as you catch. The other receivers are just as bad. Coach moves you behind the line when the team is on defense. The thing you excel at is darting in and grabbing the runner's flag, so you concentrate on that and get lots of pats on the back.

One time the mom shows up for a game, making you very nervous, and you drop a sure touchdown pass in the end zone, but try to make up for it by going crazy on the field grabbing flags and throwing them to the ground. When the game is over the mom says, Why didn't you catch that pass? It was right in your hands, Duffy. You would have had a touchdown. You look at your hands as if it's their fault. At home, she tells Pappas about how Duffy dropped a sure touchdown. Right in his hands! Pappas says, You'll never make it in football. There's not enough lead in your ass. Better stick to wrestling punks your own size, he says.

He's right about that, but when the season is over, you're voted Most Valuable Player by your team mates. Actually, Bucky is the most valuable, but since he's also captain and will get a leadership award, someone else has to get chosen most valuable. Bucky and you have your picture taken by the newspaper at an award ceremony. The next morning the picture is printed. Standing next to Bucky and wearing a Hopalong Cassidy sweater, is Duffy Pappas. Both of you are holding ribbons and smiling. When Pappas sees the picture he says not to get cocky. When he played football it was always tackle, none of this sissy flag football shit.

~~

Since Karen doesn't love you anymore, you give your heart to a girl named Connie. She is a head taller and has big brown eyes and perfect teeth and a nose that tilts upward so much you can see the insides of her nostrils. She visits you after school at your house because you've told her about how dark the attic is.

You take her upstairs and turn out the light. Black as black, what a cool place, she says, I can't see you at all, Duffy. Kiss me. You are facing each other, holding hands. It seems a good time to give her a kiss, so you stand on tiptoes and plant a liplock on her. After a second she startles you by saying, Duffy, you're kissing my nose. You pull the chain and see her crouching, making herself shorter in order to kiss you mouth to mouth. She starts laughing. It's too embarrassing. You want Connie to go home. You don't bring her to the loft anymore. Instead start meeting out back of her place.

She steals cigarettes from her parents and gives them to you in the alley behind her garage. Together you smoke cigarettes and kiss. One day you're rubbing against her and she grabs your boner, squeezes it, rubs it. Is there something about Illinois girls? Do they grow up faster than Colorado girls? More might happen, but her mother starts calling: Connie! Connie! So you decide to meet after school the next day. You're hoping she'll do the same thing again.

But the desire fades the following morning when she sees you in your gym clothes on the way back to the locker room and she says, What kinda legs are those, Duffy? Those are birdlegs! Birdlegs, birdlegs! She runs off laughing and quick as that you hate her guts and want to murder her. You don't meet her behind the garage after school no more. Let her jack her own self off.

~~

Winter 1953 the girlfriend is Ginger. She has bronze-reddish hair and is slim and the cutest girl who has ever liked the Duffer. She calls him Crocodile Duffer after he tells her it's what the mom calls him, although she hasn't called him Crocodile Duffer since the time she rubbed his belly and put him to sleep. He likes the name Crocodile Duffer because it makes him feel tough, makes him feel dangerous.

You and Ginger kiss and hug whenever you can. She's a little bit like Sarah Gramm, she'll let you rub on her. But nothing more. Kissing and rubbing, that's all, that's it, Crocodile Duffer.

You go roller skating with Ginger. You have a silver ring, a man's ring you found at the pool last summer. Someone left it and instead of turning it in to the Lost & Found you kept it. It is way too large for your largest finger, so you wrapped tape around the bottom until the ring fit. One night at the rink you ask Ginger to go steady. She's willing and she says, Aren't you going to give me your ring, Crocodile Duffer? You calculate she will see the tape wrapped around it and know you're faking because your fingers are so skinny. I'll get you a better ring, you tell her. She frowns and without another word turns her back, skates away.

Slip the ring off, unwrap the tape and skate after her. But when you try to give her the ring she says, Never mind if you don't want to. But I want to! you say, pushing the ring at her. She finally takes it. But going steady doesn't work out. Just like all the other girlfriends, Ginger starts avoiding Crocodile Duffer. She no longer calls him Crocodile Duffer. You don't understand it. You understand Karen not liking you no more because you were a coward the day Phillip of the green buckteeth beat her up. But what did you do wrong with Ginger? Did Connie tell her you have birdlegs? Or was it because you hesitated to give her the ring? He who hesitates is lost? Is that it? Who understands girls? Do even girls understand girls? Your love for Ginger stays big inside for a long time, but her love for you is obviously gone. You can see it every time you look into her eyes and she frowns. Duffy, you're only eleven but it feels like your heart is broken as bad as when you didn't get to kiss Miss Cima under the mistletoe. Ginger doesn't return the silver ring. You can't work up the nerve to ask for it back. What the hell, it was a free ring, anyway.

~~

The winter is long and very windy, very cold and snowy. You do the wrestling again and take your frustration out on your opponents. You throw one guy over your hip so hard he breaks his ankle. Coach calls you into his office the next day. You're thinking BIG TROUBLE. But it turns out okay. These things happen, Coach says. It goes with the territory. Don't let it get to you. And don't let up. I've told the junior high coach about you. They've got real teams there. They wrestle other schools. You'll tear em up, Duff. Then onto high school and onto college. You stick with it. You got talent. No telling how far you'll go. Maybe a wrestling scholarship is in your future.

~~

But none of what Coach says happens. When summer comes, Pappas is discharged from the Air Force and the family prepares to move back to Aurora, where he has a job waiting for him at the Rocky Mountain Arsenal. The night before leaving, your parents go out with some friends, and Karen comes over to say goodbye. You take her down to the spooky basement and sit on the steps. I was always scared of that furnace, you tell her. There it squats near the coal bin, its slotted gate closed, quiet now, but in winter the flames leaping in the slots looked like hell must look, its belly growling, its octopus arms reaching out and up to the ceiling. Karen agrees the furnace is pretty scary. You hug each other. And you're thinking she will give a goodbye fuck if you want to. But it doesn't feel right to do it when you're so sad about moving away.

All the furniture is gone, so that night you sleep on blankets on the living room floor. Carol Marie and Michele Renee are sleeping next to you. In the morning the mom wakes everybody up and says to get ready. And yes! Damn you to hell! Duffy, you have wet yourself again! You haven't done it for ages and now look at this! What's it all about anyway? Why, why, why? Jesus, you hate yourself and feel like bawling, but bawl and there will be worse trouble from Pappas. So you get some underwear from the suitcase and change quick in the bathroom.

And the last thing you do in that gloomy house is take the wet pajamas down to the basement and throw them inside the furnace. You rush upstairs. The mom looks at you and says, What did you do? I couldn't take them like that, you tell her. Where would I put them? She shakes her head, closes her eyes and says, Help Daddy load the car.

After the car is loaded and the family is inside and the engine starting, you're leaning forward staring at Bart's house and Karen's house, fixing them in your mind for the last time. Pappas looks over his shoulder backing out. Get the fuck out of my way! he says, slapping you hard on the right ear (a bell clap Grandma Inez would call it) and it's like he's jabbed a pencil in there. The pain makes you cry out. You hold the ear and curl in a ball on the seat, while Urbana, Illinois vanishes from your life.

The ear ache refuses to go away. That night in a motel the mom blows cigarette smoke into the canal and soothes it. But for two days driving to Colorado, the throbbing and ringing in the ear is always there.

After the family moves back into the house on Ironton Street, you're still complaining. The mom thinks it's an infection. Probably needs penicillin. When she finally gets time to take you to the doctor he examines the ear and says: This child has a ruptured eardrum. The mom tells him her son is all-boy, always wrestling and playing football and that's how he must have ruptured the ear. The doctor says it will probably heal itself eventually, maybe another week or two, but if it doesn't heal, he can put a paper patch on it. He asks if there is ringing in the ear. Yeah, it rings, you tell him. That might go away, he says, but then again it might not. Don't get water in there until after it heals.

Leave the office and ask the mom, Will I go deaf in my right ear? You are such a hypochondriac, she says. This from a woman whose every unexplained lump or pain or bellyache or backache or diarrhea (some evenings she practically lives on the throne) or dizziness or shortness of breath, or migraine or racing pulse, heart pounding, gas, gas, gas, whatever the problem, it is almost certainly cancer. The lump on her breast turning out to be a cyst. The diarrhea caused by nervous colitis. The gas caused by an overactive colon and her inability to digest milk, cheese, peanuts and peanut butter. Fruits and vegetables turn her into a goose. She needs to stick to meat and potatoes. Beef, chicken, lamb, pork, foods that will slow her digestive track. What she does eventually is eat almost nothing, drink Pepsi, scarf chocolates. Her diet keeps her slim and sexy. She could be a magazine model. Her exterior is runway ready.

Eventually the ear stops hurting, but the ringing is always there and you lose some hearing as well. The right ear will always be the bad ear, ringing, buzzing, infected, lots of infections needing antibiotics. Such, then, is the power of a bell clap.

JANICE - AGE 18

CAROL MARIE & DUFFY 1945

GRANDMA INEZ

CAROL MARIE & DUFFY
1946 or 47

CAROL MARIE PLAYS AN ANGEL
IN CHRISTMAS PLAY 1948

NICK PAPPAS & THE LADY
OF THE LAMP - 1950?

DUFFY & CAROL MARIE
1951

PAPPAS FAMILY 1953

CAROL MARIE 1955

SHERRYE - SUMMER 1956

DUFFY 1957

*How sharper than a serpent's tooth it is to have a thankless child.*

*- Shakespeare*

So the mom comes home from work and is searching through the fridge for an orange and she says, Who ate the oranges? And I say, I ate the oranges. And she says, You ate all of them? And I say, Yeah I ate all the oranges. Also thinking what a good boy am I. But the mom says, Well, Jesus Christ, what you do that for, you selfish brat! I tell her she said oranges were good for me. You said oranges give me vitamin C, I say. She shakes her head, says: But you don't have to eat ALL of them. You can save some for someone else. Oranges are expensive and I am the mom who works her ass off every damn day to put a roof over your head and food in your mouth and when the mom comes home and wants an orange she should be able to have one, but you never think about me working myself to the bone for you and your sisters. You never think about anyone but you-you-you. Get out of my sight.

So I get out of her sight. She's said a dozen times the doctor told her not to eat fruits. Fruits act on her like milk of magnesia. Also, I do not explain that I didn't really eat ALL the oranges. I gave one each to the twins Billy and Bruce. But I ate the other two and taste them when I burp and even as burps oranges taste good. One time when my Uncle Dean was visiting from Oregon, I forced out a really huge burp for him, thinking he would laugh because burps and farts are funny when you're a little kid, but he didn't think I was funny. He made a face and said, What the fuck you trying to do, chew your food twice? I didn't burp or fart around him anymore after that. He's a Pacific Campaign war hero. I want to be a Marine when I grow up.

The twins are leaning on the fence sneering, their noses running as usual. When I come out of the house, Billy says: Yeah, fuckface twat, we gonna tell what you did last night jumping out the window to smoke and run naked in the alley. So I say: If you tell on me I will tell what you were doing in bed when I stayed over. Shut up, says Billy. And I say: Yeah, your mother never changes the filthy sheets. My mom says your mom is too lazy to do the laundry and that is why the sheets are brown and gritty and that is why I slept on the floor and when I got home my mom made me take a shower. Mind your own business, Billy shouts. Yeah, shouts Bruce, mind your own business, fuckface twat, we was wrestling. Putting my hands on my hips I yell back at them, I know the difference between fucking around and wrestling, Bruce, so you better not say anything about me running naked and smoking in the alley! Actually they were giving each other hand jobs. That was the real reason I got out of bed. Well, that and their gritty sheets chafing my skin.

I remember how good it felt to be naked in the alley, the night air breathing on my whole body. When I grow up I am going to be a nudist colony. When I grow up I am going to be a nature freak and nobody can stop me because grownups do whatever they want. Nor can anyone stop my legs from getting long enough to make me six feet tall. Which is what the mom insists I be. Six feet. Anything shorter than that is only half a man, according to her. When I grow up to be bigger than Pappas, my arms will be Lou Thez AND Rocky Marciano. Arms that will crush cornholers named Billy and Bruce. When I grow up if any Billys or Bruces fuck with me I'll put a bat upside their stupid heads. Beat them to bloody hell. Put them in a gunny sack, set it on fire the way I set tomato worms on fire after I roll them inside a tomato leaf and pour lighter fluid on it and say, Burn bastard burn. They sizzle like bacon grease.

So Billy says: You know what you are, Duffy? You're an uptight fuckface twat. And I shoot back: You better not say that to me or I will kick your nuts so far up your ass they will fly out your nose. (Got that from Pappas, who said he told some guy who tried to fuck with him in the Zanzibar that he would kick his nuts so hard they would fly out his nose. The guy backed off. Because Pappas is tough. Just ask him. He will tell you.) Billy and Bruce laugh and I laugh too, because the thought of testicles shooting out Billy's nose is really funny. And then I tell them how the mom is goddamn mad because all the oranges are gone. I did not eat the orange you gave me, says Bruce. He lifts the lid on the trashcan and right on top of the garbage is a shiny orange. Bruce grabs it, throws it, bounces it off my noggin, reflexes so fast I catch the orange before it hits the ground. Buff it on my shirt, run into the house, tell the mom, Hey Mom, here is one of the oranges! She looks at me like I said, Here's some rat poison. I don't want that goddamn orange. You trying to kill me? How many times I have to tell you I'm allergic to fruit.

Allergic?

It means fruit makes me sick! Jesus, don't you ever listen? If you had a brain you'd take it out and play with it. If you had a brain, you'd be dangerous.

She isn't making that stuff up herself, she's stealing those lines from Pappas.

She turns back to her magazine, looking at the pictures and smoking a cigarette, a cup of coffee in front of her. The magazine is full of famous stars, all of them looking fabulous. I recognize Patti Page and Teresa Brewer. Recognize Sal Mineo. Recognize Donna Reed. Recognize heroic John Wayne. Recognize Debbie Reynolds, Gene Kelly, Donald O'Connor. The caption for those three says SINGING IN THE RAIN CLASSIC RETURNS. The mom stares at the movie stars so hard her eyes look like magnifying lenses. A little more heat and the pages catch fire. That could have been me, she claims, putting her finger on Debbie, if I had done that screen test it could have been me. You kids, she mutters. You kids.

So what the hell I toss the orange into the fridge. Go back outside. The guys are in the street playing dodge ball, which is what they were playing the other day when I got in a fight with them. Billy and Bruce kicking my bony butt all over the street, until Carol Marie came out with the broom and knocked shit out of those bastards. They took off for their house hollering Carol Marie and Duffy are fuckface twats! Carol Marie is strong. She seems to fear nothing.

Dodge ball bores me shitless, so off I go on my bike pedaling Aurora streets to see if there is anything to steal. Maybe get lucky and find an abandoned car on the back roads. Take its battery and sell it to the battery rebuilder for four dollars. Search trashcans in alleys, find cola bottles that bring two to five cents depending on their size. Offer to sweep the cement patio in front of Gramm's Grocery. Gramm gives fifty cents for that. He gives a dollar in winter when I shovel the snow off the walk. I could go to the driving range and shag golf balls for a penny each. If worse came to worse I can go home, get the push mower, go door to door offering to mow front and back yards for a dollar. Every Friday I deliver ads about sales at Safeway and other stores, for which I get ten bucks a month. As soon as there is an opening I'll be delivering *The Denver Post*, which will double or triple my income depending on how many subscribers I have. Life is not so bad when I am out in the world hustling. It's only when I am home with Pappas that everything typically goes to hell. So I try to stay away as much as I can. When I am home with Pappas, I move like a shadow, stay in my room with a book from the library or comic books from Gramm's Grocery.

~~

Saturdays, after the mom goes for her half day at work, Pappas calls Carol Marie to come sleep with him and orders me to get up and feed Michele Renee breakfast and do the laundry, which means taking all the dirty crap out of the hamper and stuffing it in the washer. Taking it outside when it's clean. Hanging it on the line. Which is hard because I am not tall yet. It is one of the major anxieties of my life that I won't measure up to the mom's prophecy, her six-foot insistence.

Being in bed with Pappas on a Saturday happened to me too. It was a surprise, a shock really, one morning when he called out, Duffy, wake up, come here! The sleepy-eyed boy climbing into the mom's vacant spot, turning over on his side, falling back to sleep instantly. Later feeling Pappas spooning me, his hand stroking my hip. It was like a dream, Pappas's thing pumping against my bottom. The feel of it so scary, I peed myself and Pappas went crazy. What the fuck! And out of bed I flew propelled by Pappas's size 13 (foot). Amid a shower of cuss words, I crawled away on all fours as fast as I could. Later, I stripped the bed and did the laundry.

Now nearly every Saturday, if the mom does her half day at work, I hear Pappas calling Carol Marie, she inching down the hall, opening and closing the door, creeping into bed with him. Which is when I get up, get dressed. And dress my baby sister in her jump suit. Jam her into the highchair. Put a bowl of Cheerios in front of her, so she can dig her greedy fists in there. Cram her mouth full and whine all the while because she wants out and down on the floor, where she can pull things off the tables and make a mess that I better clean up or else Pappas will slap me silly. I keep her locked in the highchair as long as possible, until the whining turns to screaming, like she is being murdered. Which is what I would like to do. Strangle her and that would shut her up for good. I wonder if other sisters cry as much as she does. As if smelling something wicked, something harmful haunting the house. Vampires. Werewolves. Demons. The Devil.

I tell her she doesn't know how good she has it. She is lucky she wasn't alive when the mom left for God knows where and put Carol Marie and me with that stinky old witch who rubbed my face in pee and said this is how you train dogs. I am sure I ruined her mattress. For which I'm not sorry, fuck her with a plumber's helper. Not that long ago I was still wetting the bed now and then. But I don't do it anymore. The mom had me pray to God on my knees, praying for Him to make the peeing stop. The mom said it would work if I really believed in the Lord. And it worked. If I had known the power of prayer before, I would have done it years ago.

When the washer stops spinning I take the clean stuff out and put it in the basket. My stomach rumbles, so I decide to eat breakfast before hanging the laundry on the lines. I eat a bowl of Cheerios. Put the empty bowl in the sink and then have to take a dump. Tiptoeing down the hall, I hear the bed squeaking. But that is none of my business. When I finish what is my business, I take the laundry and Michele Renee out to the backyard, tie her to the pole with a dog leash, while hanging the clothes up to dry. Leave her out there so she won't get under my feet when I dust the furniture. I vacuum the rug as well. Later, at the bedroom door, I knock and ask if I can go out and play and Pappas says, Sure, go on. He sounds happy and he says, Take a quarter from the ashtray and go to the movies. Pappas keeps his loose change in a big ashtray that sits on top of the new Packard Bell console TELEVISION/ RADIO/ STEREO. The Pappas family is moving up in the world.

I take a dollar in coins, enough to buy chocolate bars and Cokes for when I watch the movies. I leave my bike in the backyard. Don't want it to get stolen. All the thieves in Aurora would overflow D. U. Stadium. In the yard Michele Renee is wrapped up like a dumb puppy that only knows one way to circle a pole. So I unwrap her, put the laundry basket over her, with a lawn chair upside down on top, making a jail that will have her thrashing and whining, unless Carol Marie comes and frees her. Sometimes Michele Renee falls asleep under the basket, but other times she worms her way out, wraps herself around the pole so tight she looks like a human sacrifice ready for torching. But to hell with that I have places to go, things to do, movies to see.

Hiking down East Colfax Avenue, I note how Aurora is basically just a long street, an extension of Denver's east end, with bars, restaurants, gas stations, motels, clothing stores and grocery stores, barber shops, a movie house, Hershey's Five & Dime, Republic Drug, the street running on to Fitzsimmons Army Hospital, after which the town peters out and the plains of eastern Colorado start. Keep going and you will be on Highway 70 headed for Kansas. Some days I hike out to the plains and shoot at anything that moves. One time I had the 20 gauge and found a nest of baby rattlesnakes coiled tails up and shaking but making no noise. They struck at my boots and I blew them to pieces. Like shooting a nest of evil spirits.

Walking East Colfax, rubbing the coins in my pocket, I'm wishing I had taken more. Pappas would not have missed it. He never knows how much change he has. Look in his coat pockets and find a porno piece written about some naked guy sitting on a tree stump and a naked girl sitting on his cock and fucking him while he bites and sucks her tits. It was just one sheet of sloppy typing and since I couldn't turn the page I never knew what happened next, but I figured it out, even if I was only eleven then. In those same pockets I also found mysterious phone numbers and names like Kim and Bree and Candy. I found Sen-Sens and Juicy Fruit and Lucky Strikes (which I kept). I found pictures of naked ladies thrusting their butts or tits at me. I found a black and white picture of a naked muscleman with a half erect hard-on posing beside a gangbox full of tools. And I often found more loose change. If I didn't get greedy and stole only a little, instead of a lot, Pappas never asked where it went.

But then again there are times I loan Pappas money I've hustled, so he, Pappas, can go to the VFW club or Zanzibar and dance with the mom and get drunk and it never fails that they come home fighting because she has been flirting (or he thinks she was flirting). She always denies it. And they always end in bed making a colossal racket. And of course he never repays the money I loan him. But it is worth giving him the money just to get their asses out of the house for a while.

I stroll by lots of stores and by the dry cleaners with the 1953 Oldsmobile parked at the curb. It always has the keys in the ignition. Future plan: when I get big enough I will steal that car and drive to California, live by the ocean and get a job on a fishing boat.

I go by Hershey's Five & Dime and Republic Drugstore. They are not stupid stores. They are places to steal stuff. I never go into any store without stealing something. Maybe I'm a kleptomaniac?

The FOX AURORA is next door to Hershey's. The matinee starts at noon. Playing today is a cartoon festival. So this is one of those Saturdays that started out bad but might turn out good. An afternoon of cartoons! What more could a kid ask?

When I go inside and hand my ticket to the taker, he tears it, gives me the stub which I put in my shirt pocket. I hurry to the counter to get some snacks. At the counter is the tall girl with the black-rimmed glasses and pimply forehead. She has worked at the FOX for years and years. She was behind the counter the day eight-year-old Duffy ordered a Hershey bar and a box of Malted Milk Balls and paid for them with the pennies he had in his mouth. When I spit the ten pennies into my hand and laid them on the counter, the girl had cried out, Oh, yuck, you nasty little boy! I don't do that to her anymore, but she always looks at me warily when I come to order something.

The rest of the afternoon is kicking back watching Tom & Jerry, Yosemite Sam, Bugs Bunny, Daffy Duck and others. When I get home I am grateful to see the mom's car parked at the curb because that means Pappas probably won't be looking for some excuse to smack me. Though nothing is guaranteed, of course. Peeking in the kitchen window, I see Grandma Inez at the stove. With her home for dinner it could mean a good day gone bad, if they get drunk and start arguing and somehow I do something stupid, like get an orange out of the refrigerator and the mom reminds them of the day I ate three of them. Selfishly ate three and left only one! Or Pappas might narrow his eyes and say, Duffy, you didn't dust good, didn't clean the ring around the tub! And when are you going to learn and what do I have to do to make you learn, you little nitwit? If you had a brain you'd take it out and play with it.

I am hoping Grandma won't start drinking hard, because when she drinks hard her mouth goes south and she always says things that get Pappas pissed off. I called her an old witch one time, made her run to the bedroom blubbering. Pappas laughed and encouraged me to call her a witch some more, but the mom made me go apologize. Grandma Inez was weeping face down on the bed. I had never seen her cry before. I told her, Sorry, Grandma.

But I was not really sorry. She really looked like a witch. She had dyed her hair black and styled it like the Bride of Frankenstein. You'd think an old lady like her would have more sense.

When I enter the house, I smell saltpork frying. Crunchy saltpork delicious with fried potatoes. Pappas is on the couch, a pillow behind his head. He is smoking a cigarette, drinking a beer. The news is on TV. As long as he is not drinking at the table with Grandma Inez, things will most likely be all right.

In my room I read more *Starman Jones* by Robert Heinlein. For a while I become Max Jones stowing away on a spaceship and going through a time warp, landing on an unknown planet, where I have to figure out how to survive. I wish I had a 20-20 memory like Max has. I wish I understood what pseudo-distance means. I wish I understood about light years. I do understand what Starman Jones means when he says that as the crow flies is only vital to crows zigzagging up in the sky.

When dinner is ready, we sit round the table like a real family, bowing our heads as the mom says the prayer dear Lord, bless us. While everyone is eating, the chitchat going back and forth and the mom saying she has something important to tell us. I get a sinking feeling because that was what she had said when she announced she was having the baby. She is beaming now just like she was beaming then, her Irish cheeks flushing. She likes being Irish. She likes men calling her Red. She likes talking about her Irish temper. Having a baby is not what she was going to say. I got a raise, she says. I'm in charge of inventory.

It turns out she gets a nickel more an hour now and has to keep the books straight about what's in the storeroom. Which means she will be late coming home once or twice a month and maybe have to work all day some Saturdays.

I imagine more nights without her. More nights of Pappas. Probably no help from Grandma Inez: spending her evenings in Zanzibar, coming home staggering, falling into bed. Snoring so loud the whole house is groaning. She sleeps with me now, so I always try to be dead to the world before she shows up. Otherwise, I'll be poking and prodding her, trying to stop her snores from hammering my ears.

Pappas questions the mom about her promotion. He does not like her coming home after dark. I figured out long ago Pappas doesn't trust her. There is always some guy wanting in her pants and who knows what she does when Pappas isn't around? They fight about that plenty. They fought one time yelling and screaming about Michele Renee before she was born. Pappas lit the pilot lights in his eyes and turned the switch to high while he asked if she was sure the baby was his. Yow, did that ever make her cuss and scream and cry. You dirty rotten bastard, you sonofabitch! How dare you ask me that! I ought to get the gun and shoot you, you filthy minded moron. Yeah? Me thinks the lady protests too much, he told her. Sometimes she goes severely nutso and throws things at him or threatens him with a kitchen knife or jumps in the car and drives off, the tires screeching. Those are nights I crawl under my bed, hide with the dust balls. But the kid got born and now Pappas might find it pretty hard to deny how much she looks like him. A Greek from her nose to her toes.

After dinner Carol Marie and I are supposed to do the dishes, but Carol Marie has a habit of hiding in the bathroom dawdling, hoping her brother will get tired of waiting and do them himself. It's a trick that sometimes works because I'm in a hurry to go out and play or hide out in my room with one of my books. This night the mom comes in the kitchen and asks where Carol Marie is. Bathroom, I tell her. Not again, she says.

She goes to the door and tells her to get her ass off the pot. Let's get the dishes done, goddammit. Carol Marie shouts: Jesus, a person can't even take a shit around here in peace. You've pulled this stunt one time too many goddammit, the mom yells. Carol Marie flushes the toilet. As she is coming out she gets clipped on the back of the head. Pappas laughs. He is sitting at the table with Grandma Inez. She is nibbling pickled pig's feet for dessert. Both of them sipping after-dinner drinks. Gin for her, beer for him. The mom looks like she wants to murder Carol Marie. Carol Marie's eyes are saying fuck you, lady.

I still hate Saturdays most, but what the hell if I take away the fucked up morning and all the housework and taking care of Michele Renee, it was an okay Saturday all in all. So everything is cool except that tomorrow Pappas will still be alive. But I'll deal with that when I need to. Who knows, maybe it will not happen. Maybe Pappas dies in his sleep. Has a stroke or a brain tumor or heart attack. People do it sometimes, they up and die. Maybe I could make it happen if I only knew the right prayers to make an enchantment that would call a Banshee to come get him. The mom claims some gifted people can do things like that. If I had that gift, I would be calling Banshees right and left. Here he is! Wrap him up! Take him to hell, put his feet in the fire and ram a pitchfork up his ass.

Later, dishes done, it is kick back on the bed with a comic book to entertain my mind. In the kitchen the drone of voices rising and falling means the coast is clear, so out come the Lucky Strikes from the boot in my closet. I light up and smoke and look at the pictures of Donald Duck, who makes me laugh because he always gets so mad at everything and he has worse luck than I have. Look at that old Scrooge, the hills of millions in his vault he swims through and will not give a dime to Donald. I wish I could figure out a way to rip off that stingy bastard. Also thinking I would like to shovel Scrooge's money into a dump truck and leave him in his vault sucking a copper penny and clutching his shriveled heart.

The mom had a notion not long ago that this rich vet she met at the VFW was going to leave her lots of money when he died. Because she had made him her friend and went over to his house and cleaned and cooked for him and nursed him when he got sick and feeble with cancer. The two of them were great pals, she said. Like father and daughter, she said. But Pappas was jealous and said, That better be all you do for him, that old fucker wants in your pants. Oh, Nick, you are so sick when it comes to sex. Everything is sex with you! Pappas agreed. Because everything IS, he told her. Don't bullshit me, baby.

When the old man died he did not leave her a dime. Not a damn dime! she said. She was not even mentioned in the will and she said she could not understand that sort of ingratitude from a man with a million dollars. I understood it, though. I knew the old man knew what she was after. He knew she was being kind to him to get some of his money. It satisfied me to know that she did all that extra work for nothing. Her sneaky plan backfired. If she is going to get anything in this life she will have to work for it. Which is what she always says now. No free lunch. Better believe it, buster.

~~

In his cups one night Pappas says that his father caught his mother with another man and shot the man to death and went on trial in Denver, but got off because his wife was his property and the lover tried to steal her. Or something like that. Since it is explained by Pappas, who knows what the truth really is really? I am a liar and the mom is a liar, but Pappas is the biggest liar of all. He says things like he won a Navy Cross for taking out six Jap Zeros all by himself. He said during the war he was heavyweight boxing champ of the whole goddamn Navy. It could be true, what do I know? Maybe Pappas is as bad as he says, a heavyweight champ just needing a chance to turn professional and fight Rocky Marciano. I would give ten years of my life to see that one. How beyond the beyond it would be to see Pappas get his ass royally stomped! There are lots of phony bullies and braggers in this fucked up town, this fuckin Aurora. I hear Billy and Bruce brag up bullshit about how tough they are, but they're both lightweights when it comes to battling *mano y mano*. Hit Billy in the guts and he will run to Mama crying. Snotnose Bruce only fights if his brother is there helping him. None of the bragging boys I've met has ever lived up to his moment, at least not so far. At least not while I was watching.

Pappas also says he is a mathematical genius and that is why the Rocky Mountain Arsenal gave him an award nicely framed and with the seal of the government on it. They also gave him a bonus. He claims he invented a pair of glasses that let you look through women's clothing and see everything they got, but the war department stole the patent from him and uses it for spying. He said that the tattoo on his chest says DINAH because that was the name of his ship when he was at Pearl Harbor. He says when the sneaky Japs sneak-attacked he was manning a .50 caliber and saved the USS DINAH from sinking. He said a lot more stuff like that, but I have heard it so many times that watching dog turds drying in the sun is more interesting than listening to Pappas lying. Well, probably lying.

~~

June 1954. School out. My parents getting rid of me. Shipping me off to that gruff old Grandpa Mike who calls me Cowboy now and who wears itchy wool underwear even in the middle of summer. I am to help around that chickenshit farm that has the worst water in the world. So bad you might puke if you drink it straight. If you drink it day after day you are sure to get mineral deposits on your teeth. People all over Frederick have mineral deposits on their teeth. So to have good water, I get the gallon jugs from the garage and fill them. I put the full jugs in the trunk and pack my paper bags of clothes and an old blanket around them, so they won't smash against each other.

Pappas starts the engine of the newly purchased, barely used pale green 1953 four-door Cadillac. The engine purrs. I feel the power. Best looking car on the block, says the mom. All the neighbors are jealous of our Caddy, she says. Makes us look rich. But I happen to know that we are in debt to the gills. Pappas has said we might need a second mortgage on the house if things don't turn around. He needs more overtime. So does the mom. Hard workers those two. Nothing lazy about them. Pappas has taken a night job as a gas station attendant. I saw him wash some guy's windows and check his tires. He also called him sir. I didn't think anyone was SIR but Pappas himself.

So anyway, I'm on my way to Frederick again. Grandpa Mike will have company and I'll be out of my parents' hair for a while. The good part is I won't be around Pappas for the rest of the summer, a reprieve from his rages, his ass-kickings, his tongue-lashings. Pappas tells me that Grandpa Mike kicked his ass and his brother's ass when they were kids and that is why Pappas and George turned out so fucking tough. Pappas says (for the billionth boring time) that he is making me tough and one of these days I will be known as Tuffy Duffy and look back and be glad I had such a manly man's influence. Not a fucking chance in the world! But I nod like I agree he is the greatest. Pappas adds, You will never grow big enough to lick me, or be the heavyweight champ like I was, but I can tell from your bone structure and wiry build and the way you box that you will make a lightning fast lightweight, or maybe even a welterweight like Tony DeMarco, who is going to be the welterweight champ one of these days, mark my words.

I sort of like Pappas's mood this day. This afternoon he will get into the wine cellar and fill up on dago red and take a couple gallons home and they will have a party tonight without me there. Not that I care. I just hope the mom comes to see me on weekends like she promised she would. Not that I trust her to do it. She gets busy at work. Everyone demanding her time, she says. And she said, Duffer, you have to learn patience. Patience is a virtue. Speak for yourself, lady.

Now this: We are stopped at a stoplight. There is the old brick Purina building with wrought iron stairs leading up to a side door on the second floor. Beneath the stairs are four guys pitching pennies against the wall. A shapely woman is climbing the stairs and the guys stop pitching pennies and stare up at her. Right up her skirt, says Pappas grinning. He squeezes my thigh so hard I squeal, while Pappas guffaws, his tiny teeth barely showing behind what he calls his voluptuous lips. Women love lips like mine, he has told me. Voluptuous lips turn them on. He also says that mine are too thin and, looked at objectively, you ain't got much going for you except maybe your pretty blue eyes. All this as he was grinning. Grinning like steel rivets might grin if they could grin. His teeth are getting smaller because he grinds them down in his sleep. Sometimes I hear the grinding through the wall when I am tossing and turning, trying to fall asleep before Grandma Inez climbs in bed and starts snoring like a tractor with a hole in its muffler. Also thinking: Have I emptied my bladder well enough that no accident happens? Old as I am, I still worry about it.

Pappas drives on and we see two guys walking along the sidewalk with their arms over each other's shoulders and Pappas says, Those guys are queers, Duffy. Those guys are fags. You know what fags do to each other? Fags suck each other's cocks. They put their cocks in each other's mouths and suck them. He squeezes my knee and I squirm. And he says, They shoot their juice into each other's mouths and swallow it. Do you believe me? Seems like doing that would kill you, but hell yes I believe it. I've seen and heard plenty of shit already. I know what's up.

You got a girl? You getting any? Pappas asks. What the hell business is that of yours? I don't say that. I tell him, Not right now. Pappas shakes his head at me like I'm a loser and he says, When I was your age I was already popping cherries. Those little Mexican slots in Frederick. And he adds this: Your grandpa goes to a whorehouse in Longmont, did you know that? Only whores can handle him. Part of the reason my mother left him is because he has such a big crank that fucking him was too painful for her. I mean it's a monster. A foot long dog at least. And I am wondering: How does he know it was too painful? Did he hear his mother screaming in the night when Grandpa Mike was forcing her? Did he hear her say to him, Your crank is too big, Mike! Maybe it's another lie. Maybe it's truth. What do I know about such things? Plenty. As to his size, I've been to the showers with him at the coalmine, so I have to say foot-long dog is no exaggeration.

Pappas cocks an eyebrow and asks me if I want to practice driving the car some more. I definitely love driving the car. For a twelve-year-old I'm pretty good at it. Pappas pushes the seat back and slides me onto his lap. As I steer the Caddy past the smelly stockyards, I feel Pappas breathing on my neck. His breath quick. My bottom is waiting for the telltale sign. But then out of nowhere comes this stupid car making a stupid turn in front of the Caddy. Oh oh! Pappas tosses me off his lap, jerks the Caddy to the left. The front of the other car swiping the passenger side right by me, throwing me onto Pappas who pushes me again. Wrestling the wheel he brings the car to a stop.

Dirty motherfucking sonofabitching asshole cocksuckers!

Pappas jumps out of the car and I am thinking: Oh boy, that other driver is in for it now! Pappas' fiery eyes boiling like when he wants to murder me or the mom or Grandma Inez. Pappas will beat that driver to a pulp, no doubt about it. I watch him marching to the other car. My heart racing so hard I can barely breathe. Sic him, sir, sic him. Show him who was the heavyweight champion of the whole goddamn Navy.

But that is not what happens. There are four dangerous looking Mexicans standing outside their car. The grill is ripped off, the headlights smashed, the hood cocked like a pup tent. Pappas is nice as pie. He asks if anyone is hurt. The Mexicans shaking their heads. They and Pappas look over the damage and talk to each other calmly, until the cops come. It takes at least an hour to measure things and write a report. I hear one cop say to the other, Mr. Sandoval is definitely at fault. I check the jugs in the trunk. None of them are broken.

Also thinking: What will the mom say when she sees her car? Oh, my poor lovely Caddy, look at it! Those damn Mexicans! None of them can drive for shit. She will cry real tears. She cries if she sees a dead dog in the street. She cries over every sort of suffering except chickens losing their heads. She cries if she remembers when her daddy left her standing on the porch and never came back. She cries when she gets migraine headaches. She cries if a black cat walks across her path. She cries if a mirror breaking gives her seven years of bad luck. She cries when she hears about an airplane crashing or a bad accident on the highway and a woman got her brains laid open and a baby was crushed and the stupid driver that hit them was drunk and didn't have a scratch on him. She cries over all kinds of stuff like that. She is always saying how there is so much pain and suffering in the world it makes her cry cry cry. She cries when she sings that song by Johnny Ray, *If your sweetheart sends a letter of goodbye...* She cries over sappy movies, for Christ sake! Things not even real! Grandma Inez does not cry much. She only cries when she does her hair frizzy like an African and I call her a witch. A tow truck comes and hauls the Mexicans and their car away. The Caddy is still drivable except passengers have to get in on the driver's side now.

Pappas stops at a liquor store and buys a pint of whisky. Takes a big slug and says, Motherfucker that was close. If I didn't have such quick reflexes we would both be dead for sure. I saved the day again. I saved your ass, Duffy. Have a drink we earned it. I take a mouthful to prove that I might be just a skinny kid but goddammit I am tough enough for hard liquor. Whisky going down burns like venom. Jesus Christ WOO, I say. Pappas throws his head back howling.

And he goes: Let's call your mother and tell her about the accident.

He finds a phone booth and calls and talks in a husky voice like he is dying, telling her a wild story about this big pileup on the highway and how he maneuvered the car and saved our lives, but now Duffy has a broken leg and Pappas has eternal injuries bleeding badly, needing an operation. Yeah, in the hospital in Brighton and yeah, Duffy is going to live, but the doctors say it is touch and go with me, baby. I just called to say goodbye. I called to say I love you. He coughs. He moans. He winks at me.

I hear the mom on the line weeping. Pappas grinning his baby grin while I snigger and giggle. Who's that laughing? the mom says loudly. That sounded like Duffy. And then me and Pappas are shouting HAH-HAH-HAH! And the mom is cussing and she says: You better not have hurt my Caddy or I will blow your goddamn brains out. So Pappas has to fess up what really happened. While he talks, I hear her saying, My poor car, waah waah, we worked so hard to buy it and make the payments.

Look at the green Caddy leaning on the curb and Jesus it surely looks like shit. Like someone took a sledgehammer to the right side of it. Like the thing belongs in HOFFY'S, the junkyard we pass whenever we drive to Frederick— HOFFY'S USED AUTO PARTS. Bing yr on Tools!

Pappas tells the mom insurance will fix the car. No problem. Don't cry no more. I will be home in a couple hours and you can see the damage yourself. Hey, just be thankful I am so good at the wheel or we would be dead right now and you would be making arrangements. I should have been a racecar driver. Man, I tell you I am really that good. Ask Duffy. He puts the phone to my ringing right ear and I have to switch the receiver to the left ear before I say: Yeah, he is really that good.

Not that I believe it. Actually, Pappas is a crummy driver. In the past four years he has already had two accidents. There was that time he almost died, spinning the Dodge on ice and rolling over in a ditch, breaking his shoulder and ribs and having internal bleeding. When he came home he was bandaged head to waist. He sat at the kitchen table smoking and drinking and telling the story again and again, until it ended up that he was thrown from the car and it rolled over on top of him and he had to lift it off with his good arm and slide out from under. It was a miracle. Two men could not have lifted a whole slab of car like that, he said. But he had the strength of ten men and pushed the car off his broken bones and waited for the ambulance and when those medics realized what he had done they called him Superman. This was the story told the night Carol Marie and I heard him crying. I still can't get over it. Amazed that his eyes, Pappas's eyes, could actually shed tears.

Pappas has scars all over his body. He has an especially nice crescent scar on the back of his head that the mom gave him last Christmas Eve when they got in an argument about the existence of Jesus Christ Our Savior. Pappas saying he died the day of his accident and there was no light nor Jesus after death. She begging to differ. Who brought you back to life if there's no Jesus? Pappas said he willed himself back to life. He had to live for the kids, he said. And for her. Living for me, she said, hmm, and who else? The subject went to the women in his life. Six months after she met him, she had to haul him out of a hotel where he was shacked up with some slut. Pappas said it was not his fault. He was drunk and the slut practically broke his door down. Nor was it his fault that the nurse who took care of him in the hospital fell in love with him. He couldn't help it if women threw themselves at him. That nurse threw herself at him. She had a thing about touching his cock, doing it like it was an accident.

And the mom said she did not know what the hell he was talking about. And Pappas said, Oh fuck, my memory is playing tricks on me. It's the booze. The mom turned the table over. Everything went flying. She went to the cupboard and pulled out dish after dish and threw them at Pappas who was cowering behind the overturned table. When she had smashed all the dishes she grabbed the glasses and started tossing them too. Broken glass ricocheting off the wall, until the cupboard was empty and she picked up an empty beer bottle and broke it over his head. Geez did Pappas bleed. Fuck me! he said, I got scars all over my poor body and now you do this to me on Christmas, Janice! I don't know what's got into me, she said, her whole body trembling. Oh my God, I could have killed you!

She rushed him to the hospital and it took a hundred stitches to close the wound on the back of his head. Or maybe it was fifty stitches. If you could look at the back of his head now, you would see a scar that resembles a frowny mouth. He will have a bald spot one of these days. That scar will always be there. A memento moron, the mom calls it. And she said when he got home, his head all wrapped in a white turban, Do not tread on me. I will keel you! Later, she painted the wall pink but anyone with eyes can still see the chips where the dishes and glasses hit that memorable Christmas Eve. A lot of Christmas Eves were like that. Not as drastic, maybe, but drastic enough.

~~

When we get to the farm, Pappas tells Grandpa Mike the story of the accident again. His heroic maneuvering. How he scared those Mexicans half to death when he got out of the car and charged after them. Yeah, it was lucky the cops arrived or he would have kicked all their beaner asses. Grandpa Mike is sitting on the bench on the patio. Looking like a fireplug smoking a Roi Tan cigar. The brim of his straw hat shielding his eyes from the sun. His thickly muscled hands don't seem to have any knuckles at all. In front of me, some forty feet away, the chickens live their lives in the killing yard, walking and squawking and pecking.

Until the day they get their heads chopped off. Beneath them their droppings pile up like chalk stubs. Near the killing yard are the same three chained-up chow chows I hate with all my heart. Give me a gun I will gladly shoot them boom boom boom, shoot them down like the dirty dogs they are.

 Just like I knew he would, Pappas goes to the barrels in the wine cellar and fills a couple jugs with dago red. He and Grandpa Mike drink a glass together and smoke cigars on the patio. I am already bored to death. So I go to the coop, grab some ground corn out of the trough and get some chickens to eat out of my hand. The three dogs stir their chains, walk up and down, their slit eyes regarding me as if I'm a morsel. The dragging chains move their food and water bowls around. Sit down. Lie down. Get up. Pace. What a nothing life it is! Because of Husky nearly ripping me to death, I try not to go near the dogs now. But sometimes I feed them when Grandpa Mike orders me to. Pour Purina Dog Chow into their bowls, but stay a step or two beyond the ends of their chains, pushing the bowls toward them with a stick. The one dog I like is Klondike, a stray Grandpa Mike has taken in. He gets to live in the shade at the side of the house. He is not a chow. He is some kind of black-muzzled, blond-haired, clumsy-footed mongrel. He waits for me, his tail, his whole rump wagging. So I leave the killing yard and go to grinning, barking Klondike jumping around, his happy pink tongue panting with joy. Grandpa Mike never pets him. He doesn't believe in making friends with dogs. They earn their keep guarding the farm. I pet him, love him up, let him lick me, rub his belly while his tail pounds the ground like he's having a seizure. Attention is all he wants. Someone to reassure him. He's a people dog, not a bit like the vicious chows in the yard that would like nothing better than to kill and eat me.

 When it's time for Pappas to go home he tells me to be good and help out. Then his voluptuous lips kiss me softly on the mouth. Pappas's wet breath smelling of wine and cigar. He pats my butt like the two of us are best pals. Then he hops into the wounded Caddy and shoots down the dirt road. Turns screeching onto the paved street that will take him to the highway. And that is the end of him for awhile, at least a week. Possibly more. Maybe a month. Which would be a nice reprieve, but only if the mom comes herself and brings my sisters and more jugs of hose water on weekends.

~~

 The days drag by and you might say the living is easy. Go to bed when the sun goes down. Get up when the sun rises and the cock crows. I sleep in the brass bed with Grandpa Mike. He always wants to hold me. But his itchy underwear itches my already itchy dry skin, so I am constantly trying to quietly scratch myself without disturbing him. If I disturb him he says, Cowboy slip still! When the grandpa finally falls asleep, I am able to get out of his arms and scratch scratch

scratch my crackily skin.

~~

Wake to a new morning and chores and eating cereal and toast and drinking a glass of milk still warm from the cow. Suck a raw egg and get a dime. Afterwards, I feed the chickens and gather eggs and take them to the wine cellar where it is always cool. Take the cracked eggs upstairs for lunch time. Then hoe the garden, check the plants for slugs and bugs. Hoe the acre of corn once a week. Which is a hot job under the hot Colorado sun. When the corn ripens Grandpa Mike will make money selling some of it to the grocer. He also sells him okra, which he can have all of the okra as far as I am concerned. And he sells tomatoes. Which I like a lot, eat them like apples. And of course Grandpa Mike sells eggs and sometimes a few chickens. He has a small pension from the coalmine now and a Social Security check. His farm is paid off and he doesn't need much to keep things running. His bad back slows him down but doesn't stop him.

On the way home from shopping at the Red & White, we go in the general store, where Grandpa Mike buys a jar of sheep lanolin for my dry skin. We walk past the tiny stone house where Punch used to live. He is dead now. Died last winter from getting drunk and falling asleep in the snow. Grandpa Mike looks at Punch's little house for a long time. He keeps clearing his throat, blinking his eyes. Turning away he shoots snot through one nostril, then the other. Whenever I try to clean out my nostrils that way, the snot smears my upper lip and I have to wipe it off with my sleeve. I envy Grandpa Mike's nose-clearing talent. Poor Punch, I say. Grandpa Mike nodding and saying, God is up, looking down.

I recall visiting with Punch, the men sitting on the steps smoking cigars, drinking wine, talking Spanish. Of which I catch phrases and words here and there, putting them together to basically savvy what they were saying. I know it is best never to let grownups savvy how much you savvy. They expect children to be innocent and dumb and forgetful. But hardly any kids are as innocent and dumb and forgetful as their mothers and fathers want them to be. At least not the kids I know.

Punch was once a contender for the welterweight title but lost out when another fighter detached something in Punch's eye and it went blind. Punch went to work as a tire buster in Longmont. He liked to talk about the old days when this fighter and that fighter went down for the count. Punch would make punching and blocking gestures, while he told his stories. I heard names like Baby Face McLarnin and Barney Ross and Hurricane Hank Armstrong. I would daydream about it, how I'd get in the ring and knock shit out of all my opponents. Be the lightweight version of Rocky Marciano. After telling a story, Punch would shrug as if to say that was then and this is now. The two men would get sad drunk and their eyes would shine and they would wipe their eyes and smile and clear out their noses and look towards the dark fields beyond Punch's place. The white dot of the moon rising. Crickets telling the temperature, coaxing the world to whirl faster. Time. Life. Hardly more than the wink of an eye, Punch often told me, *guino de ojos*.

Grandpa Mike and I walk by the bar, Mexican music floating out the doorway, along with laughter, the squeal of a woman, the barking of a dog told to shut up! Saturday evening coming on. Men and women celebrating the end of the week, letting off steam. Grandpa Mike says they pull knives and stab each other. He said the stupids get so drunk they go blind. He says some of them end up in jail. He says the men go home and beat their wives and their children and their dogs. He says that some of them fall asleep outside and if it is winter they freeze to death like Punch did. God is up, looking down, he says again and again.

And yet I have heard from Pappas that Grandpa Mike has done all the things he says are stupid. Pappas said that his father was once called the Prince of Laramer Street in Denver. He owned a candy store that was a front for an extortion racket. Grandpa Mike sold protection to businesses. In those days Pappas and his brother George got all the candy they wanted. And Christmas was a big deal. And so were birthdays. And it seemed like it would always be great to be alive. But then came the killing of his mother's lover and it changed their lives forever. Pappas said a man should never trust a woman. Soon as your back is turned she will cheat on you. You will be raising children that are not yours. It happens all the time.

I know that Pappas still wonders about Michele Renee. She looks like him, but the mom could have had an affair with a man that looked like Pappas. A Greek or an Italian. Why not? I saw him backhand her once for waving at a couple of guys who were waving at her driving by on East Colfax Avenue. Pappas telling her he would kill her if she ever cheated on him and he found out. He said: You just remember what my old man did. You just remember he got away with it. You just remember I am my father's son.

So Grandpa Mike and I walk back to the farm and the old man rubs my scaly back with sheep lanolin. And I rub lanolin over the rest of my body and it feels sooo good. The mom said she used to bathe me in cod liver oil when I was an infant and that was helpful, she said. And she said that I smelled fishy and nobody wanted to hold me. No way I blame them. That stuff is disgusting, whether you rub it in or drink it. Also thinking that now I probably smell sheepish. Also thinking about getting more jars of lanolin, so I won't run out. I start worrying that when the lanolin is gone the dry Colorado air will have me scratching myself to death again. Also thinking that I will go to the store and steal another jar. Build up a stash. Have tolerable skin, soft on my belly, soft on my ass and the insides of my thighs, soft like my baby sister. And I won't smell fishy. I won't smell like codfish. Sheep don't smell so bad. They smell like earth and hay and dusty cotton.

When Grandpa Mike and I go to bed at sundown the old man says, Come co-down co-down Crampa. Which means come cuddle me. I am okay with it. My skin doesn't itch. At least not very much.

~~

So the week is over, another Saturday, another Sunday. I rise with the sun and do chores. Eat breakfast. And then swing on the gate. Looking down the dirt road. Waiting for the mom to show. The weekend crawls by, the sun high, the sun low. I finally give up, shuffle back to the house. Grandpa Mike fries thick slices of bologna to eat with tomatoes, cucumbers, goat cheese on bread seared in olive oil. He gives me watered down wine as well.

Then the two of us sit on the patio while the old man smokes a cigar, me leaning against him as he pats my shoulder and tells me about the auction in Longmont, where we will look for a pony. I have gone to the auction in Longmont lots of times. The first few times I got excited and picked out pony after pony. But they all had something wrong with them according to Grandpa Mike, who would point out weaknesses I never saw. So now when he says auction, I hardly pay attention. None of the ponies will be good enough. We will sit in the bleachers and watch while others bid on the livestock. Grandpa Mike will not bid on anything. He means well, but I know he can't afford a pony. When the auction is over we might go to the REO, watch a movie starring Cantinflas, who runs around with his pants falling down. I won't understand much of what the Mexican actors are saying. But Cantinflas is funny-looking no matter if you can understand him or not. After the movie, we'll go to the bathhouse for a shower, wash our hair with bar soap, which always makes it extra dry and wispy. Later, on the patio, Grandpa Mike might be jolly for a while and talk about ponies and saddles he is going to buy for Cowboy Duffy. And he'll say, You savvy, Cowboy, you savvy? And I'll say, Yeah, I savvy, Grampa. Though more often than not I don't savvy much at all.

~~

A month crawls by. The jugs of hose water from Aurora are empty and we drink water from the shallow well. Boiling it first and drinking only enough to stay alive. At dinner there is always wine. This, according to Grandpa Mike, is good for your blood. Most nights it makes me a little bit tipsy. Relaxes me. Helps me sleep well. Every Sunday I hang on the gate swinging and staring at the dirt road wondering where the mom is. Two months pass and she doesn't show. Maybe she's dead. We don't have a phone, so there's no way to know. Someone would have to write us. I can't see that happening. I could be stuck here for the rest of my life. But then again, there's a positive side to the farm's sluggish boredom: Nick Pappas isn't a factor. I don't have to worry about him yelling and smacking, smacking and yelling. I don't have to think about entering the house on Ironton wondering what mood he's in and if I've done something to piss him off. Yeah, quit your whining and count your blessings, Duffy. Life could be way worse with Daddy Pappas around.

Auction again and going through the motions of judging ponies. Of course, none are good enough for the Cowboy. Sunrise. Sunset. Lots of them. And tons more monotony, arid days, baking heat. Every living thing hiding from the intense temperatures. The birds come out in the morning and sing to each other, but by noon they're hiding in the trees, their feathers ruffled, their tongues panting. Once or twice a week, the clouds build up over the Rockies. The wind shifts and by four or five in the afternoon the rain patters the dirt, warning us to go inside. Thunder and lightning, high winds and sheets of rain so dense at times we can't see the well, the killing yard or the hen house. Night falls. Rain stops. Cool air carries the sweet scent of clean trees and cleansed earth. A good night for sleeping.

~~

Finally comes late-August arriving in a whirl of fine dust coating the mended Caddy. The mom is there to take me home in time for school. Pappas and Michele Renee and Carol Marie are in the car too. The mom grabs me in her arms. Squeezes the breath out of me, calls me sweetheart. This is when I love her. Love her smiling like a movie star, looking like Lucille Ball, and calling me sweetheart, bestest boy in the world. She raving about how tall I'm getting and how the garden is a jungle and it is time to harvest the rest of the tomatoes before they go bad. Instantly plans are made for October, the handpicking and baskets filled with sweet corn. This is going to be a good autumn, she tells everyone in her prophetic voice. Her clairvoyant eyes seeing the future. She knows what she knows. Which is everything. Grandpa Mike gets a hug and a kiss. She calls him Pa. He, beaming in the glow of her love, calls her Jinny, Jinny, like he is singing a love ballad.

They talk about how much weight I've gained and how good the farm always is for me, the hard work and sunshine, and how she has been working herself to the bone. And how have you been, Pa? she asks him. And he says, Fin, Jinny, fin. She wants to know how his back is doing. His back always hurts from when he worked in the coalmine, bending over, straining his spine. Someday he might have an operation, but for now he keeps doing what he has to do. It is a party atmosphere around the farm now. Chickens strutting, some pawking nervously. Dogs barking. Dogs wagging their tails. All of the animals sensing that things have changed. The air full of sun and energy radiating from the red-haired woman commanding their attention.

Pappas sits alone on the patio. Pappas doesn't look so good. Pappas is pale, has lost weight, his mouth chalky from eating Tums for the tummy. He talks about almost dying from bleeding ulcers. Yes, he was on the operating table and his heart stopped and he was dead, but they shocked him back to life again. This was the second time he died, and the third time will be the charm. The doctors took out three-fourths of his stomach and told him to never drink again. Maybe he could have a beer now and then, but he must not touch hard liquor. A drop would burn a hole right through what is left of his stomach. You see why we have not been out to see you? says the mom. We have been worried sick taking care of this poor man. I nursed him back to health. The doctors give me credit he pulled through. They tell me I have the healing touch and should have been a doctor. So true. So true.

Michele Renee is toddling all over the killing yard, chasing chickens, reaching for rabbits in their cages. She goes to the chow chows and pulls their hair and they let her. They wag their tails and lick her. She tries to pat the new calf, but he runs away. She runs to Klondike. Crawls into the doghouse with him. Later, I find her sleeping there hugging the dog. I show the mom and she says, Oh, that is so cute! She wants a picture of it, but she's forgotten the camera.

I am ordered to kill two chickens. Off with their heads, out with their guts, rip out their feathers! Carol Marie and the mom harvest green beans and tomatoes from the garden. Dig up potatoes, clean them, dice them. The mom rolls chicken parts in egg and seasoned flour. Southern fried chicken frying in two skillets on the coal stove.

Carol Marie hustling to obey orders. Table pulled out. A leaf put in the middle to make it big enough. Folding chairs brought out of the closet. Cigar smoke, the aroma of wine and fried chicken, the sun coming through the window softening the linoleum. The whirlwind mom, her sweaty face and frizzled hair. She keeps giving commands like a general. Her voice filling my grateful ears. Her laughter coming in bursts, a whinny that always makes me smile, even though I have no idea what's so funny.

I watch Pappas move to the table like a weary old man. Seeing him like that makes me feel evil. Get a cane, get a walker, get a wheelchair, poor sappy Pappy. The family sits down. The mom recites: Bless us oh Lord for these thy gifts …. The milk gravy is poured over the mashed potatoes, the chicken devoured and look how happy Grandpa Mike is! On his jowly face is a wish that the family would move back in with him, live on the farm. Keep a lonely old man company. He will be good. He will not raise his voice. He will not be any trouble. But in a few hours the kitchen will be cleaned, dishes put away, table tucked against the wall and the family will be in the car heading home to Aurora. Grandpa Mike will be surrounded by breezes nudging the trees. He will light a cigar to keep him company. He will tell himself that this one day is over and in six more days the family will be back with jugs full of hose water. That is if they come back next weekend. And if not? Then the one after. Or the one after that. God is up, looking down is what really matters.

> *Follow your most intense obsessions mercilessly.*
>
> *- Kakfa*

Saturday. Autumn 1954. The mom calling and saying she's working overtime. The news angers Pappas. He hangs up the phone and mutters, She's up to something. Women are always up to something. He goes outside. Lights a cigarette. You watch him heading towards East Colfax, the Zanzibar. You're praying the mom gets home before he does.

No such luck. Pappas comes home red-faced drunk, in a bad mood, cussing about some argument, some motherfucker giving him shit. Pappas picked a fight and got thrown out, told to cool off, told to sober up. He points a finger at you and shouts, I'll cool off when I damn well want to cool off! And he says he doesn't know how any man can stand this cock-licking life. You can't trust nobody! Look at what time it is! When's she comin home, goddamn her!

It is a bad day all around because a short time later he comes into your room to inspect it (a random inspection, he calls it) and finds dirty underwear in your underwear drawer. Pappas exploding in anger, slaps you. Bellowing, Filthy little bastard! What the fuck you think you're doing? Booze breath torching your face, vapors of death flaming inside your nostrils.

You don't know why you put the dirty skivvies there. Maybe because they had been lying around on the floor and you were too lazy to walk down the hall to the hamper and drop them in. Or maybe you didn't want to add to the dirty clothes you washed and hung that day. Or maybe you were embarrassed about Pappas looking in the hamper, as he occasionally does, and saying, Look at this nicotine stain in your crotch. Don't you ever wipe your ass? You give all these excuses because you really have no clue why you threw dirty shorts in that drawer. But it doesn't matter because Pappas has decided it is because you're lazy and stupid. Filthy little useless bastard. A bedwetter. (Though you haven't wet the bed for months and months, not since you were eleven and a half.)

Whatever the case may be, you know the drill: you scream, you cry, you give enraged Pappas the reaction he wants, cowering, trembling, snot-tears-drool running off your chin. It is easy to lose control because the guy really scares the piss out of you. In fact, sometimes you actually lose control and wet your pants, though not this time, which maybe you should have because it would have emptied your bladder. An empty bladder might have saved you from what happened next.

Cringing, whimpering in the aftermath of the beating, you stand there wiping your eyes. Pappas looking you over. He's breathing heavily, like he's gone ten rounds in the ring, and he says, Quit that crying. Be a man. He holds your face in his hand and scrutinizes it, turning it right, turning it left, and he says in a not unkindly voice, Okay, take a bath, Duffy. It'll sooth these bruises. Let's get you cleaned up before your mother gets home.

You strip while Pappas pours the water. Climbing into the tub, you sit holding your knees against your chest and nodding your head while listening to him explaining that cleanliness is next to godliness and never hide dirty clothes. That's what hampers are for. Dirty clothes, like dirty hands and faces, need to be washed in order to get the germs off. Germs kill. Do you want germs to kill you? No, of course you don't. Put dirty clothes where they belong from now on, okay? That's the point I'm making. You're a stubborn little shit, you know? You always have to learn things the hard way. Why is that? Why don't you just be good? Strange boy, stranger than strange, strange as they come. Something only a mother could love, I swear to god. My dad would have killed me if I had done half the stupid things you do.

Pappas is being real nice now, talking soft in velvet tones, washing your back with a cloth. But then dumb Duffy ruins the precious dad and son moment by going germy again. Your honor, I can't help myself! It comes out of me before I even feel it. A tiny stream of yellow urine rising through the water between your legs. Pappas sees it, his face flushing, his head hitting the ceiling. His maddened hands grabbing the pisser by the neck. The scary man enraged and bellowing all over again. Hauling pee boy out of the tub and into the hallway. Hurling him toward Carol Marie's room, raising him like a shot-put and flinging him into the wall—kaboom! Stunned by the blow, you see stars and hardly know where you are. So out of it, you don't remember to slobber scream cry. But Michele Renee cries. She is scooting down the hall as fast as her little legs can go. You feel your pipestem ankle in Pappas's hand, feel yourself pulled off the bed, bumped to the floor, dragged toward your own bedroom. Where he tosses you inside and slams the door. You're wet and sniveling, shivering and listening to Pappas stomping up and down yelling, What the fuck! What the fuck is wrong with that goddamn kid! Jesus Christ, do you see what he makes me do? Fuck! Fuck! The fucks fading as petrifying Pappas goes outside. You hear the car's engine start. Tires squealing. Where's he going? You hope it's into a lake or off a cliff.

At that moment it occurs to you that Pappas is over his operation now, back to normal. As well as can be. Well as he was before the doctor cut half his ulcerous stomach out. You look under the bed. Michele Renee is there curled in a ball. She is chewing her fist. You crawl to her, hug her, tell her, We gotta get our asses outta this loony bin before he kills us, sis. Either that or we gotta kill him. Your mind going to the .30-30 in the closet, the German luger in the nightstand drawer, the .20 gauge, the WW II bayonet, the hunting knife, the WW I saber Grandpa Mike gave you to hang on the wall. Shoot or stab him in his sleep, shoot or stab him while he is grinding his teeth, shoot him between the eyes the way they shoot cattle. Stab him in the throat the way they stab pigs. A world without Pappas. What would it be? What would it mean? Reformatory, the Boy's Industrial School at Golden. Lock Duffy up. Throw away the key. No riding his bike. No TV. No books. No Wonder Bread sugar and butter sandwiches. No Cokes, no candy, no cigarettes. The guards would beat you, as would bigger boys. One way or another, Pappas would still be there. He'll always be inside you, Duffer.

~~

When the mom and Grandma Inez get home, they make dinner. The family sits at the table while the mom says Grace. Father, Son, and Holy Ghost. She glances at your busted face, shakes her head and says, Fighting again, Duffy? Is it those twins? You tell her they ganged up on you. What am I gonna do with you? she says. Shrug your shoulders and say, I'm a hopeless case. Smile, hoping she'll smile back. Eat your dinner, she says.

Jerking her thumb towards Pappas, Grandma Inez says, You should'a saw the spectable this one made of himself at Zanzibar today. They threw him out. He come back later, but they wouldn't let him in. He ain't welcome no more, Frankie said. Pappas raises his fork and tells her if she don't shut her mouth, I'll fuckin stab you with this, you old whore. She picks up her fork and right back in his face says, I'll stab you back, you sonofabitch! I want her out of this house! he says. No goddamn respect. What's there to respect? she asks him.

That's enough! shrieks the mom. Everybody shut the fuck up or I'm leaving now and never coming back. Goddamn almighty, I work my ass off all day. I'm tired. Can't you two see how tired I am? Jesus Christ, I come home hoping for a little peace and quiet and you two have to start your bullshit again. I'm sick of it! Her eyes are blazing like little green flames. She has her own fork in her hand, threatening them with it. Push me, she says. I dare you to push me.

Silence falls over the table. Grandma Inez and Pappas are looking down at their plates. Pappas looks like he has a hangover. Grandma Inez looks older than old.

Your mouth is sore, your teeth and nose ache, your whole body is throbbing. You eat your dinner quick as you can and ask to be excused. Out of my sight, says the mom. She says it matter-of-factly, she says it quietly. You hurry to your room, close the door, take the .30-30 from the closet, load it, promise to God that if they start forking each other, you'll rush out there and shoot him. Call it defending the mom and the grandma from being murdered. You will kill him, reform school or no reform school, Golden or no Golden, you will kill him, kill him. Dream of his death. Imagine it.

~~

The next day after breakfast you bundle your sister, sit her on the crossbar of your bike and ride her around for a while, following your nose west on Colfax Avenue, all the way to Denver to the natural history museum. You walk her around inside the building looking at monster bones and great horns and teeth that could kill you both in less than one second.

Together you spend the afternoon in the park strolling, watching ducks and swans swimming in the pond, people sunning themselves, chatting, laughing, playing chess and checkers. All the usual normal nice stuff like you've seen on TV. *The Life of Riley, Ozzie and Harriet, I Love Lucy, Make Room for Daddy.*

Later, after hot dogs and Cokes, Michele Renee falls asleep on the grass. You lie beside her. Peaceful is peace.

When you wake, the sun is nearing the horizon. Autumn chill in the air, leaves whirling, crab-crawling across the cement walks. You put Michele Renee on the bike, pedal furiously. Get home in time for dinner. No one says, Where you been? Home free. Better to be lucky than good. Better to be the little shit hiding his hatred, hiding his thirst for revenge behind a smile of innocence. Duffy, you ain't been innocent since you were two. Or at least since you were three.

~~

Monday, after the parents leave for work, you don't go to school. Grabbing an extra pair of jeans, you tie knots at the bottom of each leg. Go to the kitchen and fill them with canned goods from the pantry: two cans of pork and beans, spam, fruit cocktail, bread wrapped in waxed paper. Fill your canteen with water. Hoisting the bulging legs around your neck like a backpack, you grab your BB gun and two-bladed jackknife (one blade a can opener) and head out the back door, down the alley. Going south, then east, you walk for miles, until you come to the railroad tracks at the edge of the prairie.

The plan: Hobo it. Catch a freight. Ride a boxcar to Kansas, ride it forever. You wait just minutes before a train flies by too fast to jump on. So you drop that idea and stroll east down a dirt road, a farming area, where wheat fields are bare of everything but stubble. You find an anthill and start shooting ants, blasting the bastards with BBs. After you've killed and crippled a bunch of them you move on. No idea where you're going.

Another mile brings you to some grain silos. There is an office attached to one of the silos. No one there. The door not locked, so you go inside and follow a hall that leads to a garage. Coming out of its side is a chute cocked upwards looking like the spout of a teapot. Beneath it is a big Chevy truck filled to the brim with grain. You climb inside the cab, root around, find a key in the ashtray and start the motor. Jumping out, you open the double doors. Driving to Kansas becomes the new plan. Get a job on a farm that's what you'll do.

You try different gears, but the engine keeps stalling. Finally, you find compound low and the truck slugs forward, going up an incline and out to the dirt road, where you floor the pedal and the RPMs climb to dangerous levels. Every time you shift to another gear, the truck stalls. Start it again, keep going, until at last the engine gives up, refusing to start no matter how loud you cuss and beat the dashboard with your fist. The battery dies too and that is the end of the truck and driving to wherever you're going.

Keeping up the pace, you enter a wide, grassy area. There is a mansion-type house on a hill, big trees beside the road and a white wooden fence ranch style. On the grassy plain next to a small hanger is a plane, a piper cub. You walk across the runway, across stiff ruts pounded to tufts by the little plane's wheels. You climb on the wing, look at the instruments and have the notion that if you can get it started you'll be able to figure out how to fly it. Climbing into the cockpit you mess with the switches and though a red light comes on, the motor doesn't turn over. For a while you're flying, shooting Zeros out of the sky. Winning the Navy Cross. The rest of your life is filled with warrior glory.

~~

When you arrive in Watkins it is past noon, few people around. A dog lying in the dust of a dirt road. You bend down and pat him. He thumps his tail. There is a café, four men inside, all of them looking like farmers chatting, drinking their coffee. A drugstore is next door. Then a barbershop and a Mobil gas station. On your walk through town, you see an ad for a worker to help build fences. SEE HORACE the sign says and there is an arrow pointing up a dirt road. On both sides of the road the land is open. There is an occasional cottonwood or oak. Lots of sagebrush. The air is so dry it burns your nose and your throat.

After crossing several roads and signs with painted arrows and the name HORACE, you come to a driveway, a weary house, a machine shed, a small barn, a red tractor and a gray tractor, a couple of dogs. There is a Dodge pickup parked near the porch. The dogs start barking. You call to them. Here, boy! Good boy! One of the dogs holds back, while the other keeps coming. It is small, about as big as a lunch box, and has an annoying high-pitched yip, ugly teeth crooked and full of tarter. You figure the dog is a mix of toy poodle and wiener dog. Holding still, you talk nice and let the dog approach. It's a sneaky one, coming in close like it just wants a sniff and then quick as a snake nipping your ankle.

Yowch, you little fucker! You kick at it.

The dog grins, running in circles, tail wagging, ears flapping, mouth open saying, See that? See what I did? Did you see it? Did you see it? The other dog, a black retriever, sitting with his rump lazily bent sideways, its tongue hanging out the side of its mouth, a calm, friendly look on its face. When you come cautiously close, the retriever lies down, rolls over, offering its belly. You see little balls and a sheathed prick. The other dog has circled behind and sees its chance at an ankle again and dives for it. But with a quick jerk of your heel you clip its pointy chin. The dog yelping, dashing for the porch, sliding through a hole in the slats and vanishing.

Little coward.

Climbing the steps, you knock on the door. No one answers. You call out, Anybody home? Nope. You walk around noting what a poor farm it is, buildings leaning with age, desperate for paint, the machinery rusty, the tractors (one a Ford, the other a McCormack Farmall) leaking oil. The Dodge pickup in the yard has bald tires, cords showing through like oblong targets, looking like bull's eyes.

In the barn you find stacks of rolled barbed wire sitting on pallets. On the backside of the barn is a fenced area. A water tub inside. Some anemic hay in a feed trough, four beefers standing in the sun, swishing flies with their tails. All the cows look pregnant.

There is a path leading into some woods. Following the path you come out on the other side at the edge of a pond. On the near side, looking at you is a tall, thin gawk of a man. He is fishing, his stiff pole stretching ten feet over the brown water. He's wearing a baseball cap that says JOHN DEERE. Hair falls from the rim of the cap, threadlike spears of it touching his shoulders. Beside him is a small perch lying on a piece of cardboard. The fish hardly more than a mouthful. The man's eyes slide over you up and down.

Off to see the wizard? he asks.

Huh?

Where you think you're going?

You hesitate, thinking maybe you ought to get out of there. You definitely don't like the way the man is looking at you.

I'm Mr. Horace, says Mr. Horace.

You want a worker to make fence, Mr. Horace?

Mr. Horace squinting hard, looking you over. You'll never make it, sonny. Not the way you goin. What you got in them pants? He points to the jeans you're still carrying around your shoulders.

Stuff.

What stuff?

Food.

Lessee.

You show him. Also thinking you really should be on your way, Duffy.

Mr. Horace pulls in his line, wraps it around the pole. He has dirty hands, dirty fingernails, most of them chewed to the quick. A waft of old sweat and dirty socks breezes by you. He needs to wash. He needs a shave.

Grab that fish. Come on! he says, heading toward the path. You poke the fish's pale belly. Pick it up and follow Mr. Horace.

Weaving through the trees, you end up back at the house and go inside. A man sits at the kitchen table. Mr. Horace cackles and says, This kid wants to hang fence, Strick! A coffeepot sits on the stove. Dishes in the sink. Boxes of cereal and canned goods strewn over the counter. The man named Strick eyes your rifle. The man has funny eyes. One blurry gray, rimmed in watery red. The other like an angry sapphire stuck in his head. His nose pocked and laced with broken veins. He has chapped lips he keeps licking.

What kind? he asks.

It's a air rifle, you tell him. Don't he know a air rifle from a real rifle? Maybe the one bright eye doesn't see any better than the cloudy one.

I know what it is, he says. What's the maker?

Red Ryder, you say.

He nods his head. It'll do, he says.

Mr. Horace announces, Spam and beans, Strick! I tole you I would catch some lunch! Spam and beans! he sings. Spam and beans. Never mind that fish, kid. Put him in the fridge. Open them pants. Let me at all of it, kid. Mr. Horace stabs a can opener into one of the cans, works it around the edge. Where you goin, kid? he says.

You put the perch in the fridge, shrug your shoulders. Once more you have a feeling you should trust your instincts and vamoose.

C'mon, kid, join us for lunch. My treat! What's your name, kid?

Duffy.

I'll call you Duff. Siddown, Duff. Have a cigarette, Duff. Give the kid a cigarette, Strick.

Strick pulls a pack of Chesterfield's from his pocket and shakes one up. You take it. Strick lights it.

Nothin like a smoke before lunch, says Mr. Horace. Unless it's a better smoke after. Goddamn, smell them beans! He's sniffing the opened can so close that some juice wets the tip of his nose. He wipes it off and sucks his finger. Put the pan on the fire, Strick! he orders.

Strick rubs his stomach round and round, burps once, twice. They are hard, gut-wrenching burps, like the ones Pappas makes after he eats or when he's drinking beer. Strick goes to a cupboard and pulls out a bottle of something white, drinks a lot of it. He puts a pot on the stove. Into the pot go the beans and chopped up Spam.

I'm glad you come along, says Mr. Horace. You've saved a starving Harvard man. Harvard, Nebraska, haw, haw. I was raised there and when people ask me where I went to school, I tell them I graduated from Harvard! Mr. Horace pulls a wad of hanging hair into his mouth, muffling a laugh. Then he says, Duff's gonna farm for us, Strick. Gonna live with us as our hired hand. So where you from, Duff? You ain't from Watkins.

Aurora, you tell him.

Aurora. He's from Aurora, Strick. A suburban boy. Let's see now, hmm. Ironton Street, corner past East Colfax on the north side, the knee-high picket fence with the cross carved on the first picket down low—a hobo sign. Gert Nelson and some sort of stew or soup for yard work. She's got bladder arms. Arms like old womans do. You know Gertrude Nelson?

Yeah. I know everybody just about. I live down aways from her. Is a cross always a hobo sign?

Sometimes. Sometimes not. You got to watch those crosses, kid. Some of them mean to take you in and save your soul. Got to be careful of that. Mr. Horace squints his eyes and thinks awhile. Nope, all skinflints, them Christians. Fuck em. Can't get nuthin off em. You ever have luck with Christians, Strick?

Strick shakes his head. He's staring at the beans and Spam, stirring them with a spatula.

Yowza, that do smell good, says Mr. Horace. So Duff, show me your wee-wee. Let's see what you got.

Hunh? You are now sincerely scared.

C'mon, I'll show you mine if you show me yours.

Hunh?

Your wee-wee, Duff, pull it out. I want to see.

You look at Strick, who has his good eye fixed on the beans and Spam.

Now, kid. Before lunch is ready. Hurry up! C'mon!

Setting the rifle against the wall, you unbutton your pants and show Mr. Horace. If you play along, maybe he won't hurt you.

It'll do, he says. Grub up!

The beans and Spam are put on plates and handed around. You're given a plastic fork. You eat keeping your eyes on Mr. Horace. He keeps talking with his mouth full, telling you about traveling from one end of the country to the other and how there's nothing like being free in a free country. But now he's settled down on this, his uncle's farm. His uncle dead. Over yonder under the live oak. Yes, and Mr. Horace is here to farm. To raise cows. They don't take much raising. You just keep them settled. Turn them out and let them eat. He is going to make fence all around the woods and the pond and turn the cows in there and in a few years there be beefers all over the place. He talks lots of other things too, but much of it you can't make out because he is mumbling, juice-rimmed lips and mouth open, showing chewed food, chewing and talking. Pappas would hate him. Close your mouth when you eat, you dumb bastard, he would tell him.

After the Spam and beans are gone, Mr. Horace opens the can of fruit cocktail, eats some and hands the can to Strick who burps and passes the can to you. You wave him away.

Mr. Horace takes the can, tips it, slips all the fruit into his mouth.

When he's done, he says, Sweet as pussy. You like pussy? You got a girl? You get in her snatch?

Your ears are instantly hot. You shake your head.

Good-looking stud like you, that's a shame. You gotta get started early. Spring don't last long, you know. Before you know it, it's winter and your pecker won't function. That's old age for yuh.

Cigarettes are passed around and lit. You smoke and listen to Mr. Horace babble about birds. I'm a birdwatcher from way back, he says. I know birds from San Diego to Portland, Maine. I know all them Colorado birds. You look like a swallow from Capistrano, kid. Strick here looks like a grouse. I'm a crow. Mr. Horace opens his mouth and clucks. That be the sound of the crow, he says. I get them to answer me. I cluck and cluck and they cluck back. Frankly, if I do say so myself, my cluck is prettier than theirs. Ain't it so, Strick? Aw, what would a grouse know? Brewer's blackbirds are all over the reeds at the pond. I seen a million of em, I ain't lyin. I seen a giant blue heron over there. I bet you didn't even know there was such a thing, did you, kid? What can a pecker like you know? All you know is your wee wee, that's all you know. Reminds me of a Louisiana water thrush. Sure, you'll say they don't come up this far, but I'm a lyin sack of shit if I didn't see one right there at the pond sitting on a cattail. I got an eye for a bird like nobody's business. Jesus, I can spot a bird a mile off and tell you what it is. The Canada jay, the northern raven, the southern pine siskin—they're rare but I seen em. I got a thing for water birds. That's my thing. But I hate cats. I'll kill a cat soon as look at it. They're making all the pretty birds extinct, you know. Goddamn ordinary fuckin house cats. I saw one jump a ring-necked pheasant and kill it and walk away, not even take a bite. Just killers is cats. We ate that goddamn ring-neck ourselves, didn't we, Strick? Fried him and ate him down to the bones. We sure was hungry that day. It was gettin cold and we needed sustenance. A feller's got to have sustenance or he dies. There's all kinds of sustenance, not just food and water. There's the sustenance of love. Don't ever forget it. Without love, what are we? Nuthin but animals blindly living, following our instincts, not knowing nothin, not having a soul or nothin, that's what we are without love. You listening to me?

You nod. The guy is weird and a little scary. But interesting.

Good. I'm older and wiser and I seen life. Now, how about you take them dishes and things and wash them before that crud hardens? That's a good boy.

How much you paying? you ask him.

What, for washing dishes?

That and for making fence.

Mr. Horace strokes his stubble shrewdly. What's a boy like you worth? How about twenty cent an hour? In a ten hour day you'd have two bucks.

You do as you're told, washing the dishes, the plastic forks, cleaning things up, the counter and stove. You hear Mr. Horace's voice coming from the living room where both men have gone. First you hear them whispering. Then Mr. Horace's voice gets louder. At one point he shrieks, Goddamn you, Strick! Don't you fuckin dare! That's my baby, that's mine!

Strick's voice comes back so soft that what he's saying melts before you can make it out. The next thing you know, Mr. Horace is there telling you to run. Strick's after us! he says. C'mon!

You sprint behind Mr. Horace out the door, through the woods. Find a place to hide on the other side of the pond.

Mr. Horace is giggling. Breathing hard as he says, Gotta love the crazy bastard. He do get funny that way. He puts his hand on your neck, squeezes it and says, Tell you what, honey, you let me have a taste and then we'll go back and tell Strick we forgive him, okay? Don't play the chaste little bitch, he says. He kisses you on the top of the head, fondles you, starts unbuttoning your pants. You flash on Pappas poking you from behind. Then there is a picture of the mom and Pappas. She on his lap facing him in the chair, her two hands wrapped around him, her hips sliding up and down. You peeking round the corner to watch and learn. Getting slapped and called a sneaky bastard! Running in panic to your room.

You let the man take your pants down. Figuring why not? But just when it seems something will happen, you hear the BB-gun fire. Mr. Horace jumps back, grabbing his ear and yelling, Goddammit! Ouch! Sonofabitch! Fuck!

Strick is standing there with the gun pointed at Mr. Horace. He waves the barrel, indicating you should pull up your pants.

Why you so shitty to me, Strick? says Mr. Horace. I treat you like a goddamn king and you treat me like shit. I'm a Harvard man, goddammit! Every fuckin time I pull a fraternity prank, you have'ta spoil it. You ugly bastard, you never—

Strick shoots Horace in the foot with another BB. Horace jumps around shaking his foot, cramming his cap into his mouth, stroking it and whimpering.

You buckle your belt.

As he strokes the rifle Strick says, One of these what put my eye out when I was a boy your age. He points to his gray eye. It happens more'n you might think.

The stricken eye, so cloudy. the other bloodshot sapphire blue.

Long time ago playin with my pals. We liked it real. We'd shoot hell out of each other. You go on now, kid. This ain't no place for you.

Strick gives you the gun. He doesn't have to ask you twice. The little dog yapping crazy down the driveway starts chasing you. Then stops at the road and brags to his buddy how he run you off.

You turn the wrong way and can't remember how to get back to Watkins. You are jogging along strange roads. You want to go home. You want to see the mom making dinner, glancing at you, smiling, stopping to brush her palm over your hair. How could you ever run away from the mom? You love her!

Where two gravel roads form a cross, trees and bushes look small in the distance, small and mysterious, like painted silhouettes against a blue backdrop. In front of it all stands the stick figure of a man. Mr. Horace? Maybe a scarecrow? Hello! Is this the real right way I'm going? Where's Watkins? Where's Aurora?

~~

It is late afternoon: you have circled back and Watkins finally comes into view. But before you get to town, a Highway Patrol rolls up. The cop saying, What you doing out here by your lonesome? You hunting?

Worn out and immensely relieved, you don't even try to lie. I'm from Aurora. I'm running away from home.

Empty that rifle and get in, he says. He's smiling. He's shaking his head like someone saying, You gotta be kidding me.

In thirty minutes the car pulls up at the Aurora police station and the runaway is hustled inside. By then the sun has sunk. While the cops wait for the mom to come, they decide to teach you a lesson. They lock you in a cell, one of them saying, You keep heading down the road you on, this here where you end up, little mister shithead. Either that or you dead. You want to reply fuck you, but don't dare. The cop looks like he wants an excuse to turn you inside out and eat your liver.

So the mom shows and she thanks the cops with tears in her eyes. On the way home she tells a sad tale about all the crying she has done, and you're coldly thinking yeah yeah, so what? And she says, Why would you run away? Don't you know you can't run away from your troubles? You have to stay and face them. You'll never be worth anything if you run away every time something makes you mad or sad or whatever excuse you have. That's what cowards do. They run. But you can't run away from yourself. You hear me, son?

Then she says, Why would you do this to me? Do you realize how much you have wounded me? Do you care that you're breaking my heart? You're killing me. You want to do that to the mom, Duffer? You want to kill me?

No, not at all. Course not.

Well, that's what you're doing. You're killing me. My heart can't stand much more of this. Where have I gone wrong with you? Don't you love me? Don't you love the mom?

You look at her, watch her mouth flapping, see how she looks like Lucille Ball more than ever. Red hair and lips full of creamy lipstick smeared on for the cops. You wanna give me a nervous breakdown? she asks. Is that what you're after? You wanna send me to the hospital? Choking on tears she drives in silence for a while sniffing, clearing her throat, her pretty lips glistening and trembling. In a wretched voice moaning: God oh God I'm so depressed I should just take the gun and shoot myself.

Which story you have heard plenty of times.

But the tears trickling down her cheek make you feel bad. You tell her you love her, and you add: But goddamn, I hate Daddy. Hate Daddy? she says like it's a big surprise. But why hate Daddy? So you wonder if you should unload it all. But the look on her face is saying don't hurt the suffering mother. Don't tell her nasty truths about her husband and Carol Marie and the things he does to you, the black eyes, the bruises. So you say, I hate him because he hates me. Always yelling and cussing at me for something. She says, No, you're wrong. He loves you. He just wants you to grow up to be a man. She says it like a recording. Like words written inside her head. Push a button and the words come out: be-a-man stuff. Fuck him, you want to say, but of course you don't. I will talk to him, she says. I will tell him not to be so hard on you. At that moment you panic: No! Please don't tell him what I said. You'll just get me in more trouble. You're waiting for her to push a bit, make you confess, tell her the truth. But she doesn't. She nods, she says, Okay, I won't say a word if you don't want me to.

But that turns out to be a lie, because a few days later when you're alone with Pappas he says, I told you to burn that trash in the incinerator. The fucking shit is falling out all over the alley. What the fuck do I have to do to get through to you? Don't know, sir, you answer. Pappas says, You drive me crazy. And he says, You see how you make me mad? Your mother told me what you said about me. Look, I don't give a shit if you hate me, but you are going to do what I tell you! You might hate me, but you are going to respect me. I would rather have your respect than your love. Pappas glares, eyes hot as Hades. He wishes you didn't exist, that he didn't have to share the house with another member of the male species. Whose fuckin fault is it that you make me do what I do? he says. It's not my fault. He taps your chest hard, his finger feeling like a wooden dowel. You bring it on yourself. You make me do the things I do to you. And that is how he leaves it. And you're thinking: Never trust the mom to keep her goddamn mouth shut, you fucking fool Duffer!

~~

Comes a day pedaling the streets towards Bubble Eye's house, you cut a corner of a lawn and some cuckoo shoots out of the house, stops you, slaps your face. Which is way worse as far as you're concerned than getting thrown into a wall by Pappas. This goddamn guy looks weird, looks wild! Wild as rabies, wild as Mr. Horace, weird as Strick. Most definitely nutso. He's yelling, saying, I told you not to ride your bike across my lawn! You ever do it again I will take your bike away! (Surprising things happen and you can hardly believe them!) You run the bike off the lawn. Stop on the street. Look back. Then it really hits you that this total stranger, this fairy-face half-bald motherfucker has really slapped you! You yell at him, you say, You'll be goddamn sorry you ever touched me! Sonofabitch! The man chases you, can't catch you as you ride off feeling murder in your heart. Skinny little shit like you gets no respect, Duffy.

At home you go in the parents' bedroom, grab the German Luger from Pappas' nightstand. Carol Marie comes in and says, What do you think you're doing? You tell her you're going to shoot a motherfucker who slapped you for no reason. Give me that goddamn gun, she commands. You're not shooting anyone. She yanks the gun away. You call her a fuckface twat, tell her that one of these days you'll kill her. Yeah, yeah, she says. Get lost, little man.

You take off for Bubble Eye's house again. Bubble Eye has eyes that stick out like Bosser marbles, blue bead irises, deep black pupils. It's some medical condition. But he's not sickly. Big and bad is Bubble Eye. His real name is Chuck. He robs houses. He's been in jail and done time in Golden. When you stole cartons of cigarettes off a truck parked outside Republic Drug, Bubble Eye bought them. When you stole a BB gun from Republic by stuffing it down your pant leg and limping out of the store like a poor cripple boy, Bubble Eye called you mucho bandito and bought the gun for two dollars. Almost anything you steal, Bubble Eye will buy. He once told you: If you let your hair grow you might look sexy, instead of looking like a boy trying to look like a Marine. But that is exactly what you want to look like. Like a badass Marine, like your Uncle Dean.

Picture Bubble Eye in his basement bedroom sleeping, his bulging eyelids fluttering because he's having a wet dream. Rap on the window over his bed. Rap and rap and wake him. When Bubble Eye opens the window, you crawl in, do a quick flip, stick it like a gymnast. The place smells of mildewed urine and farty Bubble Eye. On the stand beside his bed is a jar of Vaseline. The lid off. See where he dipped his fingers in and pulled out a glob of jelly. Why you wake me, man? he asks. I was putting the wood to Judy Forman, man. You got shitty timing, Duffy. What you want? You tell him about that weird motherfucker slapping you for riding your bike across his stupid lawn. Bubble Eye says, How big is he? Tall but a four-eyed, bald-domed broomstick, you answer. Nothing to be scared of. Together we can take him easy, doublebank him. Bubble Eye says, Go get Tony, he will help you take him down. No, I want to be your partner, Chuck. I want to go with you when you rob houses. I want to learn the trade. I am willing to not get paid for a while if you teach me. Bubble Eye thinks about it, looks you up and down like he's sizing up tail. You can see the wheels whirling. Next time I go, maybe I take you, we'll see, he says. And you say, I want to rip off the guy what slapped me. I will case him and then tell you when nobody's home. How does that sound? Bubble Eye is agreeable.

He wants to see where the slapper lives. Hop into Bubble Eye's blue convertible '48 Mercury V-8 flathead boogie woogie. The scene of the crime is nothing special. A corner house, the upper half white, the lower half maroon. A row of yellow marigolds in a planter box beneath the front window. Not even much of a lawn to speak of. Definitely not worth getting so worked up about. Just then the guy comes out. Grabs the hose. Turns the faucet on, waters the flowers. He spots you sitting across the street staring at him. He hesitates. He drops the hose, turns the water off, hurries into the house. You say to Bubble Eye, I told you he's a fucking punk. How about we go kick his ass! Bubble Eye is agreeable, Yeah, he looks easy. C'mon.

Bubble Eye is six feet tall. Broad shoulders. If anything, he will scare this guy plenty. Then you will cut the corner of the lawn and not get slapped for it. Knock on his door. And knock. And knock hard as a cop before the guy finally peeks out and says, Please you are going to wake the baby. She is sleeping. Fuck the baby, says Bubble Eye. Did you slap my friend? Please, pleads the guy, the baby is sleeping. Step out here a minute, man. We got business. The baby is sleeping, the guy keeps repeating. See he is really scared. He wishes he had not slapped the Duffer. In his meanest voice, Bubble Eye tells him he better keep his goddamn hands to himself. The guy whines about the baby driving him crazy. Almost out of my mind, he says. I get no sleep! I lost my job. My wife works nights and needs her sleep during the day. The baby cries all the time. I am not a man who goes around slapping little boys, but something snapped. All I can say is I'm sorry, really sorry. Really I am, honey.

Did he say Honey?

Anger evaporating, you are top dog and this skinny slapper is so far down he's groveling. In a milder tone Bubble Eye says, Well, it better not happen again. And the guy nods. Yes sir, he says. He looks like he might cry. He takes off his glasses, rubs his eyes and nods several times, nods like a Jew praying to that stupid wall they pray to. The guy is pitiful. So you say, Yeah, I got a little sister who cries her fucking head off all the time. I know how that shit can make you mental. So what the hell, you and Bubble Eye go away, the door clicking gratefully. Looking back, you see Nervous Breakdown peeking through the venetian blinds. Sad sucker, you wouldn't want to be him.

In the car you ask Bubble Eye to let you drive. He says, Sure, if you do me a favor. What favor? I'll show you later. And he adds, When my little brother was a baby he was like that too, always fuckin bawlin. He drove the whole family whack-a-doo. I ain't never havin kids, Duffy. If people only knew what they was doin they would never have any. And his look says the mom should not have had you either. But you get to drive the car, so you don't care what Bubble Eye thinks about the mom having a kid named Duffy. Who is very good at driving cars now. Last weekend he drove Pappas all the way from Frederick to Aurora because the fucker was so shitfaced from Grandpa Mike's wine he passed out on the back seat. You took the dirt roads home and did fine, even though you could barely reach the pedals or peep over the wheel.

Bubble Eye hands you the keys. You start the car, rev the engine, slam the lever into low, pop the clutch and away you go. It's a gravel road and the backend of the car sprays rocks all over like buckshot. The car shifting side-to-side as you pull a hard right round the corner, the back wheels spinning, the whole car sliding sideways making a complete circle, ending up heading the same way it was going in the first place. Ripping along the road, while Bubble Eye is shouting. Stop! You crazy fucker, you crazy fucker! He pulls the key out of the ignition and the car chugs to a stop. Bubble Eye keeps shouting, saying Get outta the car! Get outta the car! And Duffy is going, But what's wrong, man? Hey, man, what's wrong? I had the whole thing under control. I meant to donut, man. Shit was fun, don't you know?

Look where Bubble Eye is sitting and see that he has peed his pants. Think about his room in the basement smelling like urine. Think about this guy having no control of his fucking bladder and he is eighteen and maybe he still wets the bed! So you're better than he is. The mom and Pappas should have him to deal with. Put diapers on him. Spank him with the belt that gives welts. Punch his stupid face. Throw him into walls. You cross your heart and promise to God to drive nicely. After a minute he settles down. All right but go slow, he tells you.

You drive like an old nana to his house, go inside, down to the basement, where he hurries into the bathroom. The water running a long time as he washes himself. You kick back, take one of the cigarettes from the end table. When we gonna burgle, Chuck? I'm ready to learn the ropes, the secrets of first-class thievery, hah-hah. Him answering: You're too fuckin whack-a-doo, man! You'll get me killed!

When he comes out of the bathroom, he has a robe on. He flops on the bed. You see inner thigh and some penis. Propping a pillow behind his head, he lights a cigarette, starts talking about this place he knows in Derby where nobody is home all day. The place surrounded by trees. It would be easy to get in and out of there without being spotted, easy as pie.

Does he know what you see? Try not to look at it. He's blabbing while you keep grabbing peeks. His thing is big, way bigger than yours. Also thinking he must have been stroking it in the bathroom, it just don't hang natural. Remember the gangbox picture that Pappas has, the naked muscleman with his half hard boner? You finish the cigarette, stab it out in the ashtray. I have to go. Where you going? I'm going home. Hey, don't go yet. You said you'd do me a favor if I let you drive. He looks at the jar of Vaseline. Come on, help a guy out, it won't hurt nothing. Come on what? He grabs your wrist, dips Vaseline from the jar and smears your palm with it. Leads your greasy hand to his dick. Just scratch it, he whispers. All the cons in Golden help each other out like this. No big deal. It doesn't mean you're queer. His thing is flushed and curvy now. It seems to be looking into his belly button. Scratch it harder, he whispers. He clamps your hand around it. You're feeling excited. Bubble Eye is smiling and whispering faster-faster squeeze hard oh, oh. And then he spurts all over his own bare belly. The whole thing from first stroke to orgasm lasting about ten seconds. Twelve at the most. He lies back smiling. His eyes closed, eyelashes fluttering.

~~

Duffy and Billy and Bruce and Craig, Tony and Jack go to the cliffs with BB guns and play war. You've told them what Strick told you. How he played war and lost an eye when he was a little kid. Let's make it dangerous, make it real. Telling them the story makes everyone want to play war that way. Choose up sides. Duffy and Tony and Craig against the twins and Jack. One team runs away while the second team counts to a hundred. The hunt is on. It is good to be the team that hides because you can set ambushes. Using BB guns proves way better than pointing empty cap guns and saying, Bang, bang, you're dead. And the dead guy saying, No I'm not! With a BB there is no doubt. You get hit numerous times. It hurts almost as bad as a bee sting, but it doesn't kill you for real. Of course, if you got hit in the eye like old Strick, you would probably be blinded too. No one gets hit in the eye. Though everyone gets hit somewhere. Thrilling to pour BB after BB into your enemies and hear them cuss and howl. And you say, Got you, motherfucker! Hah!

Some of the guys own .22s and talk about using them. But when it comes time to actually do it, only Tony and Jack go for it. They hide behind boulders and shoot at each other until they run out of bullets. It's quite a show. It happens at the Cliffs, where a branch of Sand Creek runs below. Not the same Sand Creek of the massacre of Cheyenne women and children, which you know about because you're into biographies of the Plains Indians, the noble Black Kettle who tried to make peace but ended up dying heroically in battle, and the fearless Roman Nose who caught a flying arrow in his bare hand, strung it in his bow and killed a buffalo. If you could change your white skin for Cheyenne skin you would do it in a heartbeat and talk Indian with Grandma Inez. *Boozhoo ahnee, Giche Manidoo.*

There are numerous hiding places at Sand Creek, fallen trees, bunches of willows, ditches and ravines, the banks of the creek itself, the caves that guys dug into the side of the dirt cliffs long ago. The edges of the cliffs are good for watching your enemy slinking along. You can shoot down on him, pepper him good, but if he or they have climbed to the top elsewhere, you might get caught in the open and the only thing to do is shoot it out or run. The cliffs are paradise forty to fifty feet high and you can break bones if you jump over the side to get away. Some days you're there until dusk, BB welts all over your body, tired and dirty, smelling of boy sweat, the odor of wet chickens.

~~

When the boys are not shooting at each other, Duffy is usually off by himself. If he's out at night, he'll throw rocks at windows and run. He steals hubcaps, pries them off with a church key and sells them to Bubble Eye who fences them. He's taught you that lots of people don't lock their houses, which makes it easy to enter, no breaking a window, just turn the knob when you know the owners are gone working or on vacation. Anything not nailed down you'll steal from stores, houses, yards, garages. It's your profession. A dangerous, exciting, noble calling. Wholesale whatever you've got to Bubble Eye. Watches, rings, kitchen knife sets, silverware, bicycles, tricycles, tool boxes full of tools, a brand new wheelbarrow, a dolly, a bass guitar. At a vacant house you rip a phone out of the wall, for which Bubble Eye gives you a quarter, so you don't take him anymore of those. He'll buy nearly everything. Maximum two dollars, never more than two, no matter what it is. Sometimes he calls what you've brought him a load of crap and tells you to get your nasty ass out of his sight. He hates cheap shit costume jewelry, so you don't bother with any jewelry that's plastic. Everything else is kosher, pretty much okay. You always have spending money. You pay for all of your own clothes now, shoes, shirts, whatever you want. You eat fried weenie sandwiches two or three times a week at Republic. It's a living. No complaints. Other than you wish Nick Pappas was dead. What are the chances?

~~

Whenever Bubble Eye picks you up from school and drives around, you know he wants another handjob. The deal is he lets you drive the Mercury after. But it is not like Billy and Bruce who do it to each other. Bubble Eye never reciprocates. Even though you might let him. But if he don't want to? Well, who gives a flying fuck? Driving the car is more fun than jacking off. Thirteen years old and though your pecker gets hard, nothing ever comes out the way it gushes out of Bubble Eye. Someday though. Someday sure enough. But never anything he'll see. He is arrested again for breaking and entering. The cops search his basement, find piles of stolen goods and charge him with Grand Theft. When you hear through the grapevine that he's been arrested, you get plenty worried. Figuring he'll rat you out, cut a deal, save his own neck. Your prints are all over the stuff the cops have confiscated. But Bubble Eye stays true to the code and doesn't involve you or anyone else he fences for, which you be thinking is very cool is Chuck. He could have done business with the law. But instead he ends in Canon City, the Alcatraz of the Rockies doing five to seven. You'd burgle on your own, but with Bubble Eye gone, you don't know who to sell your shit to.

~~

Duffy finally gets hired by *The Denver Post*. He's at the paper shack by four p.m. to fold papers every day except Sunday mornings when they deliver the papers to his house. Best friend at the shack is Craig. Craig has bright blond hair and bright blue eyes. The girls love him. He is witty and funny and loves poetry and can quote Robert Service for as long as you're willing to listen. He goes into bars and says, I'm the President of any possible Viking surge in Aurora, Colorado, Craig the unworthy skallawagually phkuwagulous peckerneck personification of bullshit. Then he recites The Shooting of Dan McGrew. The Cremation of Sam McGee is his encore. When he's done the patrons throw money at him. Where did he get such a big memory? It makes you jealous. Your brain is tiny compared to Craig's.

One day Craig comes to the paper shack on crutches. He has a bandaged foot from having planter's wart surgery. He says the wart felt like a stone in his shoe. The doctor said he got it from going barefoot. Planters wart is a virus. How am I going to do my route? he says. You load his papers in the canvas bags along with your own. Pedal him around while he throws. Craig saying no one has ever been so good to him. You are his best friend forever. You and Craig prick your fingers with a pin and put them together so your blood will run into his bloodstream and his blood will run into yours. You tell him it's what Indians do. Now we are brothers. We are inseparable. You are me and I am you. For months and months this is true. And then his family moves out of state. Moves to Montana for Christ's sake! It's not the end of the world, but it might as well be.

The guy who gets Craig's route is named Bell, a big guy who outweighs the Duffer by probably twenty-five pounds. He is an inch or two taller as well. You don't like him because he took Craig's stall in the folding shack. One day when Bell is late you use that stall, fold papers there, until Bell shows up and says, That's my stall, Duffy. Move your ass. You shake your head and say, First come, first serve, Bell. I don't see your name on it. Argue! Scream in each other's faces. He pushes you. You swing on him. Bad idea. He lays you out with one punch that flattens your nose.

When you go to the faucet outside to wash the blood off, Bell comes over and apologizes. He says he didn't mean to hurt you so bad. But you sure pissed me off. Fuck you, Bell! Your broken nose and eyes are pulsing and swelling, blood soaking the front of your shirt. You want to get one punch of your own landed. What more damage can Bell do to you? Fists up again, you tell him you want a rematch. But Bell backs off. Says he doesn't want to hurt you no more. He walks away. Goes inside and folds his papers in an open stall. Not Craig's old stall, which is now yours.

Later when you're calmer you're awful glad Bell said what he said, did what he did. He would have killed the Duffer, no doubt about it. You do your route and by the time it's over your eyes are so swollen you're almost blind. For two to three days all you do is lie around until it's time to fold papers. Bell turns out to be a nice guy. He says he's not used to fighting guys smaller than he is, but you were asking for it. Which of course is true. You don't know what got into you that day. Whatever it was, it was really stupid. What you learned from it, though, is when in a fight—go for the nose.

~~

This is about the same time you find a big boy you can whale on. His name is Allen and though he is a head taller and much heavier, you find out one day when you punch him in the gut that he is big all right, a big sissy. Whining and whimpering and gasping and saying you knocked the wind out of him, no fair, no fair. You hit him again and he takes off running.

So you start laying for him, catch him when his mother sends him to Gramm's Grocery. Beat big Allen every chance you get. Go for his nose. What fun!    One day Allen tells his mother why his nose is bloody and she storms over to the house throwing a fit, and that's when the mom calls you a bully. You're nothing but a goddamn bully! Yeah, so what? Apologize to Allen. Get tough or die, you tell him, which is what Pappas has told you a thousand times. The mom slaps you, tells you she's never been so ashamed. You don't say it, but you like her calling you a bully.

Picking on Allen stops one day when you're following him, taunting him, calling him a waterhead, and he turns around and says, All right, Pappas, you want to fight, let's fight. He charges with his head down, takes you by surprise, his big head hitting you like a battering ram in the mouth, chipping two of your bottom teeth. You go berserk. Throw haymakers. Allen runs away with you chasing him, hitting him on the back. Finally letting him go, letting him get to his house. The next time you look in a mirror you see that the chipped teeth look like tiny fangs, werewolf fangs, which is pretty cool, actually. Except they hurt when you breathe through your mouth. They hurt for days, in fact. No more bullying Allen.

The two of you become friends. Allen always putting his hand on your shoulder, always following you around. Prick fingers and turn into bloodbrothers, you tell him. Allen is scared to do it, but you make him. Ow, ow, ow, he whines.

But afterwards he's proud and holds his finger up and squeezes more blood out of it. To the FOX you and Allen go and see a movie about paratroopers jumping out of airplanes, killing Nazi scum. Later, at home, you have the brilliant idea that you should make chutes out of bed sheets and jump off the cliffs overlooking Sand Creek. You can test the idea first by jumping off the roof of the house. You get a sheet from the linen closet. You and Allen climb up on the roof. Tie the sheet corners into knots and slip Allen's arms through what are now shoulder straps under his armpits. You stretch the sheet out and it fills with wind. Jump, Allen, jump! you order him. The chute is full. Go, Allen, go! Don't be scared, Allen. Jump! Allen leaps. The sheet doing a cigarette roll and falling on top of him. Allen spraining an ankle, hopping around crying. That is the end of the friendship. Allen's mother forbidding him to play with that damned cretin Duffy Pappas.

~~

Always getting bad grades, always in trouble with teachers. The principal tells the mom that she should think about putting her son in therapy. Maybe he needs a sedative, he says. She agrees but nothing comes of it. You see yourself telling some headshrinker all your nasty secrets. Maybe making up a bunch of lies to seem more interesting, which is what the mom and Pappas do. They lie and lie and the lies get so thick you can't get through them to what's real and what's not. So who are they, anyway? No idea. Except that they are the mom and sir. They are Mom and Daddy. But what does that mean? And what is with her calling him Daddy, when he is not her daddy? She does look younger, though, younger than Pappas. She likes to come home and say how this or that person guessed her age as years younger than she is and what she hates more than anything is the thought of growing old. She claims she won't do it. In your dreams, Grandma Inez tells her. Aging and heartache, that's what life is. A vale of suffering. Everyone gets old. Every story ends tragic. Every story ends in death. Get used to it, Janice.

~~

After Thanksgiving dinner, 1955, Pappas and the mom go to the Hanson's house for cocktails, leaving you and your sisters alone, because cocktail time is only for grownups. Grandma Inez is visiting Uncle Dean and Aunt Marge in Oregon until Christmas, so there is no grownup to stop you from stealing Pappas's Pontiac. The Hanson place is at the end of the block. Duffy knows what the four of them are up to. They drink cocktails and watch blue movies on the Hanson's projector and laugh. Peek in the window and see the images on the wall and know that Pappas is right about people putting their mouths on cocks and cunts and it don't kill them. In fact it looks interesting. But what gets to you is how people do it for the camera! Make these grainy black and white soundless movies and go into all sorts of contortions and not care who is watching and not be embarrassed by it. But then again you don't know them and they don't know you and what is the chance of ever meeting one of them? 100 million to one, maybe? And what would you do if you did meet a porn person? Ask for an autograph?

So on this Thanksgiving, after Michele Renee and Carol Marie go to bed, sneaky Duffy sneaks outside with the keys to the old '48 Pontiac Streamliner Pappas bought as a second car. You drive around the neighborhood. The Pontiac has only second and third gears working, but you're having a grand time, anyway. Until you turn a corner too close and scrape the side of a parked car, a Studebaker. You keep going, of course. Home is just around the corner. Park the Pontiac. Run into the house. Peek out the window. After awhile you're thinking you got away with something. But then a cruiser pulls up. The cop gets out and looks at the Pontiac's dented fender and makes some notes. Then he goes back to his cruiser and is gone. What's it mean? Why didn't he come arrest you? You have a bad feeling, a premonition. Also thinking: stupid Duffy you're going to jail for this.

Saturday: two days after the hit and run, you are at the roller rink. Carol Marie shows up and says you have to go home right now. A couple of cops are waiting in the living room. So what have you done? she asks. Ain't done nothin. Mind your own bee's wax.

In front of the house is a cop car. Inside the living room sits the mom and Pappas and two cops in uniform. Pappas looks a little pale, a little frightened, which is really surprising. Never seen that kind of glum fear on his face before. He looks guilty and you realize they're thinking Pappas did it. You decide not to fess up, fuck him. Get Pappas in trouble. Deny everything. When the cops question you about Thursday night, you claim to be in bed reading a book about Sitting Bull. I'm learning everything about Plains Indians, you say innocent and smiling. You offer to get the book and show them. One cop asks Carol Marie if she can confirm that her brother was in his room. I heard him go to bed, she answers.

The same cop tells Pappas that somebody in this house is guilty of hit and run and Pappas says, I told you I was with my wife that night at the house of a friend and I can prove it and look, to tell you the truth, Officer, when I saw the damage I thought someone had hit me in the parking lot. The mom adds this: Maybe somebody stole the car and brought it back banged up like that. Everyone looks at the Duffer again, eyes squinty, like they are trying to see inside him where the truth is hiding. The mom says, Duffy, if you took the car you have to say so or they will put Daddy in jail. Good, you're thinking, put the bastard in jail. Tell the truth, she says, did you take the car on Thanksgiving? Well, Duffy doesn't know why he has a sudden attack of honesty, maybe it's her teary cry baby eyes, but in any case he hangs his head and says, Yeah. Also thinking: Pappas is going to knock my brains in now. But he doesn't. No, he pats you on the back and says, At least you had the guts to tell the truth. His voice is full of relief. He looks at the cops and says, See?

You are taken to the station. Sit on a chair beside a desk. Tell the whole story to some cop who types it up and has you sign it. You're thinking they will take you downstairs and lock you up, but they don't. No, they turn you over to the mom. And then the mom is driving you to the house of the guy whose car you hit. This man with a gray mustache and a pitiful hangdog face comes to the door. Try to look him in the eye man to man, but you can't. You stare at your stupid filthy Ked's. The mom telling the man, Duffy is here to apologize. Nudging you, waiting for you to speak. But you don't say anything. In a kindly voice the man says, I hope you learned a lesson, son. Don't you wish the guy weren't so goddamn nice? Back in the car the mom says, You can't even say you're sorry! My God, what am I going to do with you? Why do you do the things you do? Don't you know you're hurting me? Do you care at all? Don't you have a conscience? Duffy stares out the window. Does he care? Nope. Not even a little bit. Fuck everyone. Fuck the mom. Fuck the world and fuck you too.

~~

Summer of '55: you are hitchhiking home from a dance in Denver. There was a dance contest, which Tony and his girl won because there were more of their friends clapping for them than for the other couple, who, in your humble estimation, were better dancers. You walk over to Colfax, put your thumb out and two guys from Casper, Wyoming give you a ride. The driver is named Rodney Booker, the guy riding shotgun is Mike the Knife. Rodney Booker is dark like a Mexican. His hair shiny black, combed straight back, a curl falling over his forehead. Mike the Knife has a flattop with long sides flowing into a ducktail, which looks pretty dippy. They are driving a 1955 Buick. There is a screwdriver hammered into the ignition, so you knew the car is hot.

They give you a lift all the way to Aurora. Rodney talks about Casper, how lots of kids are from farms and ranches. Tough studs all of them. Lots of fights at school. He has fought plenty of times. You brag on how tough the Aurora boys are. Most kids carry switch blades. Some even have zip guns. I know a guy named Buckner who got hit over the head with a crescent wrench, split his head open, but he kept fighting, until he knocked the other guy down and stomped him. Rodney and Mike the Knife like your story. They have you repeat it and add more details about blood and body shots and where did Buckner kick that motherfucker? In the balls? In the balls, yeah. In the ribs. In the jaw. Aurora boys are like that, killers what don't know when to quit. I'm that way too, you say. See my nose, see how it cocks left? I fought a guy twice my size, name of Bell. He broked my nose, yeah, but I knocked his fucking teeth out. You go on and on about how you beat shit out of Bell. Rodney and Mike the Knife eat it up. Rodney says, You'd fit right in if you lived in Casper. You tell him you got so strong from wrestling at school and boxing with your old man who was heavyweight champ of the whole fuckin Navy. Yeah, and I make my muscles hard as steel working summers on my grandpa's farm. Rodney says his grandpa owns a big ranch near Casper. If you ever want a job herding cattle, Rodney says, I'll get you one.

You ask why they come to Denver? Mike the Knife says they're taking a vacation. Yobo, man we got business with a chop shop, he adds. Chop shop? This car? Mike the Knife nods. It turns out Mike the Knife is an ex-con. Has done time for Grand Theft Auto. His specialty. There is no car he can't steal, he claims. How much will you get for a '55 Buick? you ask him. Yobo mint, says Mike the Knife.

And you're thinking: if I knew where the chop shop was I could steal cars and take them there. Make mint. Quit school, live large. Have my own pad, my own '48 Mercury ragtop. Girls coming out my ears. All of em gorgeous as Ginger and hot as Karen ready to trot. The good life, that's all I'm asking.

Where's that chop shop, man? They look at each other. Rodney shrugs and he says, You know the junkyard out past the stockyards?

We go by those stockyards every time we drive to Frederick. I know right where the junkyard is. It's called Hoffy's Used Auto Parts.

Yobo thinkin doin business? Mike the Knife asks. He says talk to Wally. Nobody else, just Wally. Tell him Mike the Knife sent you.

The parents aren't home, so you suggest hanging out at your house for a while. Rodney stops on the way for a case of Coors.

At the house Carol Marie is babysitting Michele Renee, who is already in bed. Grandma Inez is warming her seat at Zanzibar. You take your felonious friends to the lawn chairs in the backyard. Smoke cigarettes and drink beer. Mike the Knife takes out a little pipe and fills it with pot. Lights it. Passes it around. Carol Marie won't take any. Yobo, mellow you out, baby, Mike the Knife tells her. You take a couple of hits (a new experience), but mostly Mike the Knife monopolizes the pipe. The conversation goes to people, places, movies, music. You start bragging up all the stuff you know about Indians: Crazy Horse, Red Cloud. Tatanka Lyotaka—better known as Sitting Bull. Mike the Knife cuts you off, taking out a Stiletto, flicking it open, using the blade to punctuate what he's saying. How he hates fucking Indians as much as he hates Niggers and Chinks and Spics! His fingers do a little ballet, the knife slicing the air in front of your face.

What Mike the Knife says makes you instantly hate him. Also thinking: I don't like the way pot makes me feel. It's supposed to make you calm, right?

But you feel nervous jumpy paranoid. Especially about ex-con Mike the Knife who says Yobo before nearly every sentence. What does Yobo mean? Yo boy? Nasty piece of work is written all over his square, heavy-jawed face. His stupid haircut. His raspy voice. His pupils wide dilated. His knife corking as if skewering Indians Niggers Chinks Spics. Your delinquent mind flashes on the gun in the nightstand. Should you go get it? After Mike the Knife sucks the last wisp of smoke from the pipe, he closes his eyes, slumps in the chair. Falls asleep. Rodney explains that Mike the Knife always does that. Pot puts him out cold, especially if he boozes too.

At some point Carol Marie and Rodney go sit in the Buick. Five minutes later the engine starts and the car pulls away. You watch Mike the Knife sleeping, see the slack mouth seeping, a thread of drool running over his bristly chin. Easing out of the chair, you go into the house, into the bedroom, pull the gun out of the drawer. Tuck it into your waistband. Put on your Levi jacket to hide the evidence you're packing. Also thinking: pull that knife on me, I will blow your fucking head off. Also thinking: is it the pot or the beer or both? Or am I insane? Is Yobo Mike the Knife a mental disease?

Carol Marie and Rodney are gone over an hour. Worrying about that, worrying that the parents will be home from the VFW soon and Carol Marie better be back before then. You wake Mike the Knife and ask him if he knows where they've gone. Yobo fuck, what you think? His eyes are bloodshot. He holds up the knife that has fallen between his legs onto the chair. I stabbed a motherfucker with this for waking me with his snoring, he says. Billy the Kid did the same thing, you tell him, only he shot the snorer in the head. Opening your jacket to show him the butt of the Lugar. I shot a motherfucker with this who slapped me for crossing his lawn on my bike. Yobo no shit? says Mike the Knife. You relate how this four-eyed motherfucker slapped you and how you went home, got the gun, went back and shot the motherfucker in the leg when he was out watering his flower box. No one saw me do it. I cleaned the gun and put it away. The next time I saw the motherfucker he was on crutches.

Yobo bad motherfucker! says Mike the Knife, smiling, standing up, patting your shoulder. Why you don't come with us, come with me and Booker. Yobo, whaddaya say? Come where? you ask him. Yobo! Wherever, says Mike the Knife. We makes the money, honey.

You're listening. Also thinking: This is what you want, right? Take off with these bad hombres and live free, live a life of crime. Be yobo bad motherfucker like Mike the Knife says you are. But when actually faced with the offer, you get queasy. Palms sweaty. Mouth dry. Maybe it's the mixture of pot and beer working on you, but the future looks suddenly out of kilter, looks whacky and scary. Maybe I'll come up to Casper, you tell Mike the Knife. But right now I got my own shit, man. Mike the Knife gives the squint and says, Yobo grieving the man, Duffy? Yobo giving the man grief? Every fucking chance I get, damn straight. Grand Theft Auto? says Mike the Knife. Grand Theft Auto, you tell him, savoring the sound of the words. Yobo very cool kid, says Mike the Knife. I got a kindred spirit in Aurora, Colorado. Yobo ever want to partner up, catch me in Casper. Rodney will always know where I am. Yobo bring something for the kitty. We like Buicks. Buicks are easy. The two of you shake hands on it. Also thinking: Mike the Knife ain't so bad. And maybe something will come of it. It's all about contacts. It's all about who you know who you blow. A life of crime seems doable. All it takes is a bit of whack-a-doo, some guts, yobo desperado.

A horn honks and the Buick arrives. Carol Marie jumps out. She says Rodney and Mike the Knife better get going. Rodney shaking hands and saying, Glad to have met you, Duffy. Come up to Casper and see us sometime. They take the rest of the beer and boogie. You are relieved to have them gone.

Carol Marie saying, We need to get into bed before Daddy and Mom get here. You keeping watch at the window, asking her where she's been. We went over to Marilyn's, she says. Carol Marie looks like she's been through the wringer, but you don't say nothing. Why should you? Her business is her business.

Not long ago you came home and found her on the phone with Marilyn who was fucking a guy and describing it to Carol Marie at the same time. She held out the phone and said, Listen to this. You heard sloppy wet sounds. What's that? you asked. Carol Marie said, She's got the phone down there what you think? Marilyn is sexy-looking, big ass, nice legs and tits. She drives a Nash. The back seat turns into a bed. If Pappas is home when Marilyn visits he can't take his eyes off her. She eyes him too. You have a feeling they got something going on.

A pair of headlights probe Ironton Street. You know it's the parents. They're here! Hurry! Hurry! You run to the drawer in the bedroom and put the gun away. Then to your room, shed your clothes. Climb into bed. The front door slams. Hear them arguing. She calling Pappas stupid. He calling her a flirty fucking bitch. You hear the glasses being set on the table. Ice cubes tinkling. Highballs mixed and poured and all the while their voices getting louder. At one point he is saying he ought to divorce her. He says, How you think it make me look when you do like that? Oh, Jesus Christ, she answers, I'm just having fun. It don't mean nothing. I don't mean nothing by it. If you'd get off your ass and dance with me, I wouldn't have to dance with others. I seen how you look at other women. You ain't foolin nobody, Nick. And he says, I don't care if you dance with a woman, but I don't like seeing you in the arms of another man. And she says, You know why you're jealous? Because you don't trust me. You know why you don't trust me? Because you don't trust yourself! And so it goes. On and on, the arguing, angry voices blowing by each other.

Some nights he might slap her and she'll slap him back. Another memorable Christmas Eve he punched her so hard he knocked her down, gave her a shiner. She jumped right up, ran into the kitchen and got a butcher knife, chased him with it, shrieking she was going to stab him. Always brave when she's drunk is the mom, after him yelling, Stab you! You lay a hand on me I'll cut your throat, you goddamn bastard! He ran out of the house, ran into the winter night, jumped in the Cadillac, sizzled its tires down snowy Ironton Street. He didn't come back till Christmas morning when the family was opening presents. Pappas brought a peace offering. A surprise present, he said. The mom cried when she saw what it was: an anniversary clock. Just kidding, he said. Just wanted you to see it, baby. He had slept next door at the Williams house and had borrowed the clock to show her how pretty it was. He had to take it back. Which made the mom cry harder than ever.

Look, if you had done some stupid thing like that, wouldn't you have gone to the store next day and bought the mom her own anniversary clock? But he didn't do it. He teases her with a borrowed one. THEN: Forget it, hah, hah. As usual that Christmas, the family goes to church and makes nice on their knees, heads down praying, playing pious Catholics. *I believe in God, the Father Almighty…*

And then home for turkey dinner Grandma Inez has cooked. That night they all get drunk again and argue about God for the umpteenth time, Grandma Inez insisting God is Giche Manidoo and the mom saying Jesus is God and Pappas saying God is a scam and always has been and the mom, voice rising, saying, Listen to yourself, Nick Pappas, you're gonna burn in hell!

So all things being equal, maybe the fight and the punch and the knife and the running into the night and the clock being bogus doesn't matter. It's the drama that matters. Even though that kind of drama scares the sisters and their brother, the parents and grandma get off on it. And the clock is ticking, the second hand going round and round making everyone older, the mom and the gramma, and Grandpa Mike all alone in Frederick, and atheist Pappas, Duffy's sisters, himself, sunrise, sunset and one day death comes and what will you say then? What's the point of it all? What's it for?

Flash forward: This particular night of coming home from the VFW, the yelling doesn't lead to slapping or punching or knife chasing. In fact, all of a sudden they get so quiet you can hear the house settling, the wood creaking. Peeping Duff creeps out of bed and down the hallway, peeks around the corner past the living room into a slice of kitchen. And sees the mom leaning back. Pappas on his knees in front of her. Her skirt up. His head buried. She is rubbing his back round and round. Her other hand picking up her highball. Downing it casually. Nonchalant the mom. Very cool very.

~~

One night when you've been out looking for a car to steal, but having no luck, you give up. Go home. Climb through the window. Undress. Climb in bed with the little sister. She sleeps with you now. Grandma Inez sleeps with Carol Marie. You close your eyes. Sleep a nice escape. But then you hear Pappas's big feet booming down the hall. Door opening. Light on. There he stands, big bad man filling the doorway, voice saying, So you finally come home. Where you been? You rub your eyes. Huh? And Pappas says, Don't huh me. We been waitin for you. What the fuck you doing out there? Just taking a walk, sir. Couldn't sleep. I told you never to lie to me, Pappas says. Ain't no lie. Honest to God, sir. Get out of bed. Come to the kitchen, he commands.

So shit, Duffy, you're in for it again. Out to the kitchen you shuffle. There they are sitting round the table, your parents and grandmother. Grandma Inez has an empty jar of pickled pig's feet in front of her. The briny smell mixing with cigarettes mixing with beer and vaporous gin. She shakes her head and says, Kid, why do you do it? What the hell's wrong with you? And the mom says, We know you been gone for hours. Your sister came out and told us you weren't there. The little rat! Don't call your sister a rat. You tomcattin? says Pappas. No, sir, honest I ain't. And Pappas says, Honest? You don't know the meaning of the word. I wouldn't believe a thing comes out your lyin mouth. You and the slots, I can smell em on you. No, sir, I didn't see no girls. I swear to God, sir, took a walk, I like the night, I like to walk at night, it's quiet and cool … it's peaceful. Pappas's face: booze loose flushed red, broken veins blue over both nostrils. You just gonna make life miserable as you can for us ain't you? You just bullshit me and bullshit me till nothing but bullshit's comin out my ears! He jumps out of the chair. His hands quivering like they're itching to get at you. You lyin little bastard, you better tell me the truth right now! No more lyin. His beery breath swallows your whole head. Breathe him in and out and say loudly, I ain't lyin, goddamn you!

Pappas slaps you, takes you by the throat. Duffy doesn't know who he is this night, but the skinny fucker starts swinging for all he's worth, so shocking Pappas that he actually backs up. You're at him fists flailing before he reacts and grabs your throat again, picks you up, flies you into the living room. Tosses you over the back of the love seat. Flipping all the way over landing on your feet and the mom and the grandma are climbing on Pappas screaming at him to stop. You know better than to stand in no-man's land creating a target, so you book it to the bedroom. Start throwing on clothes. Your sister cowering under the covers and wailing. Before you can leap out the window the mom has come in and is pulling your arm. Grandma Inez and Pappas are bellowing at each other.

And Duffy is thinking: Sic him, Grandma, sic him!

The mom closes the door. She shouts at Michele Renee, Quit that goddamn screaming! Michele Renee muffles her mouth. The mom says. Goddamn you, Duffy, you have got to stop this shit! Tears in her eyes, stormy tears of anger and angst. We can't take no more. You're killing us. You're destroying this family. No family can take this goddamn behavior and stay together. You shout back at her, I hate him! I hate him! And she says, You don't hate him. Yes I do. She closes her eyes, swipes at her tears with the back of her hand. Please, she begs. Please! And she asks you to promise not to sneak out anymore and worry everyone half to death. Can you promise me? she asks. She's wrung out, exhausted, she says. Don't you love the mom? Nod your head, mumble, Yeah, I guess. And she says, Oh son, it's just got to end. We can't have all this turmoil. Life is hard enough without all this turmoil. Do you understand me? She tells you if she could afford it, she would send you to military school. They would teach you discipline. Knock some sense into you. And you're thinking you wouldn't mind that a bit. At least it would get you out of this lunatic asylum. So that's what you tell her. Hah! she fires back, you just think you wouldn't mind. You don't know what you're talking about. You counter with: Yeah, well, soon as I'm old enough I'm out of here. She nods. Says, All right, sure, but for now just go to bed. It's late. We need some sleep.

Later, Grandma Inez crawls in bed with you and Michele Renee. In minutes the old lady starts snoring. No matter how you prod her she only stops a few seconds and then she's at it again. You give up, let it go. She really stuck up for you, Duffy. Gave that asshole all he could handle. If she didn't smell so boozy and pickled-pig feety and her snoring wasn't so disgusting, you would cuddle her, give her a kiss.

~~

Flip the page and see Grandma Inez putting a pot of wieners on to boil. She gets out hot dog buns and bags of potato chips. Everyone sits round the table shooting the shit, munching chips, waiting for the weenies to cook. Carol Marie has a date with some jackass named Jerry. They're going to the movies. Jerry is a senior at Aurora High. He came in wearing a long, camelhair coat looking like a commercial for *Esquire*. His ears stick out too big for his head, but that is a minor flaw compared to the rest of him. Short curly brown hair, unblemished forehead, pretty brown eyes, straight nose, pointy chin, baby-smooth skin. Carol Marie introduced him to Pappas and the mom. He was told to sit down and have some chips and Coke and a hot dog when the wieners are ready. Sounds good, he said broadcasting a wide, friendly smile. Teeth so flawless you want to knock them out. Thing is: he doesn't belong here, not on our side of the tracks, the working class side of Colfax.

Pappas is drinking beer as usual. The mom having her highballs. Grandma Inez sticking to gin. The three of them have been worrying their favorite round-the-table subject, stuff about God again, stuff about death and the afterlife. After Jerry sat down, they went back at it, Pappas saying there is nothing beyond the beyond and when he dies just roll him in a ditch and cover him up, and the mom saying God is as real as this table, as real as this kitchen, as real as my beating heart keeping me alive. She FEELS God in her heart. The heart knows truths that the mind can only guess at. And if you don't know that, Nick, you're a fool.

He wants her to prove God exists the same way two plus two is four. She dives into the description Duffy has heard a thousand times about how could the earth be here and all the life on it without a great intelligent force? And how could there be a notion of God in our heads if he didn't exist, huh? And where do the planets come from and the stars and endless space out there, huh, huh?

Yeah? Well, where does God come from? Pappas asks her. Who created that bastard? You are going to hell for that remark, she tells him. Adding that God has always existed. Pappas saying, If he has always existed, then why can't the universe have always existed? The mom's voice wrathful as she replies: Because God had to make it! Janice, you're a bucket full of blithering idiots, says Pappas. You don't feel God in your heart at all? she asks. I feel nothing in my heart, he tells her. Neither do you. Your heart is just a pump, Janice. Just a fucking pump, for Christ sake! He points his finger at her and adds, And I'll tell you this: you say God is perfect and all-good and all-powerful and all that shit. If he's all-good, why is His world all-evil? Can't answer that, can you!

The mom throws her hands into the air. Satan! she shouts. Ever heard of him?

The all-good is going to let the all-bad run the show, Pappas says, sneering, snickering. I seen the war, Janice. Do you have the slightest clue how stupid what you're sayin sounds? Sic em, Satan. Make my children suffer, grind em up, kill em, pulverize the little punks. There's a god for you! God of the scythe.

Oh, there's no talking to a man like you, the mom says, closing her eyes, shaking her head. Hopeless, hopeless.

Grandma Inez puts her two cents in: God is the Great Spirit. Is Giche Manidoo! She snorts as if she's settled it, lifts her drink and says, To Giche! Drinks fast, drinks the whole thing. Slams the empty glass down and, reaching for the bottle, says, *Booz-hoo ahnee*, Jerry! Tee-hee! *Bonjour*, says Jerry. She points her finger at him and guffaws. He knows French! she says.

Jerry glances desperately towards the door, a sickly grin on his face. Big ears glowing like candles are burning behind them. Carol Marie whispers, Calm down, Grandma. The mom looking at Jerry, gives him the I-see-right-through-you, shakes her finger. Listen here, young man, Carol Marie has to be home by eleven. He nods agreement. Yes, ma'am. In the house by eleven. Yes, ma'am will do. And listen to me, says she. I know you two are young and want to have fun, and I want you to have fun. But I know what boys are like at your age and you just be careful with my daughter. I had a boy try something on me when I was fifteen and when he refused to quit I raked my nails down his face like a tiger. His skin curled up under my nails. I give him permanent scarring. She checks out her nails and adds: Carol Marie knows not to let boys go too far. She is saving herself for marriage. Men! blurts Grandma Inez making a face like she's about to upchuck chips of men.

    Jerry's smile is a paste-white smear. Eyes worried. Ears eternally blushing. Carol Marie stares daggers at the mom. Pappas wrinkling his upper lip, his slit eyes saying: You don't fool me, motherfucker. The mom has that same do not fuck with the Irish look on her face as she had the time Carol Marie went for a walk around the block and didn't come home for two hours and no one could find her anywhere and the mom called the police and said she must have been kidnapped and God knows what the kidnapper was doing to her. Grandma Inez told her not to worry. Everything be all right, but the mom would not believe it. She threw herself on the couch and bawled, while Grandma Inez kept saying, Janice, be brave! Janice, be brave! The boys in the neighborhood were alerted. Everyone fanning out looking for Carol Marie. An hour later most gave up and went back to see if she had come home.

    The cop car arrived at the same moment Carol Marie came strolling down the street carefree as a butterfly. There's that doofus, there she is! the twins yelling. Here comes Carol Marie! The mom storming across the lawn with her studded cowboy belt in her hand, thrashing Carol Marie's legs and screaming, You little shit you scared me to death, you little shit! The cops grinning, driving quietly away. The neighbors outside happily watching Carol Marie get a whipping, watching her hopping and bopping trying to get loose, but the mom had her wrist and kept whaling. Until finally she let go and Carol Marie ran crying into the house. In my mind I was thinking the whole thing looked phony. Another one of those big acts the mom puts on to prove she is Irish and nobody better fuck with the Irish. Later, she talked to Carol Marie: Bad men out there just waiting to get their hands on fresh meat like you, don't you understand? Carol Marie said she ran into Marilyn and they got to talking and didn't realize how much time had passed. Time got away from me, was what she offered. Her sorrowful eyes making her look honest and repentant. Duffy found out later she was with some guy in his car making out. She told you she didn't know why she did it. I don't really like him much at all, she said. He's just something for when I get bored. I fool around with him, but never let him screw me. Actually he never tries very hard. When he's kissing me he croons Jailbait jailbait. Like it turns him on. One time he pushed my head down and put his thing in my mouth and I bit it and, this is how goony he is, he said, Oh yeah, oh yeah do it. I meet the strangest people in the world, Duffy. All of em sick in the head. Everyone of em fake. People are fake. Fake faces, fake words, fake smiles, fake everything. If it was up to me, I wouldn't allow any of em to breed. I'm never having kids, Duffy. Uncle Dean said the worst thing you can do is bring innocent babies into this bitch of a world, which, when he said it, I knew it was true. Duffy said he believed it too. No kids, never!

So when the mom is telling Jerry that Carol Marie is not allowed to go to Drive In movies, he says politely, We're going to the FOX, ma'am. And maybe stop at Republic for a Coke after. Well then, the mom replies, that's okay. You seem like a nice boy. Pappas chimes in saying, Never trust a boy that age, Janice. He refuses to look me in the eye. A boy who refuses to look you in the eye is afraid you will read his mind. I was your age once, buddy.

Oh, Nick, she says, pleeease. Nick is right, agrees Grandma Inez. And Pappas adding, I know what I'm talking about. His forefinger tapping his head. You glance at Jerry who is staring at a potato chip in his hand like it's the most interesting thing he's ever seen. You elbowing him and nodding toward Pappas. Jerry gets the message and looks Pappas in the eye. And says, I respect Carol Marie, sir, and would never do nothin to hurt her. See, he says Sir, says Carol Marie. Yeah yeah, big deal, says Pappas. Perverts and pricks everywhere say Sir.

Grandma Inez: Look here, sonny let me tell you somethin. You better treat her like a lady. Yes, ma'am, he answers, his voice gone from baritone to alto. Her arthritic finger shoots out in warning. You just lissen. If you're old nuff drive a car you're old nuff careless. She come back with a scratch I'll take this bottle to your head. You hearing me? She lifts the bottle like she is going to swat him with it. He grinning like a dog gagging on a bone in his throat. Grandma! Carol Marie says, Stop it! The mom overriding her, You listen me, Carol Marie. Get pregnant you goin hell! Carol Marie puts her head in her hands and murmurs, Oh Jesus! And the mom saying, The mom was young once too. The mom knows what you kids are up to. I seen right through you. Carol Marie shouting back in her face, I ain't you! I aint doing none of that! Grandma Inez cocking an eyebrow and telling Carol Marie, A little bird told me you will. Don't be like your mother, Carol Marie. Shut up, Mom! shouts the mom at Grandma Inez. Pappas stands, wobbles to the fridge for more beer while saying, Carol Marie listen to your grandmother because many life been ruined just because some horny bastard couldn't keep his pecker in his pants and got some girl knocked up and had to marry her. You better quit grinning at me, Duffy, he warns you. It aint fuckin funny, you know.

*(Know? Orgies and incest, what Duffy knows could bring this whole goddamn house down over everyone's head.)*

This is very seris topic, insists the mom. You kids too young to unnerstand the wisdom ours experience. But someday you know. Someday when you grow up and have children, thas when you seen how worrisome they are. Kids worry me to death. Times I wunner why I ever had em. They suck you dry. Give nothin in return but heartaches and tears. If you only knew how many times I cried over kids! Pappas chiming in, saying, Listen to your mother. Listen to your mother. Grandma Inez agreeing, Thass right. Men! she spews. Men!

Out of the corner of your eye, you catch Michele Renee reaching up on tiptoes for the boiling pot of weenies, but before you can react she has the handle in her hand and pulls the boiling water down over her chest. She screaming, doing a whooping dance. Pappas jumping up, ripping off Michele Renee's shirt. Hoisting her into the kitchen sink, running cold water over her fiery chest. The mom dashing to the linen closet, pulling out towels. Wetting them. Wrapping Michele Renee in them and rushing her to the car and away, engine roaring just like when Husky nearly killed the Duffer.

A minute later you are still sitting staring at the stove, wondering why you hadn't rushed to save little sis from the boiling water. If you had just moved you would be a hero. But instead you sat there munching chips, watching her suicidal reaching. Grandma Inez gathers the steaming wieners off the floor and puts them back in the pan. She washes them under the faucet. Sets them on the table next to the buns and mustard and relish. She pours herself another drink. Lights a cigarette and says calmly, She'll have scars the rest of her life from that. When her boobs grow they will be scarred, poor little thing. Forget modeling for men's magazines.

She raises an eyebrow at you, Come on, kid, it aint end of the world. These things happen. Not your fault. Sit down have a hot dog. You wanna drink? How about you, Jimmy? Carol Marie?

It's not Jimmy, it's Jerry, says Carol Marie.

Jimmy. Jerry. They both begin with a J and end with a Y. He knows who I mean.

I'll have one, you tell her.

Shit and shinola, she says, and pours you gin and tonic. Which tastes not half-bad. A little like weak licorice and fizzy water. Pile in, eat the hot dogs, she says. It takes fifteen minutes for the drink to go to your head. You've eaten a lot of potato chips and a hot dog and now your stomach don't feel so good. Go out back. Walk around on the grass burping, trying to get the gas out of your gut. Carol Marie and Jerry come out, him saying, So does this mean forget it? Yeah, she says. I better stay home until I find out how Michele Renee is.

He leans her against the wall, starts kissing her. You watch them, watch Jerry go for a boob, she pushing him off. I thought you liked it, he says. And she says, I never told you that. Who said I liked it? Everybody says so. Like who? Like, you know... Get out of here! she says. Talking behind my back. You bastards. She breaks away, heads for the door, Jerry saying that everybody thinks she's crazy. And now that he has heard how her parents talk, he understands why she and her brother have such bad reputations and are so fucked up. He never heard any parents talk like that in his life. His parents would never embarrass him that way. You people are freaks, he says. Screw you, she answers. I wish you would, he pleads, reaching for her. Carol Marie is obviously not going to touch him. Duffy to the rescue.

You jump in saying, Go fuck yourself, Jerry fairy. Shut up, punk! he squeaks, his voice a high C now. You flip your cigarette at him and he swears he's gonna kick your ass for that! He starts unbuttoning his camelhair coat. Carol Marie steps beside you. If you don't back off we'll both kick your ass! she warns him. Brother and sister standing shoulder to shoulder, like something out of a movie you seen: *A Tree Grows in Brooklyn*, the brother and sister beside each other catching a Christmas tree on Christmas Eve. A free tree IF they don't drop it.

Jerry looks like somebody stuck a pin in him, let all the badass out. Fuck you two warped motherfuckers, he says. Wheeling on his heel, heading for his car, slamming the door, squealing out of there, yelling something sounding like FUCKINFAMILY! Or maybe it is FREAKY FAMILY!

Going back inside, you sit at the table with Grandma Inez drinking and smoking, until around ten, when the parents bring Michele Renee home bandaged up and smelling like sulfur, a whiff of Hell. The mom saying the skin peeled off this poor baby like strips of cellophane. The burn is worse on the left breast. The doctor says she will have scarring there and may have to have plastic surgery. Michele Renee awake, looking dopey, doesn't say a word. Now and then she whimpers. Though Pappas seems exhausted, he's back at the table drinking his beer. Grandma Inez staggers to the couch, sprawling out. You take the smelly sister to bed. As you put her under the covers, she says, Duffy, do you know who's sick around here? You are, you tell her. Everybody is. Climbing in with her, cuddling the poor, sulfur-stinky thing, you are soon sleeping the sleep of gin and tonic.

~~

Not more than two months later Pappas has his own equivalent of boiling water. He gets burned by mustard gas at the arsenal. Something went wrong and somehow the gas vomited over the left side of his face. When you come home from school he is sitting at the kitchen table with an amber highball in his hand, a big bandage taped over his left eye. His humped nose jutting more than ever, a notched tomahawk. A shiny red one. His cheek watery. Wow, what happened? Did you zig when you should have zagged? Pappas replies, You better shut your fucking mouth before I shut it for you.

Backing out of the kitchen, you idle in the bedroom, until the mom comes home from work and the two of them sit at the table, Pappas telling her what happened. He says he might go blind in his left eye. You close your left eye to see how it would feel. Sorry for Pappas. Not much, but a little.

Days later the big bandage comes off and Pappas is wearing a stupid pink plastic patch over the eye. His left cheek is wrinkled. He claims it was a mistake to ever leave the Air Force, but he can re-up because he's a war veteran. So that's what he's going to do as soon as his eye heals. No more working at the arsenal. He will enlist and go wherever they send him. He says he wants to get out of this fucking two-bit town.

A month later Pappas quits wearing the patch and the first thing you notice is … handsome is no longer the word for him. His face looks pitiful. From the left side he looks cruel. The mustard eye always watering, he has to keep dabbing it with a tissue. The eyelid drooping. Reddish scars distort the area around it, making the skin look waxy. Like melting wax leaving trails.

Carol Marie chooses this time to boldly go where she shouldn't have gone. She and Marilyn go out with some boys and get drunk. So drunk that Carol Marie doesn't dare come home until she's sobered up. When she finally comes in around three in the morning, Pappas is waiting for her. He slaps her. He punches her in the eye. Giving her a shiner just like the ones he's given you and the mom. So there is a coincidence-of-the-eye tying y'all together now. Is it saying no one can see straight or see what is right in front of their noses? None can see the truth? Pappas has permanent scarring, permanent but mild damage to his vision. The mom, Carol Marie and the Duffer got over the black eyes Pappas gave them, but they have a secret club residing in your mind. Call it the Pappas Black-Eye Club. Funny in a broody way, not a belly laugh, but definitely worth a chuckle. If you like dark humor. Which of course you do.

So after punching Carol Marie, Pappas sits and drinks at the table. The morning passes. His face the color of dago red and so are his eyes. The bad one sagging, weeping. After noon he comes into your room and says, Get your ass in the car, we're gonna pay that motherfucker a visit. As the two of you drive to the motherfucker's house, Pappas lectures about the sonofabitch needing a lesson in respect. He has disrespected me, Pappas says, emphasizing the DIS. No one DIS-respects Nick Pappas and gets away with it, not no punk motherfucker like that punk motherfucker fucking my daughter. Getting her drunk and fucking her. Oldest trick in the book. You ever want to get laid, Duffy, get the bitch drunk and she'll do anything you want.

At the motherfucker's door Pappas knocks but nobody answers. So he pounds on the door with the side of his fist. And finally a little voice on the other side asks, Who is it? Pappas saying, You know goddamn well who I am! The little voice tells Pappas to go away. Open this fucking door! commands Pappas. The little voice saying, No sir, I'm calling my parents and the police. Pappas pounds on the door some more. Puts his shoulder to it. Kicks it. But it won't give, won't open and let big bad wolf in. By now Pappas is cussing non-stop, every other word is motherfucker.

In the distance is the sound of sirens. A minute or so later, two police cars arrive. You're hoping to see a big fight. One of the cops has a hand on his gun and Pappas warns him, says, You pull that gun, I'll make you eat it and you'll be shitting little toy pistols! The cop grins. It's up to you, Mr. Pappas, he says, we can go the hard way if you want to. Well, you're expecting Pappas to start swinging, but to your surprise (and devastating disappointment) bad Pappas grins his baby grin and gives up meekly, puts his hands behind his back. Turns around and winks at you after the cop cuffs him. So is it all joke, an act? They take both of you to the Aurora jail, where they have Pappas empty his pockets. After an inventory of the contents, he signs the envelope and they lock him up. While they're marching him to a cell, you slip away. Nobody stopping you, so you walk out and all the way home. The mom already knows what's happened. She says, Let him sit there and rot, the dumb bastard!

The next morning you go back to the jail, down the stairs. No one's at the desk, so you stroll along the hall searching for Pappas. The walls are cement blocks painted grayish-blue. The doors are riveted sheet steel, with a slot for food trays. At the top of each door are small barred windows for looking in and out. You find Pappas in the last cell at the end of the hall. He is sitting on his bunk masturbating. Watching him awhile, you are not at all amazed at the size of the man's crank or what he's doing with it. Finally, you back away snickering, before saying, Daddy, where are you? He answers, I'm over here, come here. Going back to the window, you look in again. Pappas is standing with his face close to the bars. You can tell by the way his shoulder is jerking that he is still jacking off. You pull yourself up on the bars to get a better look, Pappas saying, Don't come up on me!

He asks about the mom. What is she waiting for? He wants to know why she doesn't come bail him out. You got no answers. Pappas paces himself as he keeps talking, saying Carol Marie's motherfucker won't fuck with the Pappas family no more. Scared shit out of him! Scared him shitless. Little punk, little bastard, he's lucky the cops came. I would have gotten in and killed him. Go home and tell your mother I said to get her ass down here and get me out.

So you leave him still pounding away at his cock. In no hurry to get Pappas out, you dawdle. Stop by the trailer lot: HOUSE TRAILERS FOR SALE. Days ago Pappas told you to steal one of the door mats and bring it home. Which you do this jailhouse day of masturbation. Rolling up a nice one, tuck it under your arm. Lay it out later on the porch at 1648 Ironton Street. The mat saying: WELCOME TO OUR HOME.

~~

Spring is over, school out and dumb Duffy has flunked eighth grade and will have to repeat. No one is surprised. Pappas laughing, saying, I'm surprised you didn't flunk sooner. The mom shaking her head. Oh, Duffy, Duffy, she says, her tone implying a death in the family. The look in her eyes, the pain there, is ... well, painful to see. But not enough to make you sorry. Who cares anyway? The law allows you to quit school as soon as you turn sixteen. You'll drive a truck that's what. Work construction. Bag groceries. Wash dishes. Whatever you have to do. Just no more goddamn school.

That same summer Uncle Dean and Aunt Marge move to Colorado from Oregon. They show up at the Pappas house. Move into the garage. They're in Colorado to find uranium. It is a new sort of gold rush, only this ore can be used to build hydrogen bombs. Would-be millionaires swarming all over the Rockies with $98.00 Geiger counters, claim forms, pickaxes, pamphlets titled *Prospecting for Uranium*, and *Reading Your Counter*. They buy tents, canteens, Coleman stoves, lanterns, sleeping bags, snakebite kits, compasses.

Uncle Dean and Pappas and you go into the mountains west of Central City, east of Berthoud Pass. You walk around with Geiger counters for weeks and actually find uranium ore in an old goldmine that is covered over by debris and will need to be bulldozed open. A claim is filed. Money borrowed, a second mortgage taken out on the Ironton Street house. For weeks there is excavating, Dean operating the dozer. Everyone seeing dollar signs. The mom saying she has a feeling her ship has come in at last. Her palm itches. She scratches it on wood and declares: We're going to be filthy rich! An entire month that summer Uncle Dean and you live in a tent during the week, while the mom and Pappas come up weekends. You and the rugged outdoorsman uncle fish the streams nearby; eat fresh trout every night; ride horses back and forth from the mine to the camp; haul up shoring and pound it into place with wedges and sledgehammers.

One night lying in your bags, your heads outside the entrance to the tent, you take in the wonder of The Milky Way, its heavenly glory, its mystery. What's out there, Uncle Dean, whaddya think? There's a pause before he says in his no nonsense tone, Nature. You tell him you love nature. You say, I love what we're doing living close to nature, being part of it like this. I wish we could do what we're doing here forever, don't you? Again he pauses. Duffy, he says, remember this about nature. Don't treat nature like your friend. Nature is NOT your friend. If you're unlucky and do something stupid, nature will kill you just like that (he snaps his fingers). You're dead and nature keeps going about its business. Survival NOT always of the fittest, Duffy, survival of the luckiest, that's what nature and the war has taught me.

You've never thought about it that way. But you know your World War Two Marine badass uncle might be on to something. But still, the stars are brilliant. The air smells sweetly of meadow grass and pine. The stream gurgles as if it's happy to be alive. Grateful for all of it, you're ready to take chances, test your luck.

Not many days later, you are running down the side of a hill, taking what you think is a shortcut. The terrain is unfamiliar. You are trying to slow down to keep from falling forward on your face, when suddenly an open mineshaft is directly in front of you, a great round hole in the earth. You can't stop, so you speed up. At the edge you leap into the air with all your might, the black chasm passing beneath you. Barely making it to the other side, you tumble forward, heart panicking, mind picturing your helpless body falling. Crawl back to the mine, looking into it, into a void that seems as endless as a midnight sky. Throwing a rock in, you never hear it hit bottom. You would have disappeared forever. Stare into death's inky depths. Survival of the fittest? Luck? Both? Or maybe God did it? The God notion fills you with elation. It hits you that your maker must be saving you for some reason. Something special! God's invisible hand boosting you over an abyss that is far farther than you ever jumped in your life. You cross yourself: Father, Son, Holy Ghost. Walk away from the darkness waiting for the unlucky, the unwary, and never tell anyone about it, not even your sturdy uncle who faced how many death-haunted days and nights of the war? Killer-cool. Not scared of nothing. You admire him extravagantly, even though you don't entirely agree with his philosophy about Nature not being your friend.

~~

In the fall it's back for a do-over eighth grade. The only classes you like are gym and science, studying the planets. Mr. Butler, the science teacher, a guy shaped like a pear, bald stroke down the middle of his head, tufts of greasy hair above elephant ears, always smells like cigarettes. The first two fingers on his right hand yellow with nicotine. When he gives the astronomy test, Duffy aces it. Knows when he walks out of class he aced it. But when Mr. Butler gives the test back he charges you with cheating. He doesn't know how you did it: But I'm sure you cheated, he says. I know your reputation. And he says: I got my eye on you, Pappas. Well, shit, that's fucking it for science. You do only the minimum in all your classes from that day on.

~~

Hunting season, Late October 1955, a new rifle from Grandpa Mike, a .30-30 Marlin. Pappas and Dean take you deer hunting for the first time. Hunting around the area where they have the uranium mine, where they have seen lots of deer out of season. Over the course of two days, only one deer trots along in sight. You spot him first, a four-pointer a hundred yards away, and start firing. Uncle Dean joins in. The deer zigzagging up the mountain grade passing boulders passing trees, bullets kicking in front of him, behind him, all around him. Miraculously, nothing hits him. He disappears over a crest above treeline. Hunting for him, you find a trail of tracks vanishing on a lake of granite. The rest of the day is anti-climatic.

Until late afternoon heading home, Duffy in the bed of Dean's 1945 Jeep pickup, keeping eyes peeled, the Jeep winding through the woods heading back to the dirt road that will take it to Central City. You have emptied the rifle as a caution, but kept one bullet in your shirt pocket. The Jeep shifts gears, speeds up. The men have spotted something. Lever the bullet into the chamber and wait to see what they saw: three deer browsing in a small, tree-ringed meadow. Taking aim you fire before the Jeep stops. One deer falls, the other two flee. Over the side and after the wounded deer, you go, while the men chase the other two. In your homicidal excitement you leave the empty rifle behind, chasing after the deer with Dean's Ka-Bar fighting knife brought home from the war and given to you as a present to commemorate your first hunt.

Catching up with the deer, you see she's a doe pulling herself forward on her front legs. Spine broken. A bewildered, terrified look in her eyes. Duffy doesn't stab her. Deflated and half-sick he goes back to the pickup. Puts another bullet in the chamber of the Marlin. Returns to the deer and shoots her between the eyes. Turning aside, the hunter vomits.

Later, after the two men gut the deer, you're in the cab sitting on Pappas's lap. Listening to his raving about the shot, how you got the deer when the Jeep was still moving. On the run, so to speak. He and Dean fuss over you, muss your hair, pat you, uncle saying the first time he shot a deer he threw up too. He says that at least you didn't get buck fever, which is what happens when you freeze and can't pull the trigger. Good for you!

The doe is hung on the T-bar holding the clotheslines in the backyard. You skin her with the Ka-Bar, a knife the marines made purely for killing. You could kill your enemies with it. Could kill Pappas. Will kill him if he ever slugs you again. When the carcass is ready, it is sent to a butcher who returns the remains as neatly wrapped packages piled in the freezer. You brag at school about what a great shot you are, how you dropped the doe on the run. A hard thing for anyone to do. But truth is: Duffy, you're a punk. You don't like shooting deer any more than you like chopping chicken heads off. Definitely rather shoot Pappas. Rather chop his head off. Sometimes at night lying in bed, you daydream how easy it would be to kill him on a hunting trip, make it look like an accident. You tell Carol Marie what you're thinking and she says, Do it, I wish you would. The two of you plan his murder, fantasize about it, various ways of killing him and not getting caught. Can Carol Marie keep the secret? Pappas has said never trust a woman to keep a secret. The mom.

*At the root of all unhappiness is a crisis of Love.*

*-Yahia Lababidi*

End of fall '55: good, bad, ugly. The mom hears a secret she can't ignore. Carol Marie. Carol Marie and men, Carol Marie and marriage. Pappas slipping into the line of fire that day. The mom saying she shouldn't have married him. Brings up the oft repeated parable: six months after she married him hauling him out of a hotel, him playing the man-slut. Moral lesson being you can't trust him, never trusted him since that damn day, she says. Where women are concerned Pappas can't be trusted any farther than you can throw him. Carol Marie blushing, nodding agreement, saying, That's for sure. The mom, her eyes shifting left-right, left-right, a rapid metronome measuring the beating of her heart as she says, Tell me something. Has he ever touched you? Carol Marie told me she almost fainted when she answered, Yeah, he's touched me all right. And then she spilled the beans on Pappas. Told the mom what had been going on since she, Carol Marie, was eleven years old back in Urbana, Illinois. He's done more than just touch me, she said. Lots more.

SON OF A BEECH! the mom freaks.

When Pappas comes home that evening the mom's hair and face are witchy. Eyes on fire. Teeth like a rabid dog. Face of a wild thing ready to kill. She has the Luger in her hand, her voice fiery dramatic as she points the barrel at him, tells him: You get outta heer before I keel you! You son of a beech! Pappas knows his sweet deal is over. No more bopping the mom and daughter. Slipping it to one than the other, fantasizing a threesome. The chance to work his will on that one is over. He doesn't say a word. His face ashen, his upper lip trembling, his hand out as if to ward off the bullet, he backs away. Abruptly turning, he runs out the back door, down the alley. To punctuate her meaning, the mom fires twice, Pappas hauling ass claiming the hundred-yard dash record to the corner and gone.

The mom comes back inside, marches to the bedroom, throws the gun back in the drawer and starts cleaning out the closet. In minutes, there's no more evidence of Nick Pappas. All his clothes over the back fence. Littering the alley.

And that's all? It's over? That simple? I mean REALLY?

That's all there is? I tell my little sister who's hugging her pillow, staring at me as if she's afraid I might hurt her. What will happen now? Maybe Pappas will come back with a gun and shoot everyone. I load my Marlin and wait with killer intentions, heroic scenarios flickering. Waiting for him to walk in the door. Fired in self-defense, I'll say. Protecting the family. No jury would convict me. I would walk. Walk out of court a hero! C'mon, Pappas, sir. C'mon try it. I'll splatter your brains all over the wall.

After an hour or so, sitting with the rifle in my lap gets boring. Heroic daydreams fading into a shadowy house, a morbid place needing light, lots of light. Turning on the lamps and the TV, I plop Michele Renee in front of the screen and tell her to watch *The Life of Riley*. The mom stays in her room. Another hour passing and I'm wondering if we're going to get any dinner. Listening at her door, I hear hard sobbing. Peeking in I see her curled on her side. The Luger is back in her hand. Is she going to shoot herself? She points the gun at me and says, Get out of here before I kill you. Which reminds me of the time Pappas lay on the same bed with the same gun in his hand. This was just after he got thrown in jail and the mom finally bailed him out and right away he took a bottle into the bedroom and said if anyone came in he would kill them. Everyone went around whispering, looking at each other, wondering if he was going to come out firing. Shoot yourself I kept thinking. And boom! The gun went off and everyone waited, hearing nothing, thinking, hoping, praying. It was Carol Marie who finally opened the door. He lay sprawled on the bed like a dead man. But he wasn't dead, he was just dead drunk. Sleeping it off now. I saw a splintered hole in the floor and fingered it, hoping to find the bullet, but it was buried. Carol Marie took the gun away.

So this night when the mom finally runs him off and is bawling about it, I go into the kitchen and make fried baloney and egg sandwiches and glasses of chocolate milk. Carol Marie stays in her room and won't eat the sandwich I made her, so I eat it and drink her milk too. Michele Renee and I watch *I Love Lucy* and even though some serious shit has happened, we laugh at silly Lucy pulling another stunt on Desi. Later, I put the rifle back in the closet and hoist my little sister into bed.

I hear the mom in the kitchen making a drink. When she carries it back to her room I follow her. So how you doing, Mom? You okay? Her eyes look pink-rimmed blurry, distracted. She says, Shit, I sure stirred the hornet's nest this time. She is breathing fast, practically panting. She downs the drink without stopping. Hands the glass to me. I'll have another. Don't stop until I turn my glass over.

What's going to happen now? I ask. She doesn't know. I feel like dying, she says. Wish I was dead, Duffy. When you're dead nothing can hurt you. No more memories. No more pain, no more migraines. I've never been happy! Why can't I be a little bit happy? Is that asking too much? Life is sorrow and suffering, you know what I mean? When you're dead there is no more sorrows and suffering. No more goddamn *men*.

I bet Pappas wishes you was dead too, Mom.

I knew that man was poison the first time I seen him. But God he was so damn big and handsome and manly! I tell you I can't stand no more! How did I stand it this long? You don't know how long it's been. Good God if everyone knew the shit that's happened to me since I was a little girl all hell would break loose. She makes a vinegary face and spits on her palm, slaps her own cheek. Slaps it hard. So hard it glows now. Don't do that, goddammit, I tell her. We are rid of him at last. You got rid of him. You are my hero, Mom. And so is Carol Marie for finally ratting him out. All these years I've wished he was dead.

In a voice filled with an odd wistfulness the mom says, But you know, Daddy has been good to us most of the time. He's a hard worker and sweet when he's sober. And I'm thinking, Hard worker? Sweet when he's sober? Big fucking deal! But then again, I can see why the mom would go there. She admires Pappas in ways beyond tall dark handsome. She admires hard workers, she admires hustlers, those who make their own way in the world and ask nothing from nobody. She's a product of the Great Depression and knows the value of a dollar, knows the value of hard work. Truth to tell, the mom is the hardest worker I've ever known. Long hours of labor seem like nothing to her, whether it's at home or on the job, she's a dynamo. I've always wished I had her energy. Work gives you worth, she would say. Without work you're nothing. Without work you add up to zero! Pappas bought into the same philosophy. They believed in each other's talents, each other's capacities. Yeah, so okay: hard worker. Sweet when he's sober: to her!

Her eyes looking elsewhere, she lies back on the bed chewing her lips, breathing harshly as she says: But he needed to keep his goddamn hands off my daughter! Why didn't she tell me earlier? Why did she let it go on so long? Years! What's wrong with her? You can't tell me she didn't know what she was doing. What's her excuse? I'll tell you what her excuse is. He said it would kill me if she told. He told her I would end up in a mental hospital. That's what she said he said. She said it would kill me! Did she really believe I'm such a pansy it would kill me? She knows me better than that. I'm tough as nails. I'm tougher than my own mother who is the toughest broad I've ever known. To get by in this world you gotta be tough as nails, Duffy. Just remember that when things don't go your way. My whole life, nothing has gone my way, but do I say, Oh poor me! Do I whine about it? Your sister knows what I'm made of. She should have told me the first time it happened. Damn that girl, she should have told me! Eleven years old! Eleven years old and he's molesting her. Eleven. My God eleven.

Oh, if you only knew the whole truth, I'm thinking. This shit goes way back. I don't say anything, but I'm wondering does she blame Carol Marie? Her tone says she does. What's the word for her? Ambivalent? Dithering? Dickering? I really wonder where her heart is in this, because over the years she has often bitched vicious about Pappas. Saying horrible things. How brutal he can be.

How he has slapped her when she barely even glances at some other guy.

Her tirade goes on awhile. But when I join in agreeing with her, getting in a couple digs of my own, she gets defensive about Pappas. It's like she doesn't really know what she feels about him, even after she knows what he's done to Carol Marie. Not to mention her son at all. Who doesn't say a word about the many ass-kickings Pappas has given him. Yeah, maybe at this point I am brain damaged. Yeah, that might be the problem. Yeah, my excuse for the idiotic things I do. Yeah, brain damaged! Where's that lobotomy guy when you need him? He's all the rage. Saved thousands of mentally fucked up people with his ice pick. It's in the papers, the magazines. Freeman. Walter Freeman the finger of God. Come on, Walter, here's a family you can work on.

Being fair I have to admit there have been moments when I've fallen under his spell and wavered about Pappas the way the mom does. Like the time I was a dog-gnawed eight-year-old convalescent and Pappas held me on his lap, caressed me kindly. Stroking my hair, kissing my cheek, rubbing between my shoulder blades and saying, When you grow up you will be a cowboy just like Grandpa Mike says. And on and on he went, until I was purring like a kitten in his lap. This happened when Pappas and the mom were in the first stages of leaving the land of sober for the land of all things possible. I loved him then and put my spindly arms around his powerful neck and gave him kisses and listened happily to what a great future was ahead for me. The mom saying college, maybe a doctor or lawyer, become someone with education, his head straight on his shoulders. Not none of these hoodlums hanging on the streets, not our little Duffy. I might have been chewed ragged by Husky, but I was living at Grandpa Mike's and things were calm in those days. The family acting like a real family, a scene that has always stuck with me. A could-have-been—IF things had just been different. A little bit.

But this is now when she is saying: I think I might be losing my mind, Duffy. Really I wanted to shoot him, but didn't have the guts. I'd be in jail if I had and then what would happen to you kids? Grandma would never be able to take care of you. And Grandpa is not really your grandpa, so you couldn't go there either.

What to make of it? Would I have pulled the trigger if the gun had been in my hand? How can you know these things? Back when Carol Marie and I were planning our stepfather's murder it felt like I could kill—pull the trigger. Blow Pappas away. One of the plans was for hero Duffy to take his rifle and shoot his stepfather when he got up at night to go to the bathroom. Afterwards, I would say I heard a noise and thought it was a burglar. Sounded easy. Sounded doable.

How about switching to beer? I ask her, wanting to slow her down. Hard liquor makes her loony, makes her maudlin. Before you know it she'll be into her childhood, her crummy father abandoning her on the porch and never coming back, Ed Nielson beating her mother, the swing of the vase that laid him low, moving in with her aunt and uncle, her mother's disappearance, how she would come back and lavish Janice and Dean with affection before going away again, the monster cancer that had Aunt Eunice screaming in agony. Death and death. More death.

You got a cigarette? she says. A beer would be good. Getting my Lucky Strikes and a couple of beers, I bring them back to her room. Michele Renee is there rubbing her eyes and saying, When you coming, Duffy? Gruffly I tell her to go back to bed, leave me alone. And of course she starts bawling. So she gets hauled up between us. Me and the mom lying there with our heads on the headboard smoking fags, sipping Coors and watching Michele Renee curled up, sucking her thumb. Until finally she closes her eyes. Drifts off. Picking her up, I put her in bed with Carol Marie.

Who wants to know what the mom is up to. Talking shit. She's drunk. She hates men. She hates Nick Pappas most of all. But then she says he is a hard worker and sweet when he's sober. Mom doesn't know what she's saying. Shit, she's still calling him Daddy!

A sick world, Duffy, Carol Marie tells me. This whole world is so sick. I ask her was she really only eleven when it started? Her voice rushes, spitting it out: It was the first fall in Urbana the day he looked at me with those eyes. It was a warm day, Indian Summer. I was wearing a bathing suit in the backyard sunning myself and I saw him standing on the porch looking down at me, looking right at my crotch. He called me in and laid me on the couch and did the same thing to me that the guy with the cabin in the mountains did when they left us with him. Same thing exactly. Had me lay there while he put his hand on me and said, Don't worry, I wouldn't hurt you for the world. This will feel good.

I ask her: And did it feel good? Hell no. I didn't feel anything. I was too scared and confused to feel anything. But that was the first time and things progressed from there. I was this body. His toy. Did it hurt? Carol Marie shakes her head. My cherry was already broken. I broke it that time my feet slipped on the pedals of your bike and I fell on the cross bar. So what he did that day didn't make me bleed. Just stretched me out a little with his finger. Then he licked me like George Allison used to. But you know something? I learned a trick as time went on. I have this trick, Duffy. I taught myself how to get out of myself. An out-of-body experience. I learned how to shut down my mind most of the time and not feel what was being done to me. I can still do it. I have a switch that I turn off and my soul leaves and I feel nothing. I'm disembodied. It's true. I swear to God it's true.

I believe you Carol Marie. Because I'm learning to do it too.

It's a survival thing, she says.

You sure got some shit to tell your psychiatrist someday, I say. Also thinking about Karen Fielding and what the two of us did in that other dimension, where anything goes so long as some part of you isn't there. I wonder if I should tell my sister what happened with Karen in Urbana. While Pappas was doing things to Carol Marie, I was doing things to Karen, only it was mutual, both of us wanting what Carol Marie went out-of-body to escape. I've avoided thinking about Karen as much as I can, because if I think about her I'll have to touch myself. And feel horribly sinful. Does it make me a pervert? Are you anything at thirteen for sure? Or could you be anything, hetero or homo, depending on what happens next?

Wish I didn't have all these weird pictures in my head, Carol Marie says. I see him, I see his thing, I see it in me, I see Allison licking me, I see that man who lived in the mountains feeling me up. I'm a magnet for perverts, Duffy, that's what I am. It's fucked up my brain. All the shit has made me mental. The things I do! I can't explain them. God hates me I'm so awful. Men have used me all my life, like I don't have any real me at all, just this body they're after. I might as well be a doll they can blow up and play with. I just do what they want me to do. I didn't want it. I didn't ask for it, but it happened anyway. My soul is dirty, Duffy. I'm filthy inside. Only God can make me clean. If He will. If He won't kill me and send me to hell. She crosses herself. I cross myself.

We look down at sleeping Michele Renee and at each other and I can tell we're thinking the same thing. One day it will be her turn. Somewhere. Someone. And then what? Also thinking: I really don't like sex.

Carol Marie wishes we could go to Minnesota. We got relatives there. A ton of cousins and uncles and aunts. They are nice as pie from what I remember, she says. They are real people, average real people. The thing of it is they're all NORMAL, Duffy. At least I think they are. Our mother should have never left there. She has been insane ever since she took off with us, and then our real daddy died. God knows why she left. I think part of it was she didn't want any more short, blond, blue-eyed men like our father. She wanted a movie star. A tall dark one. Our dad was nothing like that. Look at us. We're what our dad looked like. She rejected him and it became a parade of men, until she married that filthy Allison. Then traded him for Nick who was Tweedledum to his Tweedledee. I think Mom has one of those split personalities, don't you? She's a Gemini. One moment she can be this perfect mother all loving and telling you she would give her life for you and she loves you more than life itself and, well, you heard it, you know what I'm saying.

Yeah, I know what you're saying. One minute Mom loves you, the next minute she's saying: Why did I ever have any goddamn kids! I drive her crazy. I suppose I ought to be nicer, but I only half-like her. And sometimes I actually hate her.

We're both bonkers, Duffy. Who wouldn't be?

She closes her eyes. I'm about to get up and go to bed, but she stops me by saying, You know what he's been doing now when I go out on dates? He waits up for me and gives me the third degree and then he bends me over the table and exams my vagina and puts his thing in me and says his sperm will kill the sperm of the other guy. He said it would keep me from getting pregnant because the sperms would kill each other. That's how gullible he thinks I am. What if our mother had gotten up and caught us at it there in the kitchen? I kept thinking something like that had to happen, but it never did. She takes those sleeping pills and nothing can wake her.

I ask her if the sex was rough. Was he mean? She shakes her head no. Not at all. He's a tender lover. He wants to make me feel something and sometimes I did a little and it would make me so depressed I wanted to kill myself. Most of the time I could flip the switch and go away and all he had was my flesh to fuck. One time he said he loved me as much as he loved Mom and it was a shame he couldn't marry both of us like the Mormons can have more than one wife. He thought life would be heaven if he could have us as his wives and we could all sleep together. Can you imagine? Crazy bastard. He lives in a fantasy world, Duffy. A sick man. Sick men are capable of all kinds of things and capable of making you sick too. Always be on your guard! You hear me? Are you listening? This is a man who, even if he doesn't actually kill you, kills you.

Yeah, I'm listening. I'm burning her words into my brain. I ask her if she remembers our real dad and she says she does. She prays to him. Sometimes she feels him watching over her, an invisible angel. She prays: Our daddy who art in heaven, hallowed be thy name. He's up there, he's watching. I believe it as sure as I believe in God. Are you learning anything? I'm eager to know all of it, but then she cuts me off, saying, I don't want to talk anymore. Go to bed. Take your sister with you. I don't want her here tonight. I want to be alone. When Grandma comes home, she can sleep with you guys.

~~

Sunday morning taming the chaos. The mom gets us out of bed early. We dress in our church duds, and she takes us to the nine o'clock mass, where we bow before Jesus Joseph Mary and stand and sit and mumble and pound our chests mea culpa telling God it's our fault. Mea culpa mea culpa, the mom murmurs as tears trickle down her cheeks. Finally she stands up, she leaves. When I follow her outside she's standing on the lawn, blowing her nose into a hanky: I have to compose myself, she says. Go back inside and ask God to forgive you for all your sins. Next Friday we are going to Confession. Don't you realize you could be dead any second and in hell? Suffering the torments of the damned. She adds in a whisper: Life is hell.

When she says life is hell, I have a revelation: The mom is right. Life equals hell, the abode of Satan who rules EVERYTHING. God and Santa Claus are fakes. Satan is real. Frightened and lost I go back inside. Sit next to Carol Marie and Michele Renee and pray God forgive my monstrous thoughts. Making the motions, crossing myself kneeling standing sitting, repeating over and over, Forgive me, God. I want to believe, make me believe. When the mass is over, I go home and pray some more. I become obsessed with praying in the same way I'm obsessed with second hands going round and round the face of the clocks in our house. Tick, tick and two seconds are over and never coming back. Two seconds closer to death and standing before an angry God giving you either thumbs up or down. Each morning I kneel beside the bed with little sis praying the Our Father. Each night we do the same thing except we add three Hail Marys full of grace as well.

When Friday comes, I'm ready for Confession, but the mom doesn't say boo about Confession. She wants to talk to me about becoming a priest. Her eyes shifting back and forth in her head the way they do when she's thinking something strange. (And she is the one who has said never trust shifty-eyed people.) On and on she lectures, saying she wants me to pray hard about being a priest, how it would be a straight shot to heaven for me and for her if I became one of God's chosen. So let us pray on it. She folds her hands. I fold mine. On our knees we pray for Virgin Mary to enter my heart. Holy Mother Mary, show this boy the way. Let him know if he has a calling. In the name of the Father, Son and Holy Ghost. Amen. I feel tingly all over my head, a sense of wellbeing swelling my heart. Virgin Mary giving me a sign?

That night before bed, Michele Renee and I pray again. I murmur all the prayers I know: The Our Father Hail Mary oh God I am hardy sorry and I believe in one God Father Almighty creator of heaven and earth alleluia alleluia show us O Lord Thy mercy and grant us Thy salvation alleluia. When I've finished I wait to see if the tingling happens again. But nothing. So Michele Renee and I hop into bed and this was one night I want to cuddle her tight. But then the pressure of her butt on my crotch makes me think of Karen Fielding. So out of bed and on to my knees again thinking about my calling that has not come, won't you come won't you come. Also thinking: Jesus, what is with you, man? Maybe all the happenings have put a spell on the house and you're controlled by demons. Don't want to be this way. Pray! Pray so hard on the hardwood floor that you bruise your knees and you like the pain and want more pain. Go in the bathroom. Wash your pee hole with soap so hard it stings. That will show the damn thing to act up.

The next day when I pee it still stings, but then the stinging wears away and I'm right back at it with my hand. It doesn't matter how much I hate sex or how long I'm on my knees, how many prayers I pray, every two or three days my cock takes control and there's nothing to be done about it. So I know I'm as weird as Pappas when it comes to sex. But at least I stay away from Michele Renee. I no longer let her sit in my lap. I growl and make faces and she bursts out crying and says, Mama, Duffy hates me! And the mom tells me to be nice to my sister. She is just a little girl. She needs you.

But the mom doesn't know. She doesn't know.

~~

Church a few more times, but the mood peters out, like it always has before. A little religion goes a long way. A crucifix is hung on the wall in her bedroom above the bed. A leather-bound version of the Bible, complete with color pictures inside, appears on the coffee table. This is a Catholic Bible, she says, the true Bible, the real Bible, not like all those other bibles. Her words confuse me because isn't the Bible the Bible? And if not? Does it mean that all the Lutherans Baptists Methodists have their separate Bibles too? The mom isn't making sense and that old Santa Claus feeling creeps in again. Like I'm being had. Shining me on.

Sometimes it's too hard to believe in God, but there are days and nights when I'm so scared of living and dying I go back to praying with all my might. And, like Carol Marie, I start praying to our dead daddy (Our Father Hud who art in Heaven) and even imagine he answers, saying things like: I'm here. I'm watching out for you, son. I tell the mom my dead dad whispers in my ear and she looks to heaven: It could happen, she says. The dead are all around us. God has a Plan and the dead are helping make the Plan come true.

For weeks the mom has me and Carol Marie take turns reading passages from the real Bible before dinner. *Suffer the little children to come unto me and forbid them not for of such is the kingdom of God.* Suffer them? Why the suffer part? Grandma Inez refuses to read passages when she's home for dinner. She continues to insist God is the Great Spirit Giche Manidoo. Steadfast in her belief that the only way to pray to him is to wrap the prayer in smoke and blow it skyward while wearing a bright red or blue outfit. The better for Giche Manidoo to see you. Your way of praying is boring, she snorts.

The uranium get-rich scheme falls through next. Pappas and Uncle Dean lose all their money. The Cadillac is sold and replaced by an ugly four-door 1950 maroon Desoto, a gutless piece of scrap metal. Dean gets a job selling Triple-AAA insurance. Aunt Marge goes to work for Samsonite Luggage doing I don't know what. She's a big-boobed woman with overly large teeth and an ass too broad for her very slim waist. She seldom talks. At least not to me. Truly I don't think she likes me. She and my uncle have a nice tidy apartment in the garage, they've really fixed it up. The mom doesn't charge them rent. She says they help with the groceries and that's enough. They'll live off her for years, until they've socked away money enough to buy a Cadillac and a house. That's when they'll move out, but I'll be long gone by then.

~~

Pappas re-enlists in the Air Force with his old rank of sergeant. He is stationed at Lowry in Denver. He keeps calling Carol Marie, trying to get her to say it was all a lie. Trying to get her to say she exaggerated because she was angry and wanted to get him back for giving her a black eye. Which story only a fool would fall for. She meets him once. She tells me she doesn't know why she went. She doesn't know how he persuaded her. It is like she is a puppet and he the puppet master. Part of her told her not to go, but the other part that had always obeyed him couldn't disobey him when he said: Meet me in the Zanzibar parking lot. They sat in his car and talked. He kissed her gently, whispered in her ear that she had broken his heart. His love for her wasn't a love between father and daughter. His was a love between a man and a woman. His was a love he couldn't help. You can't stop love, he said. It happened between me and you. We didn't mean for it to happen, it just did. Can't you see that, honey? No, she couldn't see it. I don't love you, Nick, she told him. I'm sorry but I don't. Not true, he insisted. When the dust settles you'll see I'm right. You'll see what we did wasn't bad, it was love. I know you love me and you know it too, he said, trying to hug kiss her some more. But Carol Marie pushed him away, got out of the car and walked. Walked home as fast as her feet would carry her. Closed the door. Locked it. He called and called, but she wouldn't see him anymore. She told me: The look in his eyes terrifies me. His bad eye is like the eye of an evil spirit, the evil eye.

So Pappas starts working on me, calling me up, taking me for rides, buying me toasted cheese sandwiches, root beer floats and chocolate fudge sundaes at A&W, giving me money, telling me things like: You're my only son. Saying he is proud of how tough I am now. Taking credit for the badass version of the Duffer. I'm as malleable as a marshmallow in Pappas's hands. He is driving a very fine cream-colored '39 Ford. He lets me drive it all over town. The shift on the floor is very cool. Pappas is living in a rooming house not far away from Ironton Street, about five miles is all. He takes me there, introduces me to the owner, saying, This is Duffy. He's my son. The woman saying, I can tell he is. You want some banana cream pie and a glass of milk, Duffy? Sure do! She calls herself a pie-baking machine. Hers is the most humongous bubble butt I've ever seen in my life, a real Hottentot Venus.

The family doesn't go visit Grandpa Mike in Frederick. He is still Michele Renee's grandpa, but the mom quits going out Sundays with gallon jugs of water. We never have dinner with him again. Fading, he fades out of our lives because, well, he is Pappas's papa and the mom doesn't want to be associated in any way with anyone associated with Pappas.

> *I don't believe in anything anymore:*
> *god, country, money or love*
>
> *- Dorianne Laux*

She has dyed her hair platinum blond (Marilyn Monroe style) and has a boyfriend named Tommy, an officer in the Air Force, a captain. When he comes over, she takes a blanket out on the front lawn and they sit having a picnic, drinking eating talking. Lots of laughter. See us? See what a good time we're having? The neighbors know what's going on, but she doesn't care. She is flipping them off, saying fuck you, go to hell. This is Janice's life and she will live it the way she wants to live it. Live it to the hilt. She wasted seven years on Nick Pappas. Going to make up for lost time now. Seven years. A failed marriage. Seven years. Seems like SEVENTY, she says.

Tommy is a big guy. Maybe slightly bigger than Pappas. Short-cropped Air Force hair. Broad, manly shoulders. Deep chest. A chin that could chop kindling. He has a neat little mustache, two thin threads outlining his upper lip like Errol Flynn. Glad to have him around to keep the mom company. Keep her cheerful energetic vivacious. He seems to like you fine, but at a distance. Clearly not thinking of himself as a potential daddy. The two of them drink as much as she and Pappas used to. Sometimes they get the music going, push the furniture back and whoopee! Michele Renee and you joining in. Singing! Dancing! Making everyone laugh. Everyone ecstatic. Life is good! What a relief not to have Pappas home anymore.

So the two of them, Tommy and the mom, raise hell for a few weeks, maybe two months. Bar hopping and making erotic noises in the bedroom. And Duffy is thinking maybe Tommy will be the next daddy. Why not? Yeah well, unfortunately, it turns out Tommy is married. Has a wife in Chattanooga. When he quits coming around, the mom dives into one of her depressions, threatening to kill herself. She has had it with men for sure this time. Maybe she has had it with life she's saying. And she says: If it weren't for you kids I would take the gun and shoot myself, she repeats it again and again. Kids. Gun. Shoot. Myself, myself.

~~

Not long after losing Tommy, she dyes her hair carrot red and hooks up with a motorcycle baddy named Harry. Great flame of her hair blowing behind her as she hangs on to him, the motorcycle zooming down Ironton. Look at her go! Wearing sexy outfits, leather vests, black gloves, biker boots. Going to biker bars, she and Harry having a grand time. One of his buddies, Charlie, takes you riding with him. Hauls ass down Interstate 70. Prairie flying by in a blur. The power vibrating beneath your ass is arousing. You want an iron horse! Indian or Harley. When you arrive back home, Charlie rolls the bike right up on the lawn and you jump off and start begging: Let me take the bike for a spin, Charlie. Will you, huh, please, please! Do you know how to drive this thing? Charlie asks. You telling him: Hell yes I know how. Also thinking: Hey, can't be any harder than driving a car, can it? You seen how he shifted, how the gears rise and rise, how the brakes work, how the throttle cracks open and shoots the bike through the air like a rocket. Reluctantly, nice guy Charlie agrees to let you in the saddle, just a little spin round the block is all. Go slow. Be careful. You slide onto the seat, grip the handlebars. Charlie sitting behind saying, Easy now, easy now as you crack the throttle voom! voom! Pull in the hand clutch, kick the gear shift down one and bam! shazam! do a wheelie right off the lawn. Charlie flying off the back as the bike unicycles down Ironton for several yards before the front wheel slams down. The power! The fucking power! Duffy is frozen by the power, petrified hand keeping the throttle open. He don't shift, he don't pull the brake, he don't use the clutch, he don't turn the key to kill the engine. Racing down Ironton in first gear, heading for busy East Colfax Avenue. Ahead are evergreen bushes bordering some one-story apartments. Out of control heading for the evergreens, plowing through branches before veering back to the road, the loose gravel of Ironton causing the rear wheel to shift like a belly dancer shaking her hips so hard you nearly go down. You've heard there are two kinds of motorcyclists: those who have been down and those who eventually go down.

At long last you get it through your thick skull that you need to take your right hand off the throttle. As soon as you do that, the roaring is over, the bike drifting to a wobbly stop, plopping onto its side like you done killed it, killed the iron horse. Standing there looking at it in utter shock. My God, so much power it paralyzed you! Hear Charlie cussing screaming, calling you a dumb motherfucker, a stupid sonofabitch! In a minute he's beside you panting, pushing you out of the way, hoisting the bike up, straddling it, starting it, looking at startled Duffy and saying, Kid, you're too dumb to fucking live! Charlie takes off towards East Colfax. That's the last you ever see of him. And then days later Harry takes off too, no more motorcycle rides and the mom is blue, hating men with all her heart again. They're all rotten bastards, she says, eyes scornfully glaring at her son.

~~

Nearly every Friday night since January, you've taken a bus to Denver, crossed over the Adam's County line, searched for a car to steal. Crossed into

Adam's because in your steely mind it is only right that you don't steal from the county where you live, which is Arapahoe. In the thirteenth year of your carefully considered life you heist a dozen cars at least. The first one was a V-8 Chevy, which you took to HOFFY'S USED AUTO PARTS and asked inside for Wally just as Mike the Knife had told you to do. What you want, punk? he said. I got a Chevy for you, Mr. Wally. What? Come here! he said. Took you out back among the acres of junked cars. Grabbed your collar, fat face nose to nose, breath full of bile as he said, Who the fuck sent you? Mike the Knife, you told him. That asshole! You get your fuckin ass out of here before I break your neck. Settin me up, you sonofabitch! So that was that. The beginning and the end of the Duffer's chop shop life.

Kept stealing cars, though. It was like you were addicted. The adrenal rush high as heroin you're thinking. Drive them around by yourself mostly, but sometimes with a buddy, of which you don't have many left from the old days. Parents hate the Duffer. They don't want their sons hanging round him. He don't blame them. Troublemaker. Evil-evil. A girl in civics glares at you with hatred one day when you pick a fight with some stupid guy in class. She shut you down by saying, Son of Satan! You're the Son of Satan! I hate you! she said. You're going to hell!

Geez, what did you ever do to her? Ain't done nothing. The mom taught you to always be nice to girls and never hit them—otherwise you would have knocked that mouthy little bitch right on her can.

~~

Old pal Jack is game for a joyride. So one night you steal a pale blue '50 Ford off a car lot. It has Donald Duck whitewalls. The back end jacked up, so the car rides like a raked racer. Drive it over to Jack's. He sneaks out and the two of you tear up the streets of Aurora. Later, out to the arsenal, the back roads, putting the Ford through its paces, a rabbit runs out, the bumper bumping it, ending the life of one unfortunate Thumper.

You keep the car three days. Drive it too hard, burn up the engine. Probably it needed oil. Or water. Or both. Two days later the cops are at your house again. Back to the Aurora jail where you're told that Jack confessed and named you as an accomplice. You shrug your shoulders. Give a statement. When they ask about the blood on the bumper, you tell them a rabbit committed suicide. A cop slaps the back of your head. You're not funny, you little punk, he says. The lab is testing the blood, so you better be telling the truth. Did they really think you might have killed someone, a person, hit and run? In their shoes you'd probably think the same thing. No doubt about it you would.

A cop leads you downstairs, locks you in a cell right next to the one where you had watched Pappas having a honeymoon with his hand. Jack is already there. He says the cops knew you were in on it. They had your name, he says. You're famous all over town, Duffy. They called you an incorrigible criminal and said I shouldn't listen to you or hang around with you. I told em to fuck off.

Yeah?

Yeah.

Jack is full of shit, but you don't care. What you're wondering is if the mom will come bail you out, or will she finally wash her hands of you, like she keeps threatening to do? Or maybe finally send you to a psychiatrist to get the warps out of your brain. Get you on pills guaranteed to calm the Duffer down, make him behave NORMALLY. Be a good boy like you haven't been since you were eight or nine.

Jack climbs up on one of the bunks, puts his mouth to a round chrome speaker in the ceiling and says, Yoo hoo, all cops are bastards! Yoo hoo! He taps on the speaker with his knuckle. Yoo hoo! Tap, tap. All cops are bastards! A growling voice angrily says: You kids better knock that shit off right now! Jack laughing and still tapping the speaker, tap, tap. And repeating Yoo hoo! All cops are bastards. You hear the key in the lock. Oh-oh. The door opening. Two cops coming in and kicking both your asses. You cover up and don't even try to fight back. Helpless hapless hopeless.

Later, they transport the two of you to Brighton, the Adam's County jail, where they lock you in a corner cell big enough to hold eight juveniles. Jack and you are the only two delinquents there.

Two days later the mom is in court, a stricken look on her teary face, looking as if a doctor has told her she has cancer, six months to live. You can't stand her pity-me face saying look what I have to put up with. In fact you hate her guts. The judge is an old fart named Garrison. After a long, boring lecture about how you're ruining your life and the lives of those who love you, he puts you on probation. And tells you: If I ever see you in my courtroom again for anything you'll be going to the Industrial School for Boys at Golden. You give him your fuck you stare. Cock your head. Wrinkle your lip into a contemptuous sneer. The gesture saying, I'm not scared of you, you old bastard. What's with this attitude? You act like you have a hole in your head big enough for hummingbirds to fly through. Where'd this warped way of thinking come from? You used to be such a nice kid.

Not long after playing jailbird, Jack leaves town. His parents move him away and, just like Craig, you don't see him anymore. So what if grownups despise you? You despise them too! The cops and the mom and the teachers telling you you're horrible, a bad influence in need of therapy. You don't change your ways you'll come to a bad end, Duffy. But who the hell cares? You care about nothing nobody. Fuck them. Fuck everyone. They can all kiss my—

~~

Now and then a kid named Little Jake hops in for joyrides with you. And sometimes it is Big Lee, but he's new to it and not quite comfortable. His parents are good to him. Love him and he them. He has three sisters, one of them brain damaged so badly she can't speak, walks crippled, fingers bending like she's an arthritic crone. She slobbers constantly. Creeps you out. But big-hearted Big Lee is good to her. He is kind. Protective. Too nice a guy to hang with the likes of Duffy Pappas. Big Lee is five foot ten, muscular, very good at basketball. He and you had been on an intramural basketball team back in seventh grade and were chosen to be on one of the two All Star squads at the end of the season. You played guard. You could dribble equally well with both hands. Passed well too and got lots of assists. But hitting the basket was not exactly your talent. When your All Star squad played the other All Star squad, Big Lee shined. You really didn't belong there. Rode the bench. Too small for basketball. Too small for football. Don't much like baseball since the time you played catcher and the batter accidentally hit you in the back with the bat. Knocked the wind out. Screw baseball. Good at long distance running, though, and wrestling.

~~

The mom brings home a new boyfriend. Name of Earl. A cream-coffee Negro, with a thin mustache like Tommy had. He wears colorful cravats. Keeps his curly hair shiny and laid back with pomade. Always smelling sweet as peaches. Shy at the house, doesn't say much, only comes over after dark and always nervous waiting for Janice to finish dressing. She claims his people have taken to her as if she is one of their own, like she has African blood in her veins. He is a lovely man, she keeps saying. And she says, The instant I laid eyes on him I seen he was as good inside as the day is long. Don't he remind you of Duke Ellington?

He treats her like a lady, opening doors for her, standing behind her chair, pushing it in when she sits down. Pulling it out when she stands up. When she walks into the room, he rises to show his respect. Very courteous, old-fashioned, gentle darling. She says, When I seen him dance I thought he must be professional. But he's not. He taught himself. Well, you know, his people got rhythm, his people invented blues jazz, you know. I'll tell you something, God's truth, Earl reminds me of your father on the dance floor, Duffy.

Your father? This is the first time the mom has mentioned that your REAL father was a good dancer. You know next to nothing about him. Dad was a good dancer? How good? Her eyes look upward as if searching for him up there. You know, she says, I think I fell in love with him because of the way he moved on a dance floor. That's right. It's true. Hud was every bit as good as Earl. Hud's feet could fly. He was a bartender when I met him and let me tell you nobody messed with him. I saw him throw a guy out one night, a drunk causing trouble. Picked this guy right up from behind and ran him out the door. Your dad might have been a bit short, but he was thick, full of muscle. He was a man's man, your dad.

Well shit, Duffy, you're dazzled! A man's man? You want to hear more and more about daddy Hud. How'd he die? She looks away: Hud died in a fire, a tanker truck accident. Some damn fool lit a cigarette at the depot where your dad was filling his tanker. Everything exploded. He lived a week before his burns killed him. He was in New Orleans then, writing me letters. We were talking about getting back together. Let me tell you something, he loved you kids, loved you to death. He was a good man and he shouldn't have died so young. He was only thirty years old.

Thirty years old. Carol Marie remembers him, but you don't. Maybe that's just as well. Hard to miss someone all that much if you can't remember ever meeting him.

Grandma Inez skips Zanzibar one night to stay home and meet Earl. She is very polite, smiling, shaking his hand, saying, Very pleased to meet you at last, Earl.

But when they leave on their date she goes: What the hell is the matter with her? Play with fire and you gonna get burned. Mark my words.

~~

A cold winter's night, Little Jake and you steal a '56 Chevy, a very fine car, except only a six cylinder. As you drive around aimlessly you say to Little Jake, Hey, let's go to Casper, Wyoming. You talk about Rodney Booker's grandpa owning a cattle ranch. We could be cowboys! Little Jake's caterpillar eyebrows leap upward. His two front teeth grinning, reminding you of a rodent, a mouse, as he says, Cowboys? Cool!

That's all it takes. You drive over to Big Lee's house and knock on his bedroom window to see if he wants to go, but he won't wake up. Or maybe he is awake but playing possum, not wanting to court trouble. Not wanting to hurt his parents, maybe? You stop at a gas station for a map to figure out how to get to Casper. Then head into a white world, the roads wintry and ice-patched. Snow skirting the sides of the highway. The car slipping and sliding but making headway. Past Cheyenne and not too far from Casper, the car runs out of gas in a little town called Glenrock. Four in the morning and every house dark, except here and there a porch light burning. In the foggy air the streetlights hazy, electric blue. The sky obscure. Lone flakes twirling like afterthoughts.

Because of the hard freeze no one has a hose out, so you can't cut a piece to make a siphon and steal gas from one of the many cars parked at the curbs. Close by there is a trailer park. You and Little Jake push the car up to a trailer's fuel tank. There is a long piece of copper tubing running from the tank into the house into its furnace. You bend the end of the tube back and forth until it breaks and you can snake it into the Chevy's gas pipe. After you half fill the car, you turn off the tank's spigot, so the rest of the fuel won't go to waste. Push the car out of the park, back to the road. The engine starts. But its got problems. The fuel in the trailer's tank is not real gas, at least not the kind the Chevy needs. You'll learn later that the Chevy doesn't know how to run on number two diesel. It keeps stalling and re-starting. The rest of the way to Casper is done by leaps and jerks, but you manage to get there before the car dies for the last time. Won't fire no matter how much you worry the starter. Duffy, you're hard on cars. You've mangled the fender of the old Pontiac, killed the engines of the Chevy grain truck, the '50 Ford, and this brand new '56 Chevrolet. Cars are going to have to get tougher if they're to survive the Duffer.

So hoof it the rest of the way into town. People getting up. People going to work. Cars and pickups on the roads. A place called Corky's Café is open. Go inside and order bacon and eggs and fried potatoes with buttered toast and coffee. After eating, you feel capable of handling anything. In fact, you feel ... optimistic. Gonna be a cowboy! You go to phone booth in back. Look up the name Rodney Booker. There are three Bookers listed, one is R. T. Booker. A woman answers the phone. You ask if Rodney is there. She says, Rod senior or Rod junior? Junior, you tell her. Rodney! Phone! A few seconds later a sleepy voice says, Hullo. Hey, Rodney, it's me, it's Duffy from Aurora. Remember me? Carol Marie's brother? Oh yeah, he says. Hey, what's up, man? When you tell him you're in town having coffee with a buddy at Corky's he goes, No shit? Corky's? You're here? What's goin on, Duffy? We come to Casper to be cowboys. We want to work on your grandpa's ranch like you said we could. Rodney says, Shit. Sit tight, I'll be right there.

He arrives in a bitchen black and yellow '55 Ford two-door. Tools around Casper while you explain about the burned-out Chevy. Rodney saying, We need to hide that thing. The license plate will give you away. Cops will be swarming all over this town looking for you. At that moment you feel like a true desperado. Jesse James. Billy the Kid. Rodney knows a place to hide the car, an old garage nobody uses. Tow the car there, push it in, close the double doors. As you turn away, you notice a white-whiskered snoop looking out his back window on the other side of the alley. That guy is going to tell the cops, you say.

Rodney calls his girlfriend. She says come on over. You all hang at her house and make a plan to dye your hair to disguise yourselves. Rod drives to the store but brings back only enough dye to do one person's hair. That's when you become a redhead, auburn, same color the mom's hair used to be before she went platinum and then carrot. Rodney has to go home for a while. He says he'll be back later to take you and Little Jake out to Grandpa Booker's ranch. Cowboy hat, ropes, horses. You can hardly wait.

About three in the afternoon he phones and says his grandpa doesn't need any hands until summer. You ask him about Mike the Knife. Can we hook up with him? Mike said he would make me a partner if I come to Casper, you say. Rodney answers: Yeah, you can be his partner if you want to go to San Quentin. Mike got busted for running a car theft ring in Sacramento. Rodney doesn't know what to do with the two of you. He says he'll be over in a minute. But the minute becomes an hour and he doesn't show. His girlfriend has been lots of fun, but now she insists, You guys gotta go. My parents will be home soon, she says. So you leave her house as evening comes on and the cold is very cold and the only thing to do is steal another car, head back to Aurora. A block away you luck onto a pickup with the keys in the ignition. You tell Little Jake, The god of thieves is looking out for us.

Instead of going straight to 25, you detour to Rodney's house to say goodbye and to thank him for trying to help you. His mother comes to the door and says the cops have taken him away. They found the Chevy in the garage. They know all about you two, she says, and if you don't do something Rod will go to prison like that idiot Mike. So what the hell, you step inside and call the cops, tell some officer that Rodney Booker had nothing to do with stealing the '56 Chevy. You and Little Jake are arrested and locked away for several days, before being transported to Brighton, Colorado, the Adam's County jail again. Within hours, Little Jake goes in front of the judge and is given probation. His parents take him away.

There is a new judge on the bench, not mean old Garrison, but a young one named Jacobucci. Jean Jacobucci. He has soft brown eyes and thin dark hair combed back with a part on one side. He has a way of looking at you that makes you feel guilty and sad and sorry. With tears in her eyes, the mom pleads for her wayward son. She asks Jacobucci not to send her son to the reformatory. Heartbreaking sobs, her voice trembling, telling him how tough life has been since the divorce and before that when the boy's father died in a terrible fire in New Orleans. My boy needs help, not reform school. He's mixed up. Everything she is saying makes you feel awful sorry for yourself. Sorry for her too. The judge taps a pen on a file in front of him. Tapping as he listens. Tap, tap, tap. Finally, he opens the file. Reads aloud what Garrison had written recommending The Industrial School for Boys, Jefferson County, Golden, Colorado if Duffy Pappas doesn't stay out of trouble. What can you say to me, young man? says the judge.

Well, sir. I couldn't feel more bad for what I done. You tell him the mom is right, things are all screwed up in your head and ... I sure am heartily sorry for the trouble I keep causing. Just wanted to go work on a cattle ranch. Just wanted to herd cows. Be a cowboy, your honor sir. Be a cowboy? says the judge, giving a look that means get your head out of your ass, young man. Is that an excuse to steal a car? Why would you just do it? What possessed you? I don't know what made me do it, don't know why I can't stay out of trouble. In your most sincere voice you tell the judge, If you give me another chance, your honor, sir, I promise to go back to school and work hard and not steal no more cars. You don't look like a bad boy, Jacobucci says, his voice so soft so tender the sound of it makes you feel like bawling. It's obvious your mother loves you, the judge continues, and you love her. That's more than half the battle. Eyes searching. Pen tapping. He says: I'm going to give you one more chance, but if you're ever in here again, it's over. Do you understand me, young man? You nod. Yes sir, Your honor. You won't be sorry. Jacobucci replying, I certainly hope not. He gives you more years on probation, extending it to age eighteen.

When you get home you learn that Little Jake was sent to relatives in Alabama to get him away from that damn Duffy Pappas's pernicious power. Seems like an overreaction. Duffy don't have no power over nobody. Little Jake and other friends who get in trouble just do what they do. They don't need the Duffer to manipulate them. Those boys aren't puppets. Who is?

*Love, forgive us—cinders, ashes, dust*

*-John Keats*

 Janice gets burned by Earl just like Grandma Inez predicted. Actually burned by his friends and family. She wanted to be one of them (same as Grandma Inez wants to be Chippewa and I want to be Cheyenne), but Earl's people didn't want white bread in their midst. Earl wanted her, but his mother and sister were against blacks and whites dating or mating. One night having a party, boozing, dancing, Earl's sister got drunk and picked a fight with Janice. All kinds of racial nastiness spewing out. Janice always says she isn't prejudiced and she doesn't want her kids being prejudiced either. Coloreds are as good as whites and don't you dare call them niggers, not in my house. She didn't say that to Pappas when she was married to him. Blacks weren't Blacks or Coloreds to him, they were Niggers. But after she threw him out, the nigger word was banned in her presence. So at this party she tried to tell Earl's family all about how she is color blind when it comes to love.

 Ultimately, she couldn't sell that story. She and Earl broke up and she comes home saying no more men and especially no more colored men. Her eyes are swollen from crying. She sits at the table muttering about how the other women told her to keep her white ass away from Earl and stick to her own kind. Who did she think she was coming into their territory stealing their men? Earl had tried to intervene, but the women shut him down. Shamed him for betraying his people. Janice was told to get the hell out and she did. She says: Those women were dangerous. I thought they was gonna kill me, I really did. Told you, says Grandma Inez, her tone full of satisfaction. Satisfied big time, you betcha.

~~

 I go out for track in the spring of 1956. I'm good at long distances. Make the 440 my event. That and the mile relay. Try pole-vaulting, which I'm not very good at, lucky to clear eight feet, but that's enough to put me on the team. At the first track meet, there is a kid named Bill Bailey who is the fastest 440-yard dasher in the county. I line up next to him. When the gun fires, I stick to Bailey's shoulder, keeping a yard off the pace. The guy running in front has gone off the line like a greyhound chasing a rabbit, like we're doing a 100-yard dash, but two-thirds of the way round he runs out of gas and Bill Bailey and I pass him. One and two at the stretch, I give it all I have. Neck and neck, but Bailey has more reserves and at the wire he beats me. Later, my mile relay team comes in second. I don't place in pole vaulting. Still, coming in second in both the 440 and as anchor of the mile relay is an accomplishment I'm proud of. I'm given two second-place ribbons and for a while I behave myself. Concentrate on track: don't steal no cars, ponder going straight, making a name on the field, maybe win a scholarship to college. I imagine myself running into the record books. The future full of Duffy glory,

But the best laid plans and all that: when the team is getting ready for the next meet, I find myself in a fight with one of the other pole-vaulters, a kid who had vaulted higher in practice that day than I did. So Coach gave him my spot. I could have still gone as our best 440 man, but that kid beating me out of vaulting makes me mad. It was a fucking fluke, I tell him. He claims he beat me fair and square. He tells me if I don't like it, tough shit, Pappas, kiss my ass. Instead of kissing his ass I smack him. He smacks me back. We rumble. I'm a much better boxer. Really, no bragging, just fact: he doesn't have a chance. I hit him at will and slip all of his punches easily. The team surrounds us, everyone yelling. The noise brings Coach out of his office. He breaks it up and kicks both of us off the team. My season of glory is over. When the semester ends I'm passed on to ninth grade. Go back to my wicked ways.

~~

Early summer 1956, a year of many happenings. Me and Big Lee go to a carnival in Aurora and get in an argument with a carney who says he saw us stealing rides on the merry-go-round. Yeah, stealing rides is true, but I tell him he's a goddamn liar. The carney punches me in the jaw. I don't go down, but for a few seconds it's like someone has vacuumed my mind. See nothing, hear nothing. Out on my feet. Weird feeling. Lucky I don't get hit a second time because I'm wide open and helpless. The guy walks away. Long-sideburned Lee (how I envy those Elvis sideburns!) says, Hey, that fucker punched you, Duffy. What are you going to do? Well, the guy is way too big for the Duffer, but not too big for the Pappas.

So me and Big Lee bop over to the Pappas place. Tell him what happened. He drives us back to the carnival and as we're walking through he says, Which one slugged you? I see him and say, That guy, Daddy! Pappas rushes after him, but shoots right past and grabs this twig manning a booth and says: Did you hit my son? Twig all confused, and I'm saying, It's not him, it's that guy over there, the big guy, Daddy. In seconds we're surrounded by a bunch of carneys. One of them is the manager. He asks if there's a problem. Pappas tells me to tell what happened. So I do. And the manager says he don't want trouble. He says he'll fire the guy. Pappas is satisfied. I'm not, but nothing to do about it. As we walk away, Pappas says: Did you see the size of the ring that SOB had on his finger? You don't want to get hit with something like that. It would be like getting nailed with brass knuckles.

~~

Carol Marie meets a guy named Dan Shale who has a very fine '55 Ford, all white with pink interior, a pussy whupper for sure. She is sixteen and madly in love. They're inseparable. She believes Shale will marry her. She thinks God has forgiven her for all the sinful things she's done. I watch her soften. Watch her morphing into a sentimental tool her boyfriend can use. She believes in Dan Shale like she believes good people go to Heaven. She believes in love and marriage and having children and living happily ever after. This is sis? Tough, much abused, no nonsense sis? All gooey gaga over a blond-haired, blue-eyed Casanova who takes her out, parks the car where lovers park, the hill overlooking the airport, where they watch the planes land. He holds her. Kisses her. Mouth to mouth he says, Carol Marie, I think I love you. She melts, dying for him. I love you too, she says. Oh, Dan, oh, Dan, it's too good to be true. Big sis is putty in his hands the same way I've been putty when Pappas takes me for A&W dinners, gives me money and keeps saying, You're my only son, son.

Daddy Pappas wanting to turn over a new leaf, wanting to be my pappy for real. He says to tell the mom how good he is to me now. I promise I will tell her. But I don't. I've no idea why I'm betraying the family letting Pappas use me. Don't know why all the years living as if chained to the god of war hasn't made me avoid Pappas like a depth charge. I tell nothing to nobody. And then one day it don't matter no more. Because Pappas is gone. Transferred to Elmendorf Air Force Base, Anchorage, Alaska. No more free root beer floats, toasted cheese sandwiches, hot fudge sundaes. Banana Cream Pies. No more bribe money. No more driving the bitchen '39 Ford with the shift on the floor. Not that I miss any of it. Not really.

One night there's a long distance phone call for Janice from Pappas. He apologizes for any hurt he's caused her. He begs Janice to forgive him and please join him in Anchorage. He's a changed man, he says. I'll always love you, he says. Voice tender. To her he sounds … contrite. She tells us later that she felt sorry for him, sorry for everything, but it's time to move on. Some part of her will always care, she says. She doesn't wish anything bad for him. All the luck in the world. Goodbye, goodbye. God forgives and so do I. I ask her if there's any chance of moving to Anchorage. I wouldn't mind getting out of Aurora, going north to Alaska, the Final Frontier. The thought makes me long for Jack London and Robert Service, the odyssey of the north, the law of the Yukon: Send not your foolish and feeble; send only your strong and your sane— I want a life on the trail. Man tested by Nature. I want to live like my literary heroes lived, no holds barred. Wild wide borders stern as death. The mom vetoes it, says: Nope. Forget it! I was at the end of my rope with that man, just too stupid to know it. Bad blood. That's what he is. His mind is twisted. Grandma Inez puts her two cents in, saying, Men! And pretending to spit. The mom agreeing: Goddamn men.

The last thing I need in my life is another goddamn man!

~~

That fourteenth autumn of my life finds me with a horde of others partying at Julie's. Kids from school hanging out on the porch, the front and back yards, in the living room, the basement, where Julie and her big sister share a bedroom. The house is filled with cigarette smoke, perfume, the aroma of beer and B.O. A recipe I've come to equate with wild things, something exciting about to happen. Julie has a pint of Seagram's she's mixed with Seven-Up. Calling it Seven and Seven.

We get high and horny on the sofa, kissing and groping. I squeeze her butt. Nice butt. And continue drinking. In no time my world is painless. I have all the liquid courage needed to give Julie what she really wants. She swabs my mouth with her tongue. I swab hers. Warmth flushing my pants. Making me squeeze my thighs together and think of Karen Fielding. Her hand guiding me in. I want to get away from all the schizos standing around smoking drinking kissing pubic pumping caterwauling cacophonic chaos: shrill sounds making my bad eardrum bubbly. The place so crowded you can't walk anywhere without fender-bending some sweaty BODY.

Julie, I say, how bout we be by ourselves? There must be an empty room somewhere. No one is allowed in my parents' bedroom, she tells me, running a hand round and round my thigh close to the source and claiming, None of these cats care what we do. Her slick mouth swallowing me for two, three minutes, before she pulls back and whispers, Duffy, you are such a good kisser. Am I? Uh huh.

Well trained. Learned kissing from Carol Marie. She is an expert. One night with nothing to do the two of us talking about kissing. As an experiment she kissed me. Made a face. Said it felt like kissing a board. She had me open my mouth a little, create some suction, put my lips in motion. I caught on right away and she started waving her hand and saying, Whew, we better stop this right now. She went into her room and that was the end of that, but I would have kept going if she had wanted to.

So with Julie this night the two of us creating a vacuum with our mouths sucking each other's lips, tongues, earlobes. Hickey each other's necks. Sexy. Very. Her hand slipping to the seepy place, pumping me like Connie pumped me back in Illinois. I let Julie do it for a few seconds before I'm about to lose control and have to make her stop. I look up and see a bunch of grinning kids watching us. I'm a little shy about putting on a porn show for them. Also thinking: if she can run her hand up my leg and jackhammer wood, I can finger her honey pot. Julie smells musky and feral. Ready for whatever. I'm palming one of her breasts. Squeezing the spongy thing. She brushes my hand away. Jumps up. Says she has to go to the bathroom.

I stroll around. Drink Seven and Seven and cool off. On the stereo a vinyl 45 spinning. Elvis Presley singing don't be cruel to a heart that's true. It occurs to me that Don't Be Cruel is the only song I've heard all night. Lori is curled in a big armchair next to the record player sobbing. I ask pimply Joanne, What the fuck's wrong with her? Oh, Robbie broke up with her, says Joanne. Lori really looks stupid, I say. You come to a party and blubber all night? Joanne wants to know what I'm drinking. I let her smell it. She makes a face, says, How can you stand this stuff? She holds up a bottle of Coors and adds, This shit's no good either. You can have it if you want it. But I'm thinking: If I drink her beer I might get pimples too.

More of Julie is what I want. More kisses. More milking her sponges. I bump my way through the crowd and knock on the bathroom door. What the fuck you doin, Julie? She lets me in and says: What took you so long? Again my mind backs up to Karen Fielding, the basement, Bart Moore and Duffy Pappas taking turns. Leaning in, I visualize Karen while giving Julie sloppy smooches and feeling her breasts. Which seem smaller than before. Where did her bra go? Everything new. Everything fun. Everything steamy and sweet.

Jesus, they warned me about you, she says, hot whisky breath in my ear. She's slipping into droopy angles, thighs-wide. A hand up her skirt, all the way to damp panties. Goddamn you, Duffy, she murmurs, her lips nipping my neck. Her legs opening more as I rub into wetter than wetness. Trying to find that button. (I know now what Pappas does with the embedded BB in his tongue.) Leaning back she whispers, This is your fault, Duffy. I tried to cool it and you wouldn't let me. (This from a girl who was feeling me up in the living room in front of God and everyone.) Yeah, okay so it's my fault. Liplock her to shut her up and don't care about nothing. Tongue her face. Dry fuck her frantically. When she lifts my wet finger to her mouth and sucks it I come in my pants. Still wanting to go on, but after a minute I don't feel in love anymore, and, in fact, all I want is to get away. Bad Julie, bad. You made me sin.

I have to use the can, I say, pushing back, letting her go. She's flushed, her eyelids blinking rapidly. You're a piece of work, she tells me. I don't know if she's angry or what. When she slips outside, I lock the door. Clean myself with tissues. Throw the tissues in the toilet and flush it. I need air, so I open the shower curtain and reach for the window. Draped over the faucet is Julie's bra. I handle it, smell it (smell baby powder and body odor), press the padding that made her little titties seem larger. Illusions everywhere. Geez, I'm feeling really depressed now. I can't stand to be at a stupid party where that goddamn Lori is still playing Don't Be Cruel. Making me crazy!

I go back to the living room and there the dumb twat is in that chair weeping.

That's enough of this shit, I hiss. Lifting the arm off the record, I grab it, sail it into the wall, where it shatters, flying all over like chips of licorice. Lori gawking at me. Why did you do that? Fuck that asshole Elvis, I tell her. That was mean, you're mean, You better buy me another. That was mine. I brought it here. I ask her why she's crying over jerkoff Robbie? Which is the wrong thing to say because it turns the waterworks on again. She goes back to sobbing in her hands. What can you do with a dumb slot like that, anyway? You can't do nothing. And not Julie neither. She didn't live up to her advertising. Or maybe it was you, Duffy? You could have done it to her, the real thing, she was ready. Sucking your finger like that! You blew it.

Also thinking: Maybe I should go find her. Try again. A voice in my head tells me no, get the fuck out. Find her later maybe, but not right now. So I listen to that voice and dump the party and luck onto a car begging me to steal it. I take it to the golf range. Run it up the slopes, the 40, 50, 100 yard markers. Flying through the air like a skier leaving the take-off ramp. The car's a '56 Buick whose owner foolishly flipped the ignition switch to OFF instead of LOCK. So easy, these Buicks and Chevys, you don't even have to know how to hotwire them. Sailing off one of the ramps the car comes down so hard it breaks an axle and I bang my head on the steering wheel. Poor Buick. And poor dotty car thief. Spots floating in front of my eyes. Instant headache. A deep cut at the hairline. Permanent scar there. Permanent memento moron. Luckily I didn't hit the wheel with my mouth. For sure I would have lost some teeth.

~~

Come a week later, I take Julie to the FOX to see *Blackboard Jungle*, a movie about switchblade juvenile delinquents raising hell and calling their teacher Daddy-O. When the film's theme music, Haley's Rock Around the Clock, blasts from the speakers, some of us get up and dance in the aisles, until the ushers make us take our seats again.

After the show I'm walking my baby back home. When we get to the A&W, corner of Ironton and East Colfax, a carload of colored guys pull to the curb and jump us. A couple of them kicking my ass, while two others are dragging Julie to the car. I'm throwing panicky punches that aren't doing much good. I want my Ka-Bar. The Luger in the drawer. Julie is screaming and fighting back. She's almost inside the car when two other cars stop and guys from school pour out and start whaling on the would-be rapists. One of the guys is Bell, same guy who broke my nose at the paper shack. He says, We've been tailing them. We could tell they were looking for trouble. He tells me to get Julie the hell home.

When we get there, we tiptoe inside to the bathroom. Where I clean the blood off my face. Put a band-aid over a chip taken out of my right cheek (another memento moron added to the other ones). Twisted tissues up my nostrils to stop the bleeding. My face, my fists, everything hurts. My lips are mangled. There is no way me and Julie will make out this night. Our unfinished business will stay unfinished. Leaving out the back door, I don't hug her. Don't even pat her ass. She folds her arms across her chest as if saying, You don't want to hug me, I don't want to hug you.

And she says, Every time I think of you I'll see the A&W sign and see that car with those guys coming to rape me and maybe kill me and there is nothing you can do about it. The instant she says that, I'm in it again, an intolerable memory. Overmatched and couldn't save Julie. If I had had the Lugar I could have shot them. If I at least had my knife I could have stabbed the motherfuckers. What if Bell and his buddies hadn't come to the rescue? I might be dead and she would have got gangbanged at the very least. Dangerous world, Julie. Here's the thing. I do not want a girl who looks so sexy in tight skirts walking down the street that badasses like that want to rape her. Women are trouble they get you in trouble I do not need their trouble I am trouble enough on my own. Jesus Christ, my whole face is throbbing! Every bone in my body feels broke.

What are you saying, Duffy? That I brought this on us? I tell her I will always see them too. I'll always see them whenever I see you, just like you'll see them whenever you see me. I was overmatched, Julie. Damn near helpless! We've got that connecting us forever. I see them right this second. Her eyes are flaring with anger. Oh, go to hell, she tells me. Get out of my life. Who needs you? She bursts into tears as I turn away saying, I see them, I'll always see them.

~~

Monday a cold day. Spinning leaves and low sky gray. Soon the snow will come, usually by mid-November, the freezing cold, the long dark drag of winter. When the bell rings, I go inside, walk along the hall, where kids are banging by each other. Some messing inside lockers. And the world whirls while I find myself looking at Lori bending over pulling books from her locker. Lori has a very fine ass. It balloons nicely. When she looks up, she smiles and she says, I heard Julie broke up with you. I shake my head. Fuck that, Lori, I broke up with her. She is big trouble. She sure is, Lori agrees, and so is Robbie. I hate him. I hate him to death. I was such a dope at Julie's party crying all night like that. Hey, your heart was broken, I tell her. Lori gives a look, a flirty look, the girl is flirting with me.

I walk her to homeroom, sit at the same table: I'd like to see you sometime, take you to Republic and buy you a wiener sandwich and a green river. Maybe we could go to the FOX and see something. Yeah, so before the hour is over she writes a phone number where she's babysitting Saturday night. Call me so we can talk, she says, leaning her leg against my leg. Her front teeth are rabbity sort of, like Little Jake's mouse teeth, only bigger. Her mouth is so large I figure she could fit a whole apple in it if she wanted. Or a fist. She has freckles like Karen Fielding dotting her nose and cheeks. The word around school is that she put out to that rotten Robbie. Why would he break up with her if she did?

So come Saturday night I call Lori and she tells me to come over. She gives me the address. I stop at Republic and buy a 45 of Don't Be Cruel. Hound Dog on the other side. When I give it to her, Lori doesn't put it on. She plays The Platters instead, The Great Pretender. Just like Don't Be Cruel at the party, she plays The Great Pretender over and over as we sit beside each other on the sofa, smoking and talking about a fight I had with Jay Yakavetta.

Jay had been Julie's boyfriend before I stepped in. Fought him in an alley near school because Jay went over to Julie's house and made out with her, while she was supposed to be going steady with me. Two-timer Julie, what had I seen in her? Jay kept knocking me down and I kept getting back up. Thinking I might lose this one. But then I managed a left feint followed by a right cross that landed on Jay's nose. Blood gushing all over. His eyes tearing up so bad he couldn't see. Me and Jay were both panting like whipped dogs. Exhausted. Tony and Big Lee were yelling for me to finish Jay, but I didn't have the puff. For Christ's sake the guy couldn't see! Blood pouring over his mouth off his chin. He was foaming blood and gasping. I walked away. Glad the fight was over. My left cheek was bleeding. I felt a mouse growing under my eye. It hit me that if I kept fighting so much I was going to end up with a face full of scars. Ugly. Chicks don't like ugly, Duffy.

Near campus the principal, Mr. Woods, called to me. Took me to the office. Asked what was going on. Jay and I were just settling a score, I told him. In fact I like Jay. He's a cool guy, but if you don't fight for your woman no one is going to respect you. Mr. Woods changed the subject. He said, Are you going out for track next spring, Duffy? How about it? Coach says you've got potential. I feel flattered. Felt important. The principal of the school and the coach want me on the track team. Bucky Hedreth had wanted me on the flag football team and I got the Most Valuable Player Award. Not that I really earned it. But hey, I wrestled in fifth grade and no one my size could beat me. Except Bucky. But maybe not even him. I told myself, Look man, you won two second place ribbons when you were in eighth grade! You're bigger and stronger now, what might you do on the track field? I told Mr. Woods I would think about it. Mr. Woods squeezed my shoulder and said, I hope you do, son. Better go wash the blood off your face.

As I finish my version of the fight story, Lori says, Jay and Julie did more than make out that night. Like what? Julie goes down, says Lori. No fucking way, I answer. But I remember her sucking my juicy finger and maybe that was a prelude, which I messed up before things could go further. So Lori, have you ever done that?

She changes the record to My Prayer. We sing along with it: My prayer is to linger with you ... I watch her hips sway, circling slowly, strutting her stuff. Maybe I'm in love with her now. She can keep a tune. Her big mouth looking like it could swallow me whole. As she dances and sings, she takes the rubberband off her ponytail, letting her hair fall in front of her shoulders. Thick, brown, wavy. When the music ends she moves the needle back and replays My Prayer. I sing it in my head, looping it over and over as she leaves the room, going into one of the bedrooms to check on the sleeping kids she's babysitting.

When she comes back the kissing starts. Hardly a minute passes before she says, Do you want to? I don't say anything. She stretching out on the couch, me going down on my knees beside her. Playing her body like she's a piano. My hand, has a mind of its own, chooses to run up her skirt. No panties. Slipping a finger in, I find the way is easy. Her mouth, my mouth start going strange places.

It's over pretty fast. Maybe five minutes before I come and get up and go to the bathroom. Rinse my mouth with Listerine. Feeling bad about the whole thing. Sinful, sinful. Hating how the mood changes so quickly. Just like after dry fucking Julie at her party, I want to get away. My mind racing to find an excuse. Going back to the living room I say, Sorry, Lori but I gotta go. I snuck out and gotta get back before my mom comes home from the club. I'll talk to you tomorrow. She pouts and says, Promise you call me? Yeah, Lori, tomorrow. I really like you, Duffy. Did I make you feel good? Sure, you made me feel good, Lori. She kisses me. I can smell myself oozing from her mouth.

Boogying home I see a bicycle on a lawn and steal it. Stupid kid deserves to have his bike stolen leaving it out like that. I drop the bike a block from Ironton and jog to the house. To the bedroom window. Climb the chainlink fence. Open the window. Slip inside. My little sister is snoring through her nose like she always does. I strip to my underwear and ease under the covers with her. She snuggles up, wanting her arm over my belly, her head against my shoulder. I'm cold and she's warm and it doesn't take long to get toasty. Lifting my fingers to my nose, I still smell Lori. Was that a dream what we did or what?

Life is pretty exciting and things sometimes wildly wacky. A strange world out there. Who knows what people do in their houses? I have this thought, this idea that I will never feel alive like this when I get older, no longer a teenager. No, I will be struggling like my desperate mother. I'll end up like her and Pappas: trying to make money money. Keep my head above water. Now and then having a little fun that always includes drinking and dancing and fucking for love. Or not for love. Just for fuck's sake. It's not worth growing up and taking your place in the circle that goes round and round, until something comes along and pulverizes you, and God judges you and either burns you or lets you sing in the choir. What kind of choice is that? If there really is a hell I'm sure to go there. But I bet everyone interesting will be there too. All that boring noise in Heaven. Jesus loves me, this I know! God has to be sick to death of all those voices praising him, kissing up, groveling. Don't you think?

I wonder what goes wrong with me when it comes to sex. Before I do it I want it so bad I have no control. Then after it's over I hate it. Feel disgusted with myself. Disgusted and sinful. The whole human race has to fuck with such messy parts. Why is that? And why after sex is the high gone and everything turns gloomy, everything repulsive? Something has to be wrong with God designing a system that makes the act so perverted and shameful. Why can't people just fuck with their tongues in each other's mouths and get the same sweet-dying feeling? If I were God it's what I would have created. Spit out a fertilized egg and brood on it like a chicken. What would be wrong with that?

~~

I never call Lori again. Romeo and Juliet love at first sight hits me when I see you at school, Sherrye. You're new in town, have the tan complexion of what I later learn is Choctaw Indian. A shimmering black river of hair falling to your shoulders. Green eyes, green as clover. Never seen such green-green eyes ever. A Pocahontas profile. Noble nose. Righteous cheekbones. I watch you prancing the halls like a thoroughbred, tight blue skirt, bobbie socks, white bunny shoes, white blouse with a light blue sweater. Can't take my eyes off you, Sherrye. Follow you around like a bird fixating. The way I figure it, all the books I've read about Indians make you my destiny. Giche Manidoo has spoken. I trail after you from one class to another. To the lunchroom. When you go to the GIRLS, you find me waiting outside. Sometimes you glance my way and smile. Your smile: mesmerizing. I ask around about you and find out you're way above me. Your father an officer in the Army, a big shot, a captain. You live at Fitzsimmons Army Base, three miles away from my home.

One fateful Friday night I see you at the FOX. You are buying a Coke at the counter and you mention that you see me a lot at school. I see you a lot too, I tell you. I know, you answer, flashing a smile that makes me think of Elvis Presley, the way he raises one corner of his upper lip. Your smile is like that. Take a deep breath, I counsel myself. Calm down, Duffer. I sit with you in the theater and watch *Rebel Without a Cause* starring James Dean and Natalie Wood and Sal Mineo. I definitely identify with Dean. What kid my age doesn't? I comb my hair the way he combs his. I have a jacket like his, only his is red and mine is dark blue. I see you in the role of Natalie Wood, Sherrye. The two of us the coolest most rebellious couple in school. Also thinking: wish I had the nerve to lean over and kiss you, but I don't want to spoil anything by moving too fast. My mind reaches back to Julie at the party: *Jesus, they warned me about you.* What did they tell her? What do people say behind my back? Does it matter?

When the movie's over, I walk you outside. You telling me about a dance at

Fitzsimmons tomorrow night. Saying, You're welcome to come if you want to, Duff. I tell you I'll be there for sure. You giving me directions to the building inside the base. Easy to find. Just a straight walk from the west gate. It will be lit up. Follow the music. A '52 Ford pulls up at the curb. You gesturing, saying, My mother. You open the door, while I watch every inch of luscious you sliding onto the seat. Bye-bye you wave. Walking home, head whirling. Never felt quite like this before about a girl. Sherrye: very fine. Sherrye: like sherry wine. Sherrye. Sherrye.

The next night I take a shower (a rare homage to hygiene). Spread sheep lanolin all over my body to soften my skin. Brush my teeth. Rub butch wax into my hair. Comb it back into a James Dean pomp, curving the neck hair so it flows behind my ears, like Bucky's and Dean's hair flow. I wear my Levi's with my black and white striped shirt. Two pairs of white socks, with rubber bands around my ankles to keep the socks from slipping. Wearing my cool wedgies, which make me an inch taller. My blue nylon jacket. It's as good as I can do. I pimp down Montview Boulevard, all the way to Fitzsimmons, where the guard passes me through the gate when I say, Going to the dance, sir. Seconds later I hear Fats Domino singing *yes, it's me and I'm in love again*, the music sending warmth through the chilly air, a Pied Piper calling. When I enter the hall, I spy you right away. You're dancing with a cat I know from school. What's his name? His name is Gary.

Lots of kids are there. Some parents as well. Your mother is there. She's a little on the chubby side. A pretty face, a face like yours except the mother wears glasses. She flashes a duplicate of your Elvis smile when I'm introduced to her. She points and tells me where to hang my jacket. When I come back you're waiting for the music. Gary standing beside you. He won't look at me. When Tutti Frutti splits the air, you take my hand, not his. So fuck you, Gary.

*Womp-bomp-a-loop-bop-a-womp-bam-boom!* Tutti Frutti has just the beat I need to look like the coolest cat out there. Get down: Sherrye and the Duffer bopping. Other kids bopping. The floor bouncing beneath our feet. Your mother standing behind the refreshment table watching smiling nodding keeping time clicking her fingers. Gary hanging back. Glowering while I make my moves. You're obviously digging the action. I have to thank the mom and Carol Marie for teaching me how to iron out the kinks in a dance floor. Smooth. The Duffer is smooth. Moonglow Theme from Picnic follows Tutti Frutti, and I get to hold you for the first time. Dance slow. Arms embracing high-watt voltage. Hey, it's him and he's in love again. That's how the night passes. A fast one. A slow one. Everyone riding sexed-up musical currents.

Later, we break for refreshments, cookies, pastries, Coke, SevenUp. I want to take you out back and have a cigarette, but with your mother there I'm thinking: Better not, bozo. More dancing follows. Feet flying, hips shaking over Rock Around the Clock. Look for Gary but can't find him. Which is a relief. I definitely don't want to ruin this night with a fistfight. *Well get your glad rags on and join me, honey...*

At nine o'clock your mother calls you aside. When you come back you say, Mama wants to know if you'll walk me home by eleven. Yes, ma'am, I tell her. Your mother leaves and as we dance another slow one, you say that your mother said: You two look good together. That boy can really dance, no wonder you like him. Nice compliment, makes me think of my father, mysterious Hud's magical feet, what the mom said about falling in love with Hud because he was such a good dancer. Can history be repeating itself?

We rock to Blue Suede Shoes. In the Still of the Night comes on and I hold you as close as I dare, trying to absorb the whole length of your body. My cheek in your thick hair, my nostrils greedy for the sweet sexy scent of your skin, my lips giving your ear tender kisses. When The Five Satins quit singing, I tell myself In the Still of the Night will always be our song. Every time I hear it I will think of you and the sweetest night of my life. Later, I ask you to go out back and have a cigarette.

It's freezing outside. We don't light cigarettes. We sit on the porch steps kissing like desperate lovers. I've done a fair amount of kissing, but never anything like this. Your mouth a perfect match for mine. We have at each other for nearly an hour. I don't want to ruin it, so I don't try feeling you up. I do rub the side of your leg. And hold you tight in the still of the night. Who cares how cold it is? We've got our love to keep us warm. Nothing gets in the way of kissing. Not until eleven and the dance is over, people leaving, saying goodnight, had a great time, after while crocodile.

I hold your precious hand. Walk you home five minutes away. You take me inside. Introduce me to your father. How do you do, sir? I say politely. He's sitting in an easy chair spitting tobacco juice into a Folgers coffee can, while he watches television. He shakes my hand. I give him a manly grip. Thanks for getting her home on time, the captain says. And then he's back to watching the screen. Your mother also thanks me. Yes, ma'am, yes, ma'am, I say. You walk me to the front door, give me your phone number and tell me to call tomorrow night. Unlike with Lori, this time I will call.

There's a three mile walk ahead of me. It's late. It's freezing, my breath creating a mini-fog in front of my face. As I pass by the dancehall again, Gary and two guys step out of the shadows. Automatically I search for a weapon and see a weathered two-by-four lying under the hall's steps. It's as long as my arm. I pull it out. Turn reluctantly to face them. Saying to Gary, You sure you want to do this? Gary's eyes are grim slits, his mouth gloomy.

Duffy Pappas, he says, my name a cuss word. He and his friends don't do anything but stare. Maybe it's the weapon in my hand. I stand nervously waiting. Mouth dry. Heart pounding so hard I feel a pain in my throat. Jesus I don't feel like fighting on a romantic night like this, clear sky, the moon, the stars giving their blessing. I say to him, Look, Gary, Sherrye invited me. I didn't know you two were going together or nothing. I didn't come here to steal your girl. I come because she asked me. We can fight, but it's not going to change nothing. So is it really worth it? Gary glances at his pals. They look – how can I put it? They look uncommitted.

I see the anger draining out of him. Yeah, you're right, he says. Fuck her, she ain't worth it. He and his buddies turn away. Filled with relief, I hurry to the Fitzsimmons gate. The two by four hanging in my hand just in case Gary changes his mind.

~~

I obsess about you. About you, Sherrye. Every chance I get I kiss you. Things getting hot-heavy between us. You come with me after school to my house day after day. We make out in my bedroom dry fucking on the bed. And it seems that I can have my way if I want to. Part of me does. Part of me doesn't. What if I fuck you and then that ugly feeling follows after and all I want is to get away? Making love to you has to be glorious, like making love to an angel. It has to be soul mate stuff, luminous, an illumination like a dazzling light leading our souls to lovers' heaven. In the still of the night. Hold her tight. Love you ... love you soooo. It has to be ... beyond special.

Around this time I'm working at a bowling alley setting pins for fifty cents an hour and tips. I'm pretty good at it. Can set two alleys side-by-side and keep the ball rolling. One night I come to work and the owner, a short, fat greasy-haired wop with a big nose and thick lips reminding me of Pappas's lips pays me off and tells me not to come back. I'm fired? I know it was you stole my car, you little punk. I can't prove it, but I know it was you. I learned all about you. Every cop in town knows who you are. I feel my cheeks flushing. Your Caddy? I didn't steal your Caddy, honest to God. The man shows me a big fist with big diamond rings on the first, third and pinky fingers. Get outta my sight! Like getting hit with brass knuckles Pappas had said about the ring on the carney's finger that night of the almost.

Out of the wop's sight I go. But I stew on it. Stew and stew. The injustice, the unfairness. The accusation coming out of nowhere. This time the Duffer is totally innocent.

Later, I learn the Caddy was found and returned to the owner. So one night I take the K-Bar and slip out my window. Make my way to the bowling alley. Find the Caddy parked near the front door. Wait until the customers have left and the place is closing. I slash the Caddy's tires. Slash the sides so they can't be repaired. I run across the lot and hide myself behind a car on the street. Dark houses behind me, bare trees overhead looking like Rorschach's. The owner locks the bowling alley and gets in his car. Starts it. Backs out and stops. I hear him shouting, What the fuck! I giggle as I watch the wop run round his car screaming FUCK! every time he sees another flat tire. He stands there awhile huffing and puffing, his eyes searching for demons in the dark. I recall Carol Marie laying a turd on that nasty old woman's plant in the clay pot. Got her, my sister had said. Yeah, got you wop motherfucker, I tell him. Not to his face, of course

~~

I'm with Big Lee more and more. Big Lee gets into the car-thief habit with me. Together we go to Denver to Adam's County. Happen onto a '56 Ford doubleparked in the street. It has a ski rack and skis on the roof. The engine idling while its owners stand on a nearby porch talking loud enough that we hear everything they're saying about the fabulous skiing in Vail. Big Lee and I hop inside the car. I pull the transmission lever down two notches. The lights are off and it's so dark inside I can't see the indicator for Drive. When I smash the accelerator the engine roars, but the car doesn't go anywhere because the transmission is in Neutral. We hear a man's voice yelling, Hey! Hey! What the—

Big Lee jumps out, hauls ass past houses where porch lights are flicking on. The man running towards the car still yelling Hey! Hey! Hey! I grab the lever again, give it another downward jerk. The car leaps forward and I'm out of there just as the guy pounds his fist on the trunk. I find the knob for the headlights. They flash on Big Lee, feet pounding the pavement. I pull up beside him. He gets in and we're off. The two of us laughing maniacally as we drive to Colfax Avenue and go east. One of these days, Duffy, Big Lee says, you're gonna kill somebody or somebody's gonna kill you.

We head for the park. Dump the skis and the rack in some bushes. Then drive to Havana Avenue in Aurora. Where there's a party going on. You said you might be there, Sherrye, if your father will let you and if your mama will take you. The party is a lot like Julie's party was, cars making the street a parking lot, music so loud it's as if the walls of the house don't exist. Pity the neighbors. But you're not there and I'm thinking I should drive to Fitzsimmons and see if you can sneak out and go for a ride.

The twins and Big Lee are talking. I join them and ask Bruce for a fag. Behind us a voice says, Who you callin a fag? I glance over my shoulder and spy King Kong standing there glaring at me. His size reminding me of Pappas, a heavyweight in every way. I wasn't calling anyone a fag, I say. I was asking for a fag, a cigarette. The guy is eying me as if I'm some sort of alien species. And he growls, Since when is a cigarette a fag? A fag is a queer. A fag is a cocksucker. I shrug my shoulders saying, I don't know the history of the word. In fact I rarely use it and haven't a clue why I used it just now. Fag, the guy says, you the fag, motherfucker. My heart sinks. I don't mind fighting big guys, but this is ridiculous. I weigh a hundred and thirty pounds at best. This squarehead crewcut no-neck towering over me weighs two hundred-plus easily. He points a monstrous finger at my face and says: I better not hear you usin that fuckin word in my presence, you little punk. When he turns away, I sigh with relief. And then I see him talking to Lori. Talking fast, their eyes darting my way. She's telling him bad things about me. Also thinking: Probably should have called her. First Robbie dumps her, then I do. I'm sure she's mad as hell and wants to hurt me.

Bruce tapping me says, You know who that asshole is? That's Roy Sanders. He was on the football team. Linebacker. He graduated last year. He's like nineteen or twenty, man, a mean motherfucker, and if he don't like you you're in trouble. I whine a little, saying: What the fuck I ever do to him? Bruce says: Maybe you ought to ask that little bitch Lori. She's hacking you, man. I'll do better than that, I'll vamoose. Out the back door I go, Big Lee behind me. That ogre is scary, Big Lee says. We jump in the Ford and just as I start the engine a dark figure bangs through the front door of the house. Go! Go! yells Big Lee. I hit the gas and squeal out of there. In the rearview mirror I see Sanders standing in the middle of the street, a silhouetted figure thrusting two middle fingers in the air like gun barrels. Fuck you fuck you the fingers saying. Big Lee looking behind us tells me: Shouldn't have said FAG, Duffy. Fucker took it personal. I make the point that maybe the asshole is one, maybe he's a fag. And overcompensating. Maybe we should call him Suckdick Sanders if we ever see him again. Suckdick Sanders, says Big Lee laughing. We decide to have a code word for that prick. We'll call him SS. Nobody will know what it means but us. Suckdick Sanders, we sing, Suckdick Sanders, Suckdick …

I don't go to your house, Sherrye. I dump Big Lee off in front of his house. Then dump the car in the park next to the skis and rack and head home. That night in bed a feeling of foreboding comes over me. A premonition. Dangerous world. Danger everywhere. The feeling stays inside me for days. Deep depression. I don't go to school or call you or do anything except stay in bed as much as I can. Lose myself in reading Jack London's *Tales of Adventure*. Again and again I read To Build a Fire and see that poor, unlucky bastard frozen to death in that frozen wilderness, where one little mistake means it's over, baby, it's over …

Existence. All of it.

~~

Not sorry to see 1956 end. Crummy shit bad luck alignment of the planets. Maybe 1957 will be better, my miracle year. For my birthday, January 26, Grandma Inez bakes a chocolate cake. The mom brings home chocolate ice cream. Everyone sits around the table, while I open my presents. Grandma Inez gives me Mickey Spillane, her favorite author. *Kiss Me Deadly* says the cover. She tells me it's the best book he's written and it's a movie and I should go see it. The mom gives me a wristwatch. Never had one of those in my life. It's a Timex. Can take a licking and keep on ticking. Carol Marie gives me an Elvis record, Heartbreak Hotel. I'm thinking she bought it for herself.

After I blow out fifteen candles the cake is divided, put on plates with scoops of ice cream. As usual, Michele Renee sits at the table making a muddy mess of her face, provoking laughter. When she smiles, her little teeth are crammed with chocolate. She gets that look saying I'm a little devil. Which she really is. Sometimes. After she gets cleaned up, she climbs into my lap, wants me to pet her and the mom says, She sure loves you, Duffy, you are the one she's always waiting for. Guess that's true. The kid is nearly always under my feet when I'm home, tagging along, tiring me out with her affection. She's still sleeping in my bed, even though I've said I want to have the bedroom to myself. Be nice to your sister, she loves you so, the mom tells me. And I'm thinking what am I supposed to do about that? People love you and the tendency is to love them back. I guess I love the little brat. At least when she's being cute and not getting on my nerves. Curled in my lap, her fist holding my thumb, her head against my chest, I know she wants me to stroke her hair, so I do. Stroke her hair while listening to stories about my previous life.

It is Grandma Inez buying me the Spillane book that heads the conversation down memory lane. The mom picking up the book, staring at the cover, staring at the woman's terrified face, mouth screaming. The mom talks about when I was just two or three and trying to read her Book of the Month Club books. He was so cute, she says, the little towhead sitting there with an open book in his lap babbling, she says, smiling at me, her eyes gentle. Hopeful. Eyes saying, It's your birthday. I'll like you today. Today I'll believe in you, Duffy.

So on this fifteenth birthday the mom talks about me, how I pretended to read, and I feel brainy when she says I used to pile her books up and wall myself inside them, picking this or that book, turning the pages, making up the story. She says I tried to convince other kids I could read anything a grownup could read, and all of what she says is true, though I hardly remember any of it, other than taking the books off the shelves, opening them, wanting her to read them aloud. Her saying I was too young to understand.

Those years wither and I'm at Aurora Central Grade School, where I always get bad grades. My mind drifting whenever I sit at my desk and put my foot in my crayon sack hanging next to me, pretending it's a stirrup. I'm riding away, heading for the prairie. Teachers despair of my ever learning anything. Duffy refuses to apply himself: *Your son sets low standards and then fails to achieve them;*

*This child has reached rock bottom and has started digging.* I get D's most of the time. Now and then earn a C in reading. Never a B or an A in anything except gym class. Teachers shrug me off. They think I'm slightly retarded, perhaps? Definitely a slow learner

Who cares? This day is my birthday and to hell with the world. The mom puts on her favorite music. I get up and dance with Michele Renee attached to my hip, while the mom and Grandma Inez watch with drinks in their hands, smoking cigarettes, tapping their toes. The mom singing along, her voice perfectly pitched, a sweet alto. So much talent in her shapely model's body! Talent going to waste because she got pregnant, got married. Three kids later, the large life far beyond her, her voice rises, drowns out Gogi Grant singing *I was born the next of kin to the wayward wind...*

Carol Marie just sits there glumfaced. She is getting fat. She doesn't dance anymore. She stays in the chair in her robe and slippers, watches us, her eyes hopeless. Carol Marie is knocked up. Pregnant by Dan Shale, but the motherfucker won't marry her because she is from the wrong side of the tracks. White trash. His family is part of Aurora's elite, whoever they might be. Shale gets some buddies to testify against my sister, saying they all had sex with her. He's not sure the baby is his. (Later, a blood test will prove it is his baby, but he'll never pay a dime of child support.)

I switch the record to Little Richard doing Long Tall Sally: *...she got everything Uncle John needs, oh baby!* While I'm dancing, Grandma Inez tells me I'm a natural. Would have made a great jitterbugger back in the old days. I'm giving it everything I've got while she praises me. When the music ends, the mom talks about the time the movie producer wanted her to take a screen test, but she turned him down because she had children to raise, children who were more important to her than anything to do with stardom. She sacrificed a movie career for her babies. And she'd do it again, she says. But I am a big skeptic about that story. Who knows if it is true? Who knows if any story from her mouth is true? As Grandma Inez always says, Janice is a born actress, a drama queen. But mostly she means well, just wants a larger life. Just a big dreamer. Let her have her dreams. She would be heroic if she ever got the chance to go to war like a man with a machine gun, like Pappas and Uncle Dean shooting Jap enemies and piling up medals. And I'm thinking hell yeah, she could have been a movie star because she's as pretty as any of them, as pretty as Lucille Ball, goofy, talking loud and laughing. She can do that act like she's Lucy's twin and sing and dance circles around any star out there.

So, it's a memorable birthday all right, the best birthday I've ever had, until Carol Marie puts on Heartbreak Hotel and starts weeping. Seventeen. Pregnant. So heart-shattered it's killing her.

~~

What I'm thinking is this shit is going to kill me, Sherrye. But it's impossible to stop. It's as if I'm full of babble serum. But is any of it truth? Memory: who can trust it? Memories are unreliable at best. Full of fragments, daydreams, wishes, lies, blank spaces, caution. Capture the essence of what seems more nonstop mirage than reality. Did I really live such a life? Or did all that happen to someone else? Are you really you in this story? Maybe I'm dreaming you, Sherrye.

Long ago, when the mom wanted me to be a doctor, I was idealistic enough to believe such a thing could happen. One day there would be a Dr. Duffy. But little by little, the years passing, I began realizing I would end up just like my uncle predicted when I started getting in trouble and he said to the mom: That kid will never amount to nothin! When she told me what he said I was crushed. His opinion meant a lot at the time. As I've said before, Dean was a war hero. Joined the Marines June 9, 1942. Was a Rifle Sharpshooter, Pistol Marksman. Was sent to the Pacific. Survived two major campaigns, Tarawa in 1943 and Tinian in 1944. I asked him once how it felt to be in combat having enemies shooting at you. He said he expected to die any second. He just knew there was a bullet with his name on it. But he didn't die, wasn't even wounded, not a scratch. And he said: I'll tell you what, there's nothing like surviving what you didn't think you could survive. Every day after that has been gravy. I'd like to live to be eighty, but if I don't, that's okay, because it's all been gravy.

Yeah, so I admire my courageous uncle and to have him say I was no good and would never amount to nothing was hard to take. By then the mom realized it, too. Her constant refrain was: Where did I go wrong with you?

~~

In gym class Coach says everyone will participate in the Aurora High School Fitness Demonstration Program. Girls and boys are made to practice synchronized exercises, like jumping jacks and cartwheels and tumbling. I am good at walking on my hands, so as an added feature I and two other boys are trained to go from a pushup position to walking around on our hands, while everyone else pretends they've turned into an incline board. The music playing is marching band stuff. The main event is Friday evening when the parents will watch and applaud. Students who don't show up will get an F for the entire year.

The night of the Fitness Show I steal a car and park it in the teacher's parking lot and wait for you. I watch as your mom parks the car and goes inside, enters the gym to find a seat. I tap you on the shoulder. There is at least an hour to go before the performance, I say, let's go sit in my car for a while.

We sit in the back and make out and for the first time, I slide my hand all the way up your skirt, touch your warm crotch, your panties silky smooth. Geez it's a thrill, Sherrye. You open your legs. Let me work. But pretty soon we have to go inside. I'm thinking sex with you is just a matter of time now. When the next chance comes I'm thinking you'll go all the way. It'll happen because once a boy touches a girl the way I touched you tonight, willpower melts and girls turn into horndogs, can't help it, got to have it. Do I want that? Yes. No. Maybe. Got to find the right setting. Stars out. An immense moon. In The Still of the Night playing. I'll never … let you go … in the still … of the night.

Hurrying down the hall to the locker room to change my clothes, it's my bad luck to run into SS and Lori, the two of them walking with some guy I don't know. SS steps in front of me and says: Where you think you goin, punk? Patiently, I explain that I'm part of the fitness demonstration, have to get changed. And he says, Maybe I should take you outside and kick your ass. I ask him what for? I say: What have I ever done to you, SS? He blinks his piggy eyes and says: What you call me? What's SS? Who is SS? Shaking my head I'm saying, I meant to say Sanders. He gets in my face. You think I'm a Nazi, you think I'm SS? Or are you sayin I'm shit on a shingle? Wave that off with my hand and say, No, no, not at all. He doesn't believe me, but I can't very well explain that SS is our nickname for him and it means Suckdick Sanders, although Shit on a Shingle works almost as well. I'm gonna get you, he says, poking my chest with his finger. Somethin about you makes me hate your fuckin guts, you little punk.

Yes, I'm thinking, this is how it goes. I get rid of Pappas and here's Tweedledummer to take his place. No luck in this life. I try to explain to SS that he needs to pick on someone his own size. What chance have I got against a guy big as you? No fuckin chance he says, grinning. I'd need a gun to level this field, I tell him. I mean can't you see how out of proportion this is? There's no glory for you kicking my ass, man. He glowers and sputters, Fuckin punk! And then this guy with him, a guy who is more my size, says, This punk gives you any trouble you let me know, Roy. Right now I got to go. And he takes off and SS says to me: I'll see you after the show, punk.

The depression I suddenly feel seems deep as the Grand Canyon. I go to the locker room, where everyone is getting ready to show off for their parents. I sit in front of my locker and brood and wish I could find a corner to crawl into. Coach comes by and orders me to get my gym clothes on and get out on the floor. I shake my head no. Why not? he says. My legs are too skinny, I tell him. Which is true. I've been worried about everyone, especially you, seeing how thin my legs are: long distance birdlegs is what they are, legs like a secretary bird. His eyes widen and he yells, What! Your legs are too skinny! Pappas, you better get out there or I guarantee you'll flunk this class. I'm shaking my head emphatically NO as I stand up and head for the door. I mean it, Pappas! he says. Yeah, yeah, who cares, I mumble. DDT, Coach. What? Drop dead twice.

Going into the gym I stand in the shadows of the bleachers and watch the routines. Watch you putting all the other girls in the shade. You're limber and graceful and ought to be head cheerleader. Big Lee is out there and looking good too. They come to the part where everyone is doing pushups in sync and then they stop and two of the guys go up on their hands and walk around. I should be with them being cheered, instead of watching from the sidelines.

When the show is over, I wait for Big Lee to get dressed. He meets me in the hall and we head for the exit. There's a big crowd streaming out. The second Big Lee and I go through the double doors, SS is there with his sidekick. (Whose name I'll never know.) Without a word SS grabs me by my jacket. Fired by instant fear and anger I throw a punch that bounces off his belly. Before I can throw another I'm on my back, my mind suspended in a vacuum. It's just like when that carney slugged me, only this time I'm down and can't think, can't control my body. I try to get up and keep falling over. Arms and legs refusing to obey orders. In a haze, a fog inside my head, I see SS and Big Lee fighting, a crowd yelling at them. I'm underwater hearing it from far away.

A couple of guys hoist me to my feet and there in front of me is the sidekick. He starts banging away as I wave my arms around trying to punch him, but my limbs have gone spastic. I go down again, get hoisted up, get knocked down again. It doesn't hurt. Nothing hurts except the sound of the crowd yelling at me. I find myself all alone in a circle of people calling me a coward calling me yellow watching me stagger.

Mercifully, Tony appears, grabs me. Keeps me from falling. Back off! he yells. Back the fuck off! He half carries me to the parking lot. Big Lee is there. Blood all over his face. You and your mother are crying. Your mother says to get in the car. My head is clearing. Tony saying, I wish I had come out sooner, man. I tell him I couldn't defend myself, couldn't get my body to obey me. No one ever hit me that hard before. So hard my mind quit processing. Tony says, He's an asshole, man, a cornholing bitch bully. That's his reputation. It was his reputation in high school and it still is. You need to carry a knife and if he comes after you again stab him!

A knife, yes, I need my knife. Need my Ka-Bar. Tony puts me in the back seat of the car. Your mother is raging, Sherrye. I shut out what she's saying. Snow is falling. Large flakes drifting serenely out of the sky. I'd like to go somewhere and let the snow cover me. Put me to sleep. Forever. It's a gloomy world. Why put up with it? I'm mortified. I'm feeling more humiliated and ashamed than ever before in my infamous life. Far worse than when Pappas beat me and made me scream and cry. At least he didn't beat me in front of the whole goddamn school! The only audience for Pappas's beatings were my sisters sometimes, but mostly those beatings were done in secret, his secret, my secret, our secret, a conspiracy.

The next day I get out of bed only to use the bathroom. My face is battered. I feel achy all over. The mom says, Kid, grow up and stop picking fights. You could end up with a brain injury, end up punch-drunk. Look at your face. Won't you ever learn? She goes off to work and I spend the next three days in my room with my books. My escape. A sanctuary that never lets me down. I don't know how I will ever go outside again and face the world. There is definitely no way I can go back to school. School is over for me. The only thing left to do is hunt SS down and shoot him with the Luger. I fantasize about it. I blow him away again and again. Until my honor is restored. What honor is that? You lost it long ago and it will never come back, dopeface.

Early on the third morning of my wallowing in despair and self-pity, the mom comes in and says: At 1:17 a.m. Carol Marie had a healthy baby girl. Her name is Janis Marie. Good for her, I say. The date is March 11, 1957. When the mom goes to work, I roll over and go back to sleep. Around nine o'clock, you and Big Lee and a girl named Judy, a skinny twit with low eyebrows, tiny eyes like bird beads, come into my room. You tell me to get up, announcing, We're running away. I see sack lunches and am told there is ten dollars between the three of you. Okay, I know where we can get a car, I say.

For years now the man who owns the dry cleaners a half block east of Republic Drug has always left the keys in the ignition. Not long ago he traded up from a 1953 Oldsmobile to a four-door, two-tone green 1955 Oldsmobile Rocket 88. Big Lee and I hoof it down East Colfax, while you and Judy wait in the house. Big Lee wants to steal this one, so I go around the corner and wait for him. In seconds he's there and I'm in the car. We pick up you and Judy and boogie out of Aurora. Go east. Don't know why. Just driving. Stop and buy gas and then head south. New Mexico, Texas? Neh. California: sunny days, sandy beaches, warm winters. You and I will get married there. Big Lee and I will get jobs on fishing boats. West is best. So we head for the mountains. Remember that, Sherrye? Course you do.

All day we drive up and over the winding, snow-skirted roads of the Rockies and by late afternoon arrive in Gunnison nearly out of gas, hatch a shrewd plan to go in a grocery store and steal the March of Dimes card off the counter. Big Lee and I stay in the car, while you and Judy, less conspicuous, go inside to do the deed. But all you bring back are Oreo cookies, a bottle of milk and some candy bars. The check-out lady was right there, you say. The March of Dimes right under her nose.

A woman walks by with a bag of groceries. She's bundled for winter, parka hood up, furry boots, mittens. A purse hangs from her elbow. Situation: desperate. Someone has to do something. Get out of the car, go after her and mug her. Round the corner I trail her. At the end of the next block we stop to let a car go by before crossing the street. She looks at me. Her glasses are foggy. Her cheeks and nose rosy with cold. She smiles as she says, Freezing out here, isn't it, son? I smile and nod and say, Yes, ma'am. Cold as a well-digger's ass. It makes her laugh and I laugh too.

Now here's the thing: how you going to mug someone who smiles at you and calls you son and laughs at a joke you tell her? When I get back to the car you want to know if I robbed the woman. She got to her house before I could do anything, I say. But I have another idea.

Driving back to the main street, I pull into a gas station. The attendant comes out and I say, Fill her up, please. Watch him in the side mirror. Wait till he screws the gas cap on and turns to hang up the hose. Drive off casually. In the rearview I see him, his mouth hanging open, a look on his face that says, What the?

~~

Drive drive drive over snowy white mountains west, go through Grand Junction, through rain hitting the ceiling so hard it sounds like glass pellets shattering, the rain following us all the way to Utah. All night moving moving, headlights probing black pavement, probing million-year-old craggy formations, some of them looking like the prows of ships plowing through high desert shrubbery. It is moving that counts. Moving is a destination. If you keep moving you don't have to think about the future. Moving IS the future.

You and Judy curl up together on the back seat and sleep. Big Lee and I take turns at the wheel. Whenever the car needs gas, we pull in and have the attendant fill it. And then leave. It works pretty well until the next day at the bottom of Whitehorse Pass in Nevada. I pull up to the pumps as usual. The attendant puts the gas in and I drive off. But this guy hops inside a '57 Ford two-door station wagon and comes after us.

He's chasing us, I say. Everyone looks back. He's gaining! I've got the hammer down and the Oldsmobile's 202 horses are roaring as we enter Whitehorse Pass. Up and up the car climbs around tight curves and switchbacks. There is snow covering the sides of the hills and blanketing the evergreens. Patches of ice dotting the road. Slipping on one of the patches, the car barely makes it around a tight spot, going out onto the snow and gravel and nearly over the side, a long way down, eighty feet at least, into a canyon.

The man in the Ford has dropped out of sight, so I slow down. A few miles more a Highway Patrol appears, its lights flashing, its siren insisting we pull over. Not a chance. Next second I'm watching in the rearview as the cruiser slides sideways, turning around and coming after us. But he's not willing to keep up the pace I'm setting. It's way too stupid, too risky. After a short chase he falls back. I tell you and the others: That cop is radioing ahead.

Up through the mountains we continue, twisting and turning all the way to the top and down the other side. I tell Big Lee there will be more cops at the bottom of the pass, maybe a roadblock. He looks at the map and says there is a highway running north and south coming up soon, Interstate 93. It will take us to Idaho north or Arizona south, he says.

When we get to the crossroads, I turn north. At the top of an overpass we look down at what was waiting if we had kept going west. In the distance a gathering of cruisers, red lights flashing. We need to get off 93 and into the hills. Searching for a dirt road we find one. There is a gate and there is barbed wire fencing running far away in both directions. Big Lee gets out, opens the gate. I drive through. He latches the gate and jumps back in.

The car is rolling over the hills, plowing through mounds of snow. Tires spinning. Lots of lurching side-to-side. Lots of bouncing up and down. The Oldsmobile responding as if it's a carnival ride. A happy carnival ride. A ride full of invincible power and thrills.

Around a turn, blinded for a second by a shower of snow scooped into the air by the front bumper, we plow into a three foot drift, the car cocking askew, it's ass-close to a drop of thirty feet into a gully. Spinning the tires, I try to rock the car backward and forward, but it's no use. We get out and see the frame high-centered. Going nowhere. Unless we can dig it out. Which, with night and the cold and more snow coming on, is something that will have to wait until morning.

We sit in the car. Listen to the radio. Eat Fritos. Munch snow for water. The motor is running, the heater is on, so all in all it's as comfortable as the situation allows. Big Lee and I are confident about digging the car out tomorrow. Right now it's time to sit tight, stay warm, get some sleep.

You and I lie together on the back seat, Sherrye. Holding each other. It is soon dark outside. An angry wind seeking flaws in the window seals. A zithering sound. In spite of it all, we make love to each other. There is no holding back when I raise your skirt, pull your panties off and, for the first time, enter you, thinking it will be painful, but it doesn't seem to be. I don't ask about it, about whether you're a virgin or not. What does it matter? Nothing matters now. We fuck for a while, even though I'm not feeling very passionate. And neither, it seems, are you.

Think about where we are, Sherrye—some snowbound dirt road in high desert Nevada. This is not the way it's supposed to be! This is a stupid location for making love to each other. How could it happen that such a bizarre setting is where we fuck for the first time? Very goddamn unromantic, Sherrye! In fact that long anticipated moment of ultimate teenage bliss is a bust. Wanting to stop I ask you if I'm hurting you, Should I stop? No, you whisper, raising your legs higher. The gesture saying get on with it, Duffy. But truth is I'm so exhausted I can't keep it up and I can't come. So finally, I pull out, cuddle you, while I stare out the side window into the night, billions of stars staring back at me ferocious as wolf eyes.

Early morning we try it again. There is blood on your panties and you tell me you're sore. So you were a virgin after all. We go easy and this time I come, but the motion doesn't seem very pleasurable for you. We lie there and whisper. You ask me why I'm so bad, such a bad boy. What makes me do the things I do? I tell you I don't know. You want to know what my home life is like.

I tell you about Pappas. I tell you how he regularly kicked my ass. When I tell you about what he did to Carol Marie, you say your father molested you too. But not as bad as Carol Marie molested by Pappas. It turns out to be more like what that anonymous man in the mountain cabin did to Carol Marie. Your father got drunk and came into your bedroom and groped you one night. He masturbated while he was fingering you. Just as Carol Marie had done, you pretended you slept through it. After he got himself off and stood up a scorpion stung his foot. Which felt like supernatural payback to you because your sign is Scorpio. You tell me your father is a lot like my stepfather: hardcore military. Daily you have to polish his army shoes. Keep his uniform brushed. Your mother starches his shirts and ties. You tell me he liked me because I called him Sir.

The sun is up. It's do or die time.

~~

The gas gauge reads half empty. Big Lee and I get busy. There are golf clubs in the trunk, which we use to dig snow from under the car. It's freezing work and from time to time we have to get inside to take a breather. There is no food and it doesn't take long before we're both worn-out. We try jacking up the hind end of the car, putting brush under the wheels. Everyone pushes while I slip the transmission into gear. It almost works when I gun the motor and the car jerks backward, the tires sizzling, going about five or six feet before getting stuck again. Noon finds us still working to dig ourselves out.

It's a crisp day. Morning clouds have left a dusting of new snow, but at the moment the sky is crystal. The white sun doesn't warm anything. When it falls west the cold wind becomes fierce and drives everyone back inside. That evening we stupidly play the radio too long without starting the engine and the battery dies. There's nothing more we can do. But huddle together on the back seat, all four us trying to keep each other warm.

Through the windshield I see a moon like the blade of a scythe, its beams falling diagonally on the hood of the car. It's a godless landscape of wind. The wind. Always the wind. The wind sharp as a knife blade. The voice of the Grim Reaper humming. I doze fitfully. Having hallucinations of being chased, of losing the keys to the car. I keep muttering, I'm cold, give me the keys. Nobody knows what I mean. I don't know what I mean either. When it's finally morning, Big

Lee and I walk down the road to see where it leads. At the top of a rise we can see houses so far away they look like toys. They are painted bright colors, red, blue, green, yellow. It's not really a town. Maybe it's housing for ranch hands. Whatever it is, it appears to be our only chance for survival. Big Lee goes back to the car to protect you and Judy. I head for the houses.

It's a slightly downhill slope all the way and a much longer walk than I expected. The sky above stays cloudless. The sun a cold circle of pitiless light. The wind feels like invisible razors flicking my skin. My cheeks and ears burning, eyes filling with tears that freeze on my lashes. I have to keep rubbing the ice off in order to see. I'm isolated. I could die out here. Sleep the stone sleep of the forever dead. Easily! A frozen corpse no one would find until spring. If then. If the coyotes don't find me first. Scatter my bones all over their territory. You, and Big Lee and Judy might die too. Someone would travel that ranch road one day and find all three of you huddled in the car, your bodies blackened by frostbite, dried out and shrunken by the unforgiving cold. Mea culpa. I led you to this God forsaken vale of frozen misery. Jesus, forgive me. Have mercy, Jesus, on this stupid sinner. I promise I'll be good if you get me out of this. I'll go to church every Sunday. Honest to God. In the name of the Father, Son and Holy Ghost I plod through the snowy, brush-dotted plains, my feet frozen to numbness. It's like walking on blocks of wood. Fear hurries me. Fear keeps me going. The imagined headlines I see: FOUR FROZEN BODIES FOUND WEST OF INTERSTATE 93.

The trek takes maybe two hours or maybe it's shorter and just seems like two hours. But when I finally get there I go to the closest house, a blue house. Before I'm past the gate a woman comes out, two dogs with her charging and barking, their fangs bared and I'm thinking this might be a replay of Husky on a rampage. What do you want! the woman yells. How did you get here? I'm so weak and woozy I can barely talk. The dogs are barking as I'm whispering, Good boys, good boys, holding out my hand for them to smell.

I point behind me, up the miles-long grade, and croak out the words: Stuck, ma'am. Stuck three days up there. Stuck in the snow. Please help us. I put my frozen hands over my frozen face and burst into tears. The woman abruptly changes her attitude. She rushes down the steps, her arms open, her voice sympathetic, calling me a poor thing, telling me to come with her. By now the dogs are wagging their tails.

The woman is tall and slim. Her hair dishwater blond. She's not wearing makeup, but she doesn't need any. Her beautiful, healthy face is glorious, a spring flower, a daisy. She's wearing an apron and some sensible pants and boots. She takes me inside. Sits me at the kitchen table. Fries me some eggs and makes me some toast, slathers it with butter. Gives me cup after cup of coffee. And listens to the story of how my friends and I were exploring the back roads and got stuck in a snowdrift.

She makes a few phone calls. Tells me not to worry about my friends. Help is on the way. I learn from her that the little community is filled with railroad workers. There are train tracks nearby and the men from the community maintain them, riding railroad carts, going miles in both directions repairing problems they find.

The men come home. Two of them fire up their four-wheelers and head up the road. In an hour they're back with Judy and you and Big Lee. You're so weak you need to be carried into one of the bedrooms and laid on a bed by two of the men. I notice the man holding your ankles is looking up your skirt, a lustful leer on his face. I sit with you. I hold your hand. You tell me: I thought we were dead, Duffy. I thought you were out there turning into an ice cube and we were next. You weep, turn your head away. The savior lady makes you and the others fried egg sandwiches. Glasses of milk too. You tell her: This is the best fried egg sandwich I've ever had in my life. Oh my God it is so good!

Out in the living room the phone rings. The woman answers it. When she hangs up she says to her husband: They want you to meet them at the car with these kids. Her husband, a stocky fellow, much shorter than his wife, cusses, says: Fuck me, I gotta drive em the hell back up there? Shit!

Out to the four-wheelers we go. My arm supporting you as I tell our beautiful angel: I'll never forget you, ma'am. Can't thank you enough. You saved us. You saved our lives. God bless you, ma'am. Tears brimming in her eyes she is smiling. God bless you too, she says, and good luck, Duffy.

We head back to the Oldsmobile slipping and sliding, engines roaring, the four wheelers finally arriving where a government car is waiting, two men inside it, one old and one young. Both wearing suits and ties, winter overcoats, fedoras. They are plain clothes police officers from Elko, Nevada.

~~

They take us to a café in Elko and treat us to hamburgers, fries and Cokes. We sit in a booth eating, not saying anything, while the two men sit at a table talking. The younger one calls me over, has me sit down. And he says: Whose car is it? Is it your car? I shake my head no. Did you steal it? he asks. I nod my head yes. The older man says, Oh no. The younger one looks at him and, in a satisfied voice, says, See, what did I tell you? The older man looks at me with eyes that remind me of the mom's eyes the day I told her I had flunked eighth grade. Sad and disappointed. As if I had personally hurt him somehow.

Big Lee and I are locked up in the drunk tank in Elko. You and Judy are locked up somewhere upstairs. There are no bunks in the drunk tank, just a cement floor to sleep on, but we're so tired it doesn't matter. At least the place is warm.

It's the midnight hour when the steel door crashes open and a scraggly, gray-haired old man with one eye is ushered in. He is mumbling and pacing and staggering from one wall to another. The socket of his missing eye looks like a small, red-rimmed vagina. What's wrong with that guy? Big Lee says. I tell him the guy is a goddamn wino. The wino starts yelling I ain't no goddamn wino! I ain't no goddamn wino! He is banging on the door, kicking it with his foot, insisting he ain't no goddamn wino. I tell Big Lee: If he comes for us we'll doublebank him. You hit him high, I'll hit him low. The door flies open, two cops come in and kick the wino's ass and drag him into a cage farther down the hallway. We can hear him but not see him. He won't let it go, the litany that he ain't no goddamn wino!

The next day an officer takes down our statements. When it's my turn I sit in the chair next to his desk. He stares at me for several moments before he says, You got a hell of a record already. He taps some papers, waits for me to answer. I shrug. And he says, I'm just curious, but can you tell me why? I shrug again. You don't know? he says. Ain't got a clue? Let me tell you something, kid. You're headed for reform school. It's no picnic in there. They'll make you wish you were never born. I nod my head and tell him I've already wished that a thousand times in my life.

The same afternoon we're transported to Reno, the county jail there. Big Lee and I are lodged on the top floor. We don't know where they take you and Judy. There is only one other juvenile in the cell. He's an Indian locked up for stealing a pickup. He's fat and friendly, has black, smoky-smelling hair hanging to his shoulders, a round Navajo face. He tells stories about a cave in the mountains loaded with gold. He says he stole the pickup to go into those mountains and bring the gold out. When they let me go, he says, I'll buy off some guards. Give em a share of the gold, so you guys can escape, eh? We go along with what he says. Maybe he's telling the truth. What do we know? I try out Grandma Inez's Chippewa phrases. A plane flies over, so I say, *Be-mis-a-gak*. No reaction. Try *Booz-hoo ahnee*. No reaction. Try Giche Manidoo. The Indian shakes his head and squints at me as if I'm delirious. The next day he's taken away.

~~

Days later chains are locked around our waists. Our hands and feet are cuffed to the chains dangling down our legs. We're led outside to a Nevada State Government car. We watch as you and Judy shuffle in chains to another car and climb inside. In tandem, we head back to Colorado. Big Lee and I try to talk, but the officer riding shotgun turns round and tells us to shut our fucking mouths. At one point he says to the other officer: If it were up to me we'd dump these punks in the desert and leave em to rot.

For the two days it takes to get back to Colorado, Big Lee and I only talk at night in a cell in some strange town. Rock Springs the first night. Laramie the next, where you and Judy are put in a cell next to us. There is a solid steel wall between us. But by reaching out through the bars and curving our arms around to the other cell, you and I can touch each other, hold hands and whisper how much we love each other.

At the end of the journey we're driven to Brighton, the county jail. This is Big Lee's first time, but it's all too familiar to me. Up the dimpled stairs, a U-turn and then down the hall to the end, turn right and step through the steel door, hear it slam, hear the keys jangling, hear a key turn and the bolt slick into place. The same maroon blankets on the bunks, the same blue striped pillows and blue striped mattresses. The same three toilets and washbowls. The same silver steel table in the center of the room. The same two recessed lights in the ceiling. The same silver bars looking out on the jail's lawn and trees and a street full of parked cars. Across the street are houses, sane-looking houses with yellow grass poking through scraps of snow.

Big Lee asks me what I think will happen now. I tell him, They'll let you and the girls go probably tomorrow. As for me, the Industrial School in Golden is my destination. He wants to know if I'm scared to go there. Maybe I'm too stupid to be scared, I say. Or maybe it's just that I don't give a damn anymore. I really don't care what happens to me. He says he wishes we hadn't done any of this. He says it's his fault. Mine and Sherrye's, he says, the two of us egging each other on, and then Judy saying she would run away too. She hardly even knows us. All this trouble, Duffy, and I didn't even get laid. He laughs and shakes his head. I stare across the street at a cozy-looking house, with a small apple tree in the front yard. Amazingly there is still one apple hanging on a branch, shriveled up dark and looking dead, but somehow hanging on, even though the other branches are bare.

The authorities don't wait until tomorrow. You and Big Lee and Judy are turned over to your parents before nightfall. I'm left alone in this large eight bed cell. For the first time in my life I'm really, really lonely. I miss you more than I've ever missed anyone, even more than I missed the mom when I was sent to Grandpa Mike's each summer.

~~

In the morning I'm given oatmeal and milk with a slice of bread that is toasted on only one side. Also a cup of coffee, no cream no sugar. I don't like the coffee. It's bitter. I drink it anyway. I ask one of the guards if he could give me a cigarette please, sir. He says: Shut your shit hole or I'll shut it for you.

A day later he takes me downstairs to see a detective. Walking along side-by-side, his hard hand gripping my biceps, he starts stepping on my feet. I haven't a clue why he's stepping on my feet. But it hurts, so I shove him away and say: What the fuck wrong with you, man? He slams me into the wall, puts his hand on my throat and bangs my head a few times. Then, without a word, he continues ushering me downstairs. Puts me in a room with a table and two chairs.

I sit there an hour before a man comes in and questions me about my part in the theft of the '55 Oldsmobile and the ride to Nevada. He says, You know you can be charged with the Mann Act. What's that? The interstate transportation of females for immoral purposes, he says. They can charge me with that? You really did it this time, Pappas. The judge is going to throw the book at you. Now, tell me the truth, did you steal that car, or did Lee steal it? I did, sir. I tell him everything was my idea and the others just went along. And he says, That's how we figured it, Pappas, even though your friend said he was the instigator. The detective looks at me a long time, like the inquisitor in Elko, his eyes curious. He says: Why do they follow you? That's what I don't get. Why do they listen to you when all you do is get them in trouble? Shrugging my shoulders I reply, I have no idea, sir. And it's true, I don't. I'm not big, not very strong, not witty, my personality and intelligence seem borderline brainless to me, so why some kids do what I tell them doesn't make any sense at all.

Except maybe they're all as stupid as I am and living for kicks, living for excitement, the impulse that creates something wild and scary out of our measly lives. Our measly boring lives. Lives where tomorrow is miles and miles away. Lives where NOW is all that matters, because it won't be long and we're all dead, anyway. LIFE: a vale of heartache and suffering, just like the mom and Grandma Inez say it is. That's the way it feels when I'm not distracted stealing cars or stealing from stores or fighting or fucking. I'm fifteen and young enough to know these things.

~~

Come Saturday, my sister shows up with her new baby. This is Janis, Carol Marie says. Janis reminds me of infant Michele Renee all wrapped and red-faced and squished. Isn't she cute? says Carol Marie, holding the baby up against the bars for a kiss. My lips touch a downy head soft and warm, smelling like something fresh and natural popping out of the earth.

Don't know why but I suddenly feel like crying. Thanks for coming, I say, but you better go now. Carol Marie says in a voice almost a sob, Oh, Duffy, I'm just so sorry. God knows what will happen to you. I nod my head. I go back to my bunk. I want her to leave. She stands there hesitating. What shitty lives we've had, she says. Then, cradling her baby, Carol Marie goes away. I hear her footsteps fading. I imagine her at home with her baby on her breast tonight. Grandma Inez and the mom are there. The three of them watching TV. Something making them laugh. Also thinking: First time I see my little niece I'm behind bars. Duffy, who the fuck are you? What the fuck is your problem?

A few more days go by before I'm taken to the judge. It's Jacobucci again, those same soft brown eyes regarding me like I'm a riddle, as if my face doesn't fit the idiotic things I do. Don't let the exterior fool you. The mom is there too, her eyes brimming with tears. I sit next to her. Across the table Jacobucci has my file in his hands. As he and the mom discuss my case, the consensus I hear is a cliché: my behavior is mostly the product of a broken home and what I need is a man's influence. The judge looks me in the eye and says that my mother has been fighting like a tiger for my life. He hopes I appreciate the effort she's making to keep me out of Golden.

Once again I am presented with a decision about you, he says. Your mother thinks if she sends you to Alaska to live with your former stepfather that he'll keep you out of trouble. He's volunteered to take you. My understanding is that he's always been able to control you and that your worse behavior came after he and your mother divorced. Is that how you see it, son?

Hell no, that's not how I see it! But that's not what I say. Hope has entered my head, a way out, a way that leads to the Final Frontier. Sure, it leads to Pappas too, but he doesn't scare me anymore. At least not much. And also, I know what he's up to. He wants to use me. He thinks that by coming to my rescue, he'll be able to win the mom back. A delusion. But that's all right. Because I'm going to use him to get me out of this mess. So I tell the judge what he needs to hear to justify sending me out of state, to the Alaska Territories, to the Pappas who will keep my sorry ass in line. It's true, I say. Yes sir, I wouldn't dare cross Daddy.

*I want the final rending of my flesh from yours.*

- *Steve Davenport*

When the plane makes its approach to Anchorage it flies low over a marshy island. I am staring out the window, watching the shadow of the plane darting over a moose standing knee-deep in a pond, dipping its head beneath the water and bringing up moss. Seeing the moose is thrilling. A live moose just like that! It's a good omen. The plane lands at the airport. In the waiting area is a man wearing a blue uniform. Pappas. His face puffy, a little reddish. He no longer has an olive complexion. But standing before me is essentially the same Pappas I had hoped never to see again in my life. Maybe he is a different person now. He's told the mom he is. Told her the loss of her has humbled him. Made him see things more clearly. Made him gentler. More caring. More loving. He'll be a real daddy this time, he's told her.

Pappas gives me a soft kiss on the mouth. He smells of Old Spice and cigarettes as usual. He says, Well you made it, Duffy. Look how tall you are now. But still too skinny. Need to fatten you up. Are you hungry? I tell him I saw a moose standing in a pond. Pappas winks his good eye. Which makes his droopy eye more noticeable. The heavy eyelid swollen. Eyeball bloodshot weepy. One side of his face is distorted. The other side still handsome. A Jekyll and Hyde face. Oh, lots of moose round here, he says. Sometimes they come into town and check it out, walk right up Fourth Street. Game everywhere, hunting and fishing like you wouldn't believe. Don't worry we'll get out in the boonies soon and I'll show you around. This is God's country. Alaska puts anything in the lower forty-eight to shame. He smiles. His little teeth are still bright. His lips thick and velvety voluptuous. His right eye smiles. His left eye continues weeping. He wipes it every few seconds with a hanky. He used to call Colorado God's Country. But now Alaska is God's Country. Maybe it is.

Pappas has a purplish-blue 1950 Chrysler Imperial with part-time power steering, automatic transmission and what is called a safety clutch. The car has power to spare, he says. He drives towards Elmendorf Air Force Base on a narrow road bordered by pines and brush and ferns, thick foliage. Anchorage in late April is cool and clear. I don't see any igloos. Trees trees trees. Leaves budding, branches dressed in multiple shades of green. Lots of bridges with rapid water running under them. To the east there is a range of mountains capped with sunshine and snow that make them look vaguely like the bald domes of old men. Everything about the countryside is restless, a restless wind making the trees sway, the restless land rolling with hills, the hills climbing higher leading to other mountain ranges that Pappas says run all the way south to Juneau, east to the Yukon and past Skagway. These particular mountains in front of us are called the Chugach, he says, and wait until you see them at sunset. Those peaks pink as flamingos! Unreal, Duffy. Unreal. This is a country for men like us. Pappas waves his hand at the land. Not many white women are tough enough to handle Alaska. Most the women you find here are First Nation Indians. Lots of them. Lots of Inuit. Eskimos. Problem being natives in Anchorage don't have enough to do to keep out of trouble. So most of them drink like fishes. You can see them staggering along the streets day and night. Sorry-looking boozers. You'll see. You'll see what I mean.

At the airbase he parks and leads the way inside a hanger. He is the master sergeant in charge of pulling maintenance on some planes. He is also a flight engineer. Two men are working on a B-25 in the hanger. He introduces them. This is Carl. This is Norman. This is my son Duffy. Carl is short and wiry like me. He looks me up and down and says, Welcome to Alaska, young man. Norman says, Grand, grand! He is taller than Pappas and what you might call rangy. He has humped shoulders and long arms. Bony wrists. Both men's hands are black with oil.

Pappas takes me to a base cafeteria, feeds me a hot dog and potato chips. Then he stops by the PX and buys a case of Budweiser. Drives me into Anchorage, through a downtown teeming with people and cars, just like Denver except not nearly as big as Denver. A sign announces: POPULATION 49,000. On Fourth Avenue, a banner overhead says ANCHORAGE FUR RENDEZVOUS. I see the Anchorage Grill, Royal Bar, the D & D Bar & Café, Gilman's Bakery, the Gitchell Hotel, Ship Creek Market, Lois Beauty Salon, Victory Lounge, the National Bank of Alaska and Stolt Electric, lots of stores of all kinds, just like any city would have, and I'm thinking the Final Frontier may be in Alaska but this Anchorage ain't it.

Down Third Avenue, then turn round and drive back along Fourth. Pass the 4TH AVENUE THEATER and D & D Bar & Café again. Pappas saying, This is where I hang out when I come to town. Take you there and introduce you to Jimmy the Greek someday. At the corner he stops for a stop sign. I see three Indians on the sidewalk passing a bottle in a brown paper bag. Sure enough one of them staggers and has to put his hand against a wall. He grins naked gums totally toothless. Pappas drives up First Avenue and takes a left at Sitka. Goes about a hundred yards, pulls up in front of what he calls the cabin.

Home is not a real cabin with notched logs and four-pane windows and a shake shingle roof. This place is basically a shack made of plywood and covered in red asphalt siding, the paint oxidizing. Across the road cater-corner is a patch of woods, mostly evergreens and birch. We take the luggage inside. There is a couch against the left wall. Two armchairs. End tables with shade lamps on them standing next to the couch and chairs. There is a radio, but no TV. Wood floor. No rugs. To the right of the main entrance is a long, narrow kitchen. In its center are a Formica table and four chairs. There is a refrigerator. Inside it are two cans of beer, a block of fuzzy cheese, a bottle of spoiled milk. In a cupboard is a box of Cheerios. Other cupboards have dishes and cups and glasses. Empty spaces. Pots and pans clutter the oven of a four-burner propane stove. All of the windows have blackout shades to blot out the midnight sun in June July August.

At the other end of the cabin are two bedrooms sharing a wall. There is a bathroom at the end of a short hall. The bedroom for me has two singles in it. A closet to the right of the doorway. Both beds have cartoon comforters, Peter Pan on one, Tinker Bell on the other. Those were here when I moved in, Pappas says, chuckling, shaking his head as he adds, Why would they leave them? There's a story there. And he says: Go figure. And then he says: Let's go shopping. Let's fill the fridge. He pats me on the back. Squeezes my neck gently. His hand a lingering caress. His good eye asking for understanding. His weepy eye asking for sympathy. His small smile saying I hope you like me. See how good I am? This is not the Nick Pappas you used to know.

~~

The next day after he goes to the base I clean house. Sweep the floor with a broom. Dust with a raggedy old dishcloth moistened with wood oil. I do the laundry at a Laundromat a block away. Fold towels and clothes. For dinner I slice and fry potatoes. Throw in some wieners and fry them too. Over the course of the next few days I fry hamburgers and sliced potatoes, fry pork chops and sliced potatoes, scramble eggs and slice more potatoes. I usually have dinner ready when he gets home. It's like Pappas and I are married. This is our honeymoon period.

I never would have thought we could get along so well together. There are even moments when I think maybe I've misjudged Pappas a bit. Just a tad, I mean. I mean, what was it like for him marrying a woman who already had two little snots, a tight little readymade family? Did he feel like an outsider most of the time, none of us his? Strangers really, a man-child, a girl-child calling him Daddy, when he wasn't one drop their daddy, not a shred of him in them. This is what he fought for? A track home in East Aurora, a woman who had two husbands before him and who knows how many others, a stormy, crazy wife who drank and smoked and cussed like the sailors he bunked with during the war, a woman who would chase you with a knife or smash a bottle over your head if you slapped her or made her jealous, a righteous mother pointing a gun at you, threatening to shoot you for touching her daughter. His woman was never his woman, not really. She was a man-magnet who came with tons of luggage, not the least of which was a pair of tow-heads to deal with. Is this it? Is this all there is? I wouldn't have wanted to do it. No, I wouldn't have done it no matter how sexy she was, no matter how fascinating and wild in bed.

I had already come to the realization that the man hadn't a clue about himself and what he really wanted—except all the gorgeous women in the world, of course. Especially a mother and her daughter. Would that have been enough? I wonder if he felt sort of wistful (was he capable of feeling wistful?) for his youth and freedom and the excitement of the war and all those adrenalin experiences that made him feel fully alive and vital. I bet he did. But he got married to a divorcee and got stuck. Every time he looked at me, he saw the men in his woman's life. Plenty of them, no doubt about it. I probably would have hated to see me too. As the years went by how boring it must have been for him. Her too. No wonder they fought so much. At bottom: everything too familiar too fast. It wasn't him. He wasn't made for that particular American dream. And neither was the mom. And yet ... there it is. And seven years later it's the two of us, an odd couple no doubt about it. But I'm thankful we're getting along. Maybe this will turn out for the best after all. Be an optimist, Duffy. Think positive.

~~

One night Pappas spells it out for me, his psychological relationship to the mom. We're sitting at the table drinking Budweiser and talking about going fishing with Norman and Carl. Pappas tells me stories about fish so big they snap your line or break your pole and sometimes even pull you into the water. Fishermen have been known to drown because they're too stubborn or stupid to let go of their poles. By the end of my third beer I'm feeling idyllic and his words sound sensible wise ... fatherly. The rhythmic lilt of his voice hypnotic. He runs his hand through my hair. You remind me of your mother, he murmurs. If you let your hair grow a little longer and dyed it auburn you would be her spittin image. As long as you're alive, so is she, he says. (Pappas is off his rocker if he thinks I look like her. Almost no resemblance at all. But I don't tell him that.) It kills me, he says. It kills me every time I think of her. You don't know what you have until you lose it. I wish I had understood how I was my own worst enemy. How could I have treated her that way? Don't know. What a fool I was in them days. Whoever that man was he is not me, not the real Nick Pappas, nuh-uh. I think a lot of it was being so insanely jealous. Jealousy can drive you crazy, did you know that? She would walk into a room and every man in that room would want her. Women too. You could see it. And she could feel it and I would watch her flirting and it would drive me fuckin nuts. Drive me to drink it would. She'd slip into her femme fatale here-she-comes, and I would want to kill her and everyone near her. Love is no good if there's no trust, know what I mean? We drove each other crazy. No bullshit, Duff. I really believe it. It took getting away from her and coming up here to clear my head. I know we could make it work now. Nobody can love her like I do. When you write her, tell her that, okay?

His bad eye is leaking and he keeps dabbing at it with his sleeve as if he is crying. I find myself not minding how ugly the one side of his face is compared to the other. The overall effect is of a man punished by life but not defeated. It doesn't seem possible that who I'm looking at now could have been the one who beat me savagely for peeing the bed, for throwing my dirty skivvies in my chest of drawers, for any excuse handy at all. But then I flashback on Carol Marie and what he did to her and my heart hardens. He doesn't talk about her, hasn't mentioned her name once. It's as if she doesn't exist. Maybe listening to him is making me schizophrenic.

He gets out of his chair, opens two more beers, finds a pen and a ruled tablet. Let's write it right now, he says. The letter to your mother, he says, shoving the tablet towards me, handing me the pen.

*Dear Mom,*

*Daddy and I are settled in a neat cabin not far from downtown. I am learning to cook and make dinner. I do the laundry. We go to bed early and get up early just like we did at Grandpa Mikes farm. This Alaska is real beautiful more beautiful than Colorado. Bigger looking than Colorado and wild boonies like it was when mammoths lived here.*

Pappas reads over my shoulder. Tell her GRANDER, he says with emphasis. Put down that it looks GRANDER. So grander gets in there. Then he says to write about how much he has changed. Tell her I don't drink like I used to. Tell her I don't go out. Tell her we stay home and talk and read and listen to the radio. Tell her I'm reading a history book about King Minos at Knossos on the island of Crete, my ancestors my father's ancestors. (Pappas actually does have a book about Knossos, but I've never seen him reading it. He also has a paperback called *The Greek Way*.) Tell her I'm improving my mind. Tell her how good I am to you. Tell her I talk about her all the time and that I love her. Tell her I said I will love her till the day I die. Tell her, Duffy. Write it down. I'll mail it for you tomorrow.

I write exactly what he wants. Also thinking: I've never heard him talk like this before. Geez, maybe Nick Pappas really has changed. We salute each other by clicking our beer bottles and drain them without stopping. By the time I go to bed I'm drunk as a skunk. Next night too. And every night thereafter.

~~

One morning at dawn Pappas and I grab the fishing gear and the rifle. I strap on my uncle's Ka-Bar fighting knife. Its seven-inch sheath hanging halfway down my thigh. Did he ever kill Japs with it in hand-to-hand combat? He never said. Norman and Carl pick us up in Norman's 1957 Buick station wagon. Head out to the Kenai Peninsula. Go south towards Seward over a mountain pass and then along the Kenai River close to Resurrection Bay. To a place where the ocean washes over a beach full of gray stones and pebbles. No sand at all. A tributary runs into the sea there. The river is not as big as the Kenai, but big enough, shallow where it fans out and kisses the ocean. Little inlets dot the path running past massive boulders and massive trees and dense undergrowth. Upstream the river is deeper. The bottom of the river is a quilt of smooth, multicolored stones. The water so clear I can see fish nosing along doing fish things. There are creeks and thin waterfalls pouring into the main body of water. Everywhere the landscape seems to be posing. This is Alaska, Pappas keeps saying. This is Alaska!

A mile or so later we stop hiking and set up camp. We grab the poles. Bait the hooks. Spread out along the bank to try our luck. We catch plenty of fish: some salmon, some Dolly Varden trout. Some of which we eat for lunch, roasting trout on green sticks over the fire, peeling the skin off, pinching the meat with our fingers. Popping it into our mouths like popcorn. I eat a whole trout and still feel hungry. Norman gives me a hunk of black bread from a round loaf and says: If all you had to eat was fish you would starve to death. You know why? Because fish is all protein and you need to balance it with fat and carbohydrates. Pappas says that Norman used to be a nutritionist in a hospital. Dietitian, right, Norm? So here he is back in the Air Force changing oil. Pappas laughs. Norman laughs. So does Carl. And Norman says: Life, she is a grand bitch, a grand bitch. You never know one day to the next where you is. You can't predict a thing. It's all a crap shoot.

Life, she is a grand bitch, agrees Carl. But at least we got each other. Us is family, Duffy. Now you are family too. We drink to it, ey? Out comes a bottle of Old Crow he hands around. I take a sip that burns my throat, digs a hole in my gut before it settles into what feels like a steaming sewer. Within thirty minutes the men have finished the bottle and are working on another and that is the end of fishing. Overhead gray clouds are edging in.

Pappas loads his rifle. Starts shooting at birds. In seconds they've vanished. Then he shoots and shatters the empty Old Crow bottle. He sets up stones on the trunk of a fallen tree and tries to shoot the stones off. He finally gets one to scatter. Carl tries his luck but keeps missing. He says he needs another drink to steady his eye. Norman waves off the offer of trying his luck and says he hates guns. What about you, Duffy? Carl says. Ever shot a rifle? Pappas brags on me, saying, Hell, yeah! This kid is a deadeye. Hit anything. I trained him myself. Hell, yeah. He hands me the rifle. I aim and bam! Miss the stone. The kick of the rifle hurts my shoulder. I rub it and Pappas says fiercely: See? See? What have I told you? You gotta hold the butt tight, goddammit. Be a fucking bruise there. He pokes my already sore shoulder and adds, Bet on it, stupid. His eyes are the old boozer eyes I've known for years, the hard liquor eyes that always make me imagine being clubbed to death. By missing the stone I've made a liar of him. He snatches the rifle and shoots into the water at fish swimming by. He reloads and hands the rifle to Carl who is eager to shoot at the fish. Neither one of them hits a thing as far as I can tell.

To get away from Pappas in his flush-faced Pappas mood, I head downstream. Even when I'm far away I can hear them talking and laughing. Every few seconds I hear the report of the rifle, a clash of air echoing all the way to the beach. Sitting on a boulder, I'm watching the ocean curling, slapping smooth slick pebbles polished for millennia. The bay water is gray as a brain, same color as the clouds from here to the horizon. A fine haze films the air. Behind me is glistening old-growth forest. Thrusting above the trees are jagged young mountains collared in more clouds. Snowcaps never melt on those peaks. This Alaska is glorious enough to satisfy nature-lovers-hunters-fishers-of-fish-loners-dreamers. Anyone afflicted with adventure of the heart. I get moony about the scenery, the waves splashing the shore at my feet, the far reaches of water west to Russia and mountains east to the Yukon, where Jack London and Robert Service were inspired to become wordsmiths. The cool, damp air makes me feel as if my lungs are growing larger. Multiple shades of green so vivid and glossy they look painted on by the god of the forest. Thick moss greener than Emerald City clinging to the north side of the trees.

At that moment, with Emerald City in my mind's eye, it hits me as hard as anything ever has that I will survive, I will grow up, I will become a writer. Novels and short stories. Adventure tales. I'll make up stories about Alaska! Write about my life too. Not long ago I read Irving Stone's biography of London, *Sailor on Horseback*, and now I decide that's how I'll live my life—I'll be Jack London, take chances, have adventures, see the world and write about it. Live life like the mom wants to live—live it to the fullest. Yes, Duffy, that's what you'll do. Whatever comes your way you won't be afraid. A voice tells me that the writer's life is the point of everything that's happened to me. What else could it mean? What's it for otherwise? As the mom is always saying—what's it all about, anyway? Why am I here?

But first I'll have to read more and read faster. Still haven't finished the Mickey Spillane Grandma Inez gave me months ago on my birthday. Have to do more than simply read, though. Have to study the books and really see into the heart of how stories get done. Learn to write by imitating others. Sit with a book and look at a sentence and write a sentence like it. Easy enough. I see myself becoming rich and famous. My stories eagerly anticipated by thousands of adoring fans like James Michener has. I've read his *Tales of the South Pacific*. I'll connect my stories like he did, some of the same characters showing up in each tale. Mine will be *Tales of The Final Frontier*. Oh yeah, oh yeah. This is a fine daydream I'm having sitting on a rock staring at an ocean, telling that ocean what kind of life is waiting for me as I grow older. If I grow older. My dad died at thirty. I might not live even that long. I might die in my teens! Eighteen. What if I die when I'm eighteen? How sad that would be. What a waste. I'd always be remembered as an incorrigible criminal. A bum. A stupid bastard. Bedwetter. Jailbird. Worthless. That kid will never amount to nothing. Quit fucking around with your life and stay alive. Get to work! Get the work done, Duffy.

I stretch my hands toward the water and start praying. Make me a great writer, I pray. And I pray: Grant this wish, oh god of the ocean. His name is Neptune. His name is Poseidon. Sprinkle your power all over Duffy, baptize him. Give him your blessing. Give him a sign. If you grant his wish he will give you his life. When the time comes to leave this earth he will drown himself like Martin Eden did. Feed the fishes. Become their wafer, their Eucharist.

Walking to the edge of the water, I dip my face in, baptize myself, prove my sincerity to Poseidon Neptune. Make a covenant. Behind me Pappas is asking, What the fuck you doin? He laughs. Norman and Carl laughing too. You can't drink that, you goose! says Pappas. C'mon, get your ass in the car it's raining!

All three men are happy drunk. They stop at a store along the way and buy a six-pack of Bud and drink it before we get to town. Norman parks on Fourth near the theater. We go into the D & D. Walk through the café section to the bar behind the beaded curtain. Pappas saying loudly, Jim, a pitcher of Bud! Pappy, where you been, says Jim. He's tall and slim, bald on top. Has a gray handlebar mustache, waxed tips curling upward. We sit in a booth. Been fishing, Jim. This is my son Duffy. He come to live with me now. Duffy, this is Jimmy the Greek. He's as Greekily Greek as I am. Welcome, Duffy, my bar, Jim says, his accent reminding me a little of Grandpa Mike's accent. I tell him I'm glad to meet him.

Sitting on a stool is a man with the widest shoulders and biggest arms I've ever seen. He is anvil-jawed like Rocky Marciano. He could be Lou Thez. Deep-eyed and ruggedly handsome. Blondish kinky hair cropped close. A neck as thick as my thigh. He and Pappas size each other up. The man smiles, his teeth as even as pegs in a crib board. He nods at Pappas. Pappas nods back. Jim brings the pitcher and says, Pappy, you see heem here, no? Pappas says he doesn't know him. Jim says that the man is Kris Karvonis famous from Macedonia. This Kris Karvonis calls himself Kris Karr. He has his picture in muscle magazines. Mr. Los Angeles. Kris gets off the stool. Shakes hands with Pappas, Norman and Carl. When he shakes my hand his deep-set eyes look into mine and instantly I love him. He is wearing one of those wool pullover sweaters with leather patches on the elbows. His muscles straining against the cloth. He says that he and his girl came up from Los Angeles. Got here a month ago. Staying at the Gitchell. Cocking his arms he tells me to squeeze his biceps. Biceps so big that both of my hands together can't go all the way round them. Kris says he needs to get me into the gym lifting the weights. And I'm thinking, okay, sure, pump me up and then I'll go back to Aurora and kick Roy Suckdick's ass. Pappas is giving Kris the eye. He doesn't like this guy. Or me staring at him worshipfully, wondering what it would be like to be him, so handsome and manly. Pappas says: Duffy has always been too thin. Weightlifting will be good for him.

The curtain parts behind Kris and a woman walks in. Tall thin, what you call willowy. She's dressed in a form fitting black dress, wearing it like a model. She has orange hair, wavy and luscious. Eyes lined with thick black mascara. Thickly curling lashes. Smiling eyes smiling at Kris. Her skin silky, her cheeks pillow pale. Grand, says Norman, his eyes welcoming. Carl is blinking as if he can't believe what he's seeing. Kris says to us, This Joy. She sure is, says Pappas. All of us gawking at Joy. Her lipstick orange slick moist matches her hair. She has a nibbly slope to her lower lip, pouty. Any man would want to kiss her and more. No doubt about it.

Pappas has brightened. He scoots out of the booth, stands up, shakes her hand, introduces himself as Sergeant Nick Pappas and asks if she would like to sit down. No, she wants to sit at the bar, but thank you very much, Sergeant Pappas. Call me Pappy. Everyone calls me Pappy. She looks at me and says: And who is this? Kris introduces me and says, Heem Pappy's son. I take her slim hand. Relish its warmth its smoothness. Close up I see she has lots of freckles saddling her nose, fanning over her cheekbones. I think of Karen Fielding and Lori and wonder if freckles are omens. I'm as much in love with Joy as I am with Kris. But dumb as a tree knot I can only stand there mouth open speechless. Joy is an Olympian goddess my mind tells me.

So glad to meet you, Duffy, she says. You been long in Anchorage? I shake my head. Pappas tells Joy I've been in Alaska two weeks. I'm thinking: Has it been that long? Really? Is he a good father? she asks nodding towards Pappas. I mutter, Yeah. And she says, Good. My old man's a stinker. Wouldn't live with that bastard again for a million dollars. Good dads are rare as pity.

She and Kris go back to the bar, sit on stools, heads leaning together talking in voices so low I can't hear what they're saying. She crosses her legs, her skirt riding up. I see bare knee. Trim ankle leading to a stiletto heel, the tip of the shoe perched on the end of her toes. All I want is to gawp at the two of them. Envious and heart-struck, I know I'll never look like him, never have a woman like her.

~~

One evening I walk to the store and buy a few groceries and head back. It's past nine but faint reddish light still suffuses the sky. The days are getting longer, the sun not falling off the edge of the earth until past ten at least. An Eskimo girl in tight jeans and a suede vest walks by crying into her hands. Has somebody done something bad to her? Duffy to the rescue? I take the groceries to the cabin. I tell Pappas about the crying girl. He wants to know what she looks like. She's a small thing hardly more than five feet tall. She has hair hanging all the way to her wing bones. Raven. Pappas thinks a second and says: Go get her. Bring her here. Tell her we can help her. We must help maidens in distress. Right?

I hurry back. Spot her a block away staring at some squalling seagulls riding currents in the sky. When I catch up with her, I see her shoulders shaking. I ask if she's all right. She won't look at me. She hurries down the street. I have to move fast to walk alongside her. Do you need a place to stay? We have plenty of room and you're sure welcome to come and have a beer. Would you like a beer? Are you hungry? She looks hard into my face and says, No! Faster and faster, she walks. As I continue to coax her, a car pulls up and a big Indian jumps out and grabs her arm. Steers her toward the car. Get the fuck away from her, you pimp! he says. I tell him I'm just trying to help. And he says: Don't gimme that shit! They get into the car and leave. I wonder what it was all about. What made him call me a pimp? Is that how I look now? Like a pimp? What do pimps look like?

~~

Mornings after Pappas leaves for the base I often walk to the D & D for coffee and sometimes breakfast. One day I'm sitting at the counter eating eggs and hash browns and toast when Joy walks in and sits on the stool next to me. She smells delicious, like a vanilla cookie. I'd give a testicle if I could bury my face in her hair. She wants to know if I've seen Kris. No, I haven't seen him. I stare at her, look away. And stare again. Throat so dry I can't swallow. She says she got a job as a B-girl, and Boris, the owner of the bar, needs a bouncer. She told him about Kris and the guy wants to see him. Ain't you gonna eat those eggs, Duffy? she says. What? I say. Your breakfast, she says, you gonna eat it? There is no way I can bring myself to eat in front of her. When I push the plate away she pulls it to her, grabs my fork and starts eating. Can't let good food go to waste, she says, shoveling eggs in her mouth as fast as she can.

Her hungry, earthy act snaps me out of my love trance. Joy ain't no goddess. She's a beautiful long-legged orange-haired girl with a big appetite. For everything. In less than a minute she is wiping the plate with a piece of toast. Washing it down with my coffee. She gets up and says: If you see Kris, tell him to go to the Sourdough. Maybe he's at the hotel? I offer. I been there already, says she. This morning he was complaining of a toothache. So maybe he's at the dentist. She heads for the door. And I'm thinking: Mr. Los Angeles gets toothaches?

A few days later Joy is at the counter again, but this time I eat my own breakfast. When I ask about Kris she says he's in bad shape. The tooth has been bothering him a long time and the dentist had to pull it and now his jaw is swollen. He has a fever. The hotel is threatening to kick them out because they can't pay the rent. We might have to sneak out, she says. But Kris is in no shape to go, so what to do? Won't your boss give you an advance? I ask her. Boris? she says. Not a chance in hell, she says. We'll have to live on my tips for now. Everything is twice as expensive in this damn Nowheresville. Well … it's not nowhere, but you can see nowhere when you reach the city limits. You got any money, Duffy? About twenty dollars, I say. Her eyes brighten. Can you loan me ten?

Later, I tell Pappas about Kris being down with a fever because of his tooth and Joy is working as a B-girl at the Sourdough. His eyes shift, become cunning. Come Friday night I know where he'll be.

~~

Carl and Norman show up for a celebration. With them are two Eskimo girls. I'm flustered because the petite one in jeans and suede vest is the same girl I saw crying on the street several days ago. The other girl is very fat. She has greasy hair, a round face. She is missing her two front teeth. Her name is Martha. The other is Mary. I saw you, I tell her. Hoah? she says, looking me over. You were crying and I tried to help. Some guy came in a car and made you get in. He called me a pimp. She frowns and says: Shee that bastard. And that's all there is. No talking about him. She wants to party. She turns the radio on. Tunes it to a local station. Chuck Berry singing *all hail rock and roll*. She winks at me. Does a little shimmy. Says: You dance?

There is a store-bought cake in a box. Norman cuts it up and passes slices around and says: Here's to Carl's promotion to staff sergeant. Thanks to you, Pappy. Here's to Pappy, too, for recommending Carl. TO PAPPY! There is plenty of beer and Carl has brought a tall bottle of whisky. Which he hands me. Saying, Have a snort, my boy. So I have a snort and chase it with beer. The music is loud. Mary and I are looking real good, I'm thinking. Dancing my best for her, making the moves that remind me of dancing with Sherrye at Fitzsimmons. You cute, Mary says. When she smiles her eyelids almost completely close. I see tiny twin sparks surrounding dark pupils. Miniature stars. You have beautiful eyes, I tell her. You cute, she says.

Song after song is played. Everybody dancing. Everybody drinking. I'm not a bit drunk. Holding my liquor like a man. Slow dances fast dances. I can do it all for Mary. Carl is giving me hard looks, but I don't care. She wants me not him. To hell with Carl. She kisses my cheek when I hug her. My lips find her lips, her whisky tongue slipping inside my mouth. Our tongues dueling. Thighs pressing. Norman has fat-as-a-panda Martha pinned to a wall. His hands all over her outrageous boobies. Pappas is watching. His eyes a pair of pin pricks. He wants to watch somebody do it. Carl wants Mary. I want Mary. Let Norman have Martha. Things are under control. One more dance and I'll work Mary towards the bedroom. Up and at em. Also thinking: You're drinking whisky straight from the bottle and you don't feel a damn thing.

Well hardly a thing.

Maybe something.

Most definitely heat in my belly. The nausea coming on so quickly I barely make it to the bathroom. Upchucking chocolate cake and whisky. I'm there for who knows how long clinging to the throne. Every time I try to get up, the heaving returns. I hear the party going on without me. Carl's promotion party. And I've lost my chance with Mary. But who cares? I'm too sick to care.

At some point in the evening she comes in. Grabs my hair, pulls my head out of the toilet and says: Hoah! I want you! And I say, You got me, baby! I try to stand. Can't. Can't do anything. She lets go of my hair. Goes out slamming the door. I doze. Time flies. I wake on the floor and hear people leaving. A car starting. Pulling away, gravel spraying. Horn honking. It takes maybe an hour before I can crawl on all fours out of the bathroom. No one is in the living room. To my right the bedroom door is open. A dark figure pumping another dark figure on the bed. They look like two seals mating face to face. Or two walruses, maybe. Using the wall to stand, I get closer. And see Pappas giving it to Martha. I hear her murmuring, Hahnee I luff you. Hahnee I luff you. I close the door, go to the couch. Pass out.

In the morning I hear Pappas shouting, Duffy! Duffy! Come here! Get in here! I open my eyes to a fuzzy, gut-churning world. Staggering to the doorway I see Martha on top of Pappas holding him down, kissing him and saying, But hahnee I luff you. I luff you, hahnee. Get her off me! cries Pappas. I grab Martha. She finally stands up, holds her head and weeps and says again, But hahnee I luff you. Her breasts sag onto her saggy belly, a belly creating a skirt behind which her pubic hair is hiding. Jesus Christ, says Pappas, get this fat bitch out of here. Take her down to the corner and get her a taxi. He rolls over and I'm left to dress Martha and lead her weeping out of the house. At the corner I hand her a five dollar bill and tell her to go home.

~~

That night Pappas and I go to The D & D for dinner. Joy and a haggard Kris come in. The left side of his jaw is still swollen. He orders a bowl of beef broth. Joy orders a steak with baked potato. Oh, jaw it is so sore, Kris keeps whining. Poor darling, says Joy. Ohhh, moans Kris acting like a big baby. Be a man, I want to tell him.

After we all finish eating we go into the bar. Pappas orders a round of drinks. His treat. This will cure what ails you, Pappas tells Kris. We got kicked out of our hotel, says Joy. They kept our luggage. We don't know what to do. I need clothes for work. There's a pause. Looks of sympathy. And then: Listen, says Pappas, you and Kris come stay with us. You can have Duffy's room. He can sleep on the couch. That's so good of you, says Joy. You are such a sweet man. But what will I do about clothes? They talk it over with Jimmy the Greek. He agrees to front Joy some cash if he can put the money on Pappas's bar tab. Joy will pay him back soon as she and Kris get their first paychecks. A couple of weeks max. Magnanimous Pappas agrees to it. Everyone happy. Kris says his jaw has gone from sore to numb now. Buy me nudder drink, Pappy? I'm high and glad to be alive. I've been high every night since Pappas and I have been together. I understand why he likes it so much. The world is not so scary. I'm full of optimism about my future. Not a drop of anxiety in me.

~~

Next morning I'm sitting at the counter when Jim asks me to wash dishes for him. His main dishwasher hasn't shown up. So I wash dishes Monday and Tuesday. Make a few bucks. Wednesday the regular dishwasher guy comes back and I'm out of a job.

Jim introduces me to a fellow named Paul. He has a rug cleaning business. He hires me to work for him. He's fortyish, with the ropy forearms of a man who works hard for a living. There is a shock of grayish hair hanging on his forehead. He has a prim mustache, long, gray sideburns and a crooked grin. His eyes bulge like maybe he has a bad thyroid. Very intense eyes looking at me as if he's trying to look inside, examine my thoughts. He's married and has three daughters.

The first day at work, I'm on my hands and knees scrubbing a huge rug stain. Paul comes in and says: What you got there? He kneels and says: That's wine. People are so fucking careless. He grabs a brush and starts scrubbing. We're both scrubbing. His hip bangs my hip. Hips touching. We continue to work on the stain. Paul presses. I pretend not to notice. A moment later he throws the brush in the bucket and hurries away.

The next day we take the now stainless rug back to its owner. Move the furniture. Spread the rug out. The owner, a golden-haired lady in pearls and a silky purple dress, holds a yapping poodle in the crook of her arm and says she is satisfied with the job. She gives us a two dollar tip.

Driving back to the shop in Paul's rattling old station wagon, he tells me to open the glove box. There's a surprise in there. I take out a bottle of vodka and some rolled magazines and open one and see naked women in lurid poses. Instantly I get wood. What you got there? Paul says laughing as he pokes my crotch. He opens the bottle, takes a big slug and passes it to me. I down a mouthful and tell him vodka tastes like medicine. The bottle goes back and forth and before I know it, I'm drunk and slurring my words and giggling.

Paul drives the station wagon to a pullout spot next to the Eagle River. I can hear the river rushing as Paul makes comments about the girls in the magazine. I'd eat a mile of her shit just to see where it came from, he says of one woman reclining on a couch fingering herself. One picture shows a guy eating pussy. She's grinning. She has her hand on his head. The next picture shows her giving him a blow job. We've finished off the bottle and my eyes are blurry. I roll the window down to get some air. Paul tells me to climb in the back and stretch out. So I do. I'm nearly asleep when I feel him rubbing my penis. Worrying it to wood again.

And he says: I jack you off, you jack me off. No hesitation, he goes right for my buttons with one hand and releases himself with his other hand. He takes my hand and puts it on him. I recall Bubble Eye and how I would do it for him if he let me drive his car. So what the hell I do Paul too. And he does me and after just a few strokes, I tell him I'm going to come. And he says: Already? Want me to suck it? No! But he sucks it anyway, shoots my sperm right into his mouth. And swallows it. My hand has stopped moving, so he takes over and gets himself off.

As we're driving home he wants to talk about what happened. He can't believe I've never sucked a cock or been sucked before. I shake my head. I keep my mouth shut. Feeling queer and ashamed and uneasy to say the least. It's one thing to masturbate a guy when you're eleven or twelve and have hardly an ounce of sense, but it's something else when you're fifteen and totally aware of what it all means. Why didn't I stop him? Why didn't I get out and leave? Is this what happened to Carol Marie when Pappas did what he did to her? A paralysis of the will? Or was it the vodka? Pappas wasn't bullshitting when he said the way to get laid is to get your date drunk.

When Paul pulls up at my house, I tell him I don't want to clean rugs no more. I go inside and start drinking beer as fast as I can. Get drunker than drunk and throw up again.

But I'm not so drunk or sick that I forget Paul calling me up and saying: So fuck you then! Don't come back, you fucking little cock teaser!

What is there about me that attract guys like him? Like Carol Marie I seem to be a magnet for strange men. Am I somehow putting out signals? Am I queer and just don't know it yet?

~~

Pappas is in debt to a guy who fixed the Chrysler when Pappas hit a guard rail, smashing the right fender, some months ago. This guy keeps threatening to write Pappas's commanding officer. One evening he drives me over to the man's house. Gives me $40 dollars. Tells me to knock on the door and give the money to the man. I knock on the door and when I try to give the man the payment he goes bananas. He says: That bastard owes $400 not $40! I'll sue him! He shakes his fist at me.

I get my ass out of there. Run round the corner, where Pappas is hiding in the car. When I tell him what happened he says, Well, I made a good faith gesture, so he can kiss my ass now! And then he gets this idea that money runs through his fingers like water and he says that I should handle the money. You're old enough to take that responsibility, he says.

So, on the first of the month he gives me cash to pay the rent and utilities and groceries. He calls me, Head of the household.

~~

The master cylinder goes out on the Chrysler. No brakes and Pappas has no idea how to fix it. Norman sells him a '51 Pontiac for $50. The clutch slips but the car is drivable. When Pappas is at work I use the Chrysler to go to the store and visit D & D for breakfast. Sometimes I drive around sightseeing. For braking I use the emergency handbrake. It slows the car down and stops it well enough. Works pretty well, actually. The days are getting even longer and Pappas and I stay up late drinking every night of the week with Carl and Norman. It is always around two in the morning before Kris and Joy get home from the Sourdough.

They are making money, but they haven't paid Pappas back yet. Both of them have new clothes. Every morning Kris pumps iron at the basement gym on Fourth Street not far from the theater. He takes me there, teaches me about biceps curls and bench presses. Most of the guys who come in are bursting with muscles. They make me so self-conscious I quit going.

~~

Pappas starts spending more time at the Sourdough and I'm left on my own a lot. Late into the night I sit at the table drinking beer and trying to write stories. The more I drink, the better I write. Booze makes me creative. Booze makes me clever. I write one called Brute. It's set in Egypt. Brute is a slave who is helping build a pyramid. He kills the man who is beating him with a whip. He runs away and the Pharaoh's soldiers hunt him. Most of the story is about the hunt and the heat in the desert and deadly snakes and scorpions almost biting Brute. When at last he can't go on he turns round and charges the soldiers and dies heroically. I was really excited when I was writing the story, but after it's finished and I read it sober, I hate the damn thing and tear it up. I don't know anything about Egypt or Pharaohs or Slaves and it shows. I try to write about Grandpa Mike and the farm, but can't think of anything to say after writing about going to the auctions in Longmont and never bidding on a pony. So I write about my grandma. I describe how she eats pickled pig feet, drinks gin, smokes Pall Malls, speaks Chippewa. Then I run out of things to say about her as well. The writing eventually loses its charm. The beer doesn't.

~~

At noon one day while I'm fixing lunch, Kris brings a girl home. He winks at me and leads her into Pappas's bedroom. I've seen her before, the ash-blond waitress from the Eagle River Diner. I hear the bed creak. And then it's quiet. And then I hear her saying, No, Kris, no. And I'm wondering what she was thinking coming home and falling on the bed with him? Kris is obviously a guy you do not say no to. While they're tussling I make myself a fried egg and baloney sandwich. Open a can of Bud. Sit at the table eating and drinking. Noises coming from the bedroom: kisses, panting, groaning, heavy breathing, clothes rustling and the girl saying, No, no! And she says, Slow down will you? I can hear her whimpering as if his mouth is muffling hers. I'm sure his hands are all over her body, his knee between her legs pushing her skirt up as she breaks her face away and says sternly: I said no, Kris! Now stop it! Baby baby, he breathes. She keeps saying no and the tone of her voice is that of a woman who really means it.

The struggle shifts into a higher gear. The bed banging. She is slapping him and I think he slaps her back. I hear a crack! And her crying out, Goddamn you! That hurt! Get off me! The springs are squeaking and there is the sound of clothes ripping and she says, Oh! Oh, my god! This is followed by a rhythmic creaking. It doesn't last any longer than it takes for me to eat my egg and baloney sandwich and finish my beer.

Hear her climbing out of bed, standing up, slipping into her shoes and she is out of there. Her heels clicking across the wooden floor. She glares at me sitting at the table. She looks ... she looks fucked. Her hair tangled and damp, looking like ragged ribbons clinging to the sides of her face. Her lipstick gone. Her mascara smudging her cheekbones and part of her nose. Her twisted mouth and eyes are a contorted mask of outrage. Her voice furious as she says: You can tell your friend I'm going to the cops! He is going to jail if it is the last thing I do! She heads for the door, slamming it hard as she leaves. Maybe Kris better get out of town, I'm thinking.

But when he comes into the kitchen he is calm. His kinky blond hair is tidy. He is shoeless and shirtless, his chiseled muscles looking invincible. He's the cleanest, healthiest looking man I've ever seen in my life. She's going to the cops, I tell him. And he says that she won't go to the cops. He didn't force her into the bedroom. She wanted him to fuck her. He says that women like her want you to force them to fuck. They feel guilty about fucking unless you force them. Every woman likes a bit of rape, especially when your cock is new to them. You make them take it to the hilt and they say they hate you, but you can feel them loving what you doing. The more they struggle the wetter they get. And he says that this bitch got her rocks off, he guarantees she did. He tells me that as soon as she gets home she will finger fuck herself. And think of him while she's doing it.

He has a satisfied smile all the while he's talking. Everything he says sounds reasonable. Big strong Kris from Macedonia. She looked mad as hell, I say. And he says that she teased him in the taxi, slipping her tongue in his mouth, letting him pinch her nipples. And moaning about it. He says: You catching one like her, you fucking her good. You hear what I say I tell to you? I reply: Fucking her good. He laughs. I laugh. Together laughing and laughing and saying fucking her good, fucking her good.

Maybe he's right. What do I know? He gets behind me, squeezes my shoulders. Feeling his face next to mine. His breath in my ear. Smelling sex on his breath. You like it me? he says. And I say: You are very cool, Kris. I wish I had your body. He says he's worked hard to have a beautiful body. And he says that if I want to be like him I have to pump tons of iron. He squeezes my biceps and tells me, Tomorrow we go gym.

He goes into the bathroom. I hear the shower running. Later as he's leaving he says I should come to the Sourdough and he will buy me a drink. He says the girls there would like young stuff like me. Pappas won't be home until late, so it would be a good night to visit the Sourdough and meet the girls and finally watch Joy dancing naked on stage.

~~

As I enter the Sourdough I see Kris checking IDs. I tell him I don't have one. He takes me outside, digs in his wallet, brings out the military identification card of a private stationed at Fort Richardson. There is no picture. The name on the card is Peter P. Pearson. He is 21. Kris tells me to memorize the serial number and then come to the door, show him the card, tell him the number. Say it loud. I sit in the Chrysler and memorize the number. When I go to the door, Kris takes the card, asks me to quote my serial number. Which I do easily. Just inside the entrance, I walk past a potbellied man in a black suit who I figure is Boris. Close-set eyes, flaring nostrils and wearing what is obviously a toupee. He ogles me up and down. I feel his eyes following me and wonder if he's another cocksucker with porn magazines and a bottle of vodka in the glove box. I keep repeating Pearson's serial number, so I won't forget if Boris asks me.

The music is loud! Girls and guys sit at tables talking, practically yelling. Some are propped on stools at the bar chatting with each other. Stroking arms. Hands stroking. Leaning knee on knee. The girls are dressed in skimpy outfits. They wear heavy makeup, especially on their eyelids, blue black shadow sprinkled with silver glitter. Some of them look way too young. A plump one is dancing nearly nude on stage. She wears a g-string that barely hides anything. She has pasties on her nipples. Men sit on stools staring up at her. She has platinum hair and eyes that look at the men as if she knows what size it is. And she's not impressed. Big knockers swaying. Call her bovine. She squats and her vagina flashes pink around the thin edges of the string. She rises and shakes her can-do. When the music stops, men throw money on stage. As she picks it up, she bends from the waist and gives them a look up her backside. Her hanging tummy forms lazy washboard rolls.

Angie is her name, says Joy. Joy is standing behind me. Come sit with me, she says. We sit at a table and watch the girls working the men, getting them to buy drinks. I hear the man at the next table ordering champagne. A forty-dollar bottle. The girl with him winks at me and sticks her tongue out. The name of the game, Joy says. These are mostly service guys. Lonely. They want a girl to talk to. That's all that happens most of the time. You wouldn't think men would need to talk so much. Where have all the strong, silent types gone? She laughs softly. Bats her fake eyelashes at me. Since she's being so frank, I ask her if the girls are prostitutes. She answers that some of them are part-time prostitutes, but the majority make their money on tips. Get a guy drinking, get him high, get him talking, lean your boob on his arm, maybe touch him under the table, and nine times out of ten you will get a very fat tip when he leaves. He'll empty his pockets. Liquor and longing make men generous, she says.

Angie sways out of the back room. Comes dressed in spiked heels and what look like painted-on chinos. A tank top shows off her mighty cleavage. She weaves past the other tables and sits at ours and says in a Mae West voice, Hello, handsome. Her upper chest is sweaty. I smell musky armpit and talcum. I smell beer whisky champagne cigarettes fusing. All of it delicious. She talks to Joy. Tells her that so far the slugs are being stingy. Joy should get up there and move her toot-toot. See if she can inspire them. Angie turns to me. You dance? she asks. How old are you? I tell her twenty-one. She throws her head back, laughs. Yeah, and I'm fifteen. I turn away so she won't see any more lies in my eyes. Wondering if fifteen was a guess. Wondering if experienced women can tell a kid's age just by looking. Yeah, I can dance, I say. My mom taught me. She could have been professional, my mom. Angie's smile is friendly, eyes twinkling. She doesn't look at me with the half sneer she gives other men. We talk about where I'm from and what I'm doing in Anchorage.

Nick Pappas is your father? she says, eyes dubious. Sort of, I say. And she says: He don't look a thing like you, honey. She tells me she came to Alaska because she heard men outnumber women six to one. She says she never made this good a living when she lived in Kansas City or Seattle. You don't even have to know how to dance, she says. Hell, all I do is wiggle my ass and tits at them and they start salivating. You like my hair? I'm really blondish like you, but platinum works magic on these sex-starved cheechakos. It makes them think of fucking Marilyn Monroe.

There is a long pause as she stares at (into) me. I can feel my ears reddening. Reaching across the table, she cups my chin in her hand and says, Jesus, baby, I'd sure like to plank you. I feel my penis shriveling, feel it looking for a place to hide. My mouth is smiling, but good lord she scares me. I want to get away from her. Buy me a drink, she says. I shake my head. Sorry, Angie, I only got a couple of bucks. Well then, buy yourself one. She gets up, goes to another table, sits with a lonely looking airman in uniform.

Joy is on stage stripped to panties and pasties. Her sluggish breasts hardly bounce at all as she moves slow and easy. The music is full of yearning violins, a woman sighing in the background. Joy stretches her body as if it, her body, is yawning. Turning around and bending over, her arms reach out, the fingers swaying up and down in a talkative way as if she's Hawaiian. Legs scissored, gluteus max looking hard as sheathed boulders. It's almost as if she is doing slow motion calisthenics, a kind of sleepy ballet. The men are mesmerized. No one shouts or whistles. They watch her. Joy the floating wetdream. A guy close by says to no one in particular, Jesus, what would you do for some of that? He starts nibbling his forefinger. When her dance is over she gathers her tips. Comes back to the table. There is the same sheen of sweat on her that there is on Angie, the same flowery armpit aroma. Not at all unpleasant. Arousing actually.

Kris comes to the table and tells her that Boris wants her circulating. Duffy, you need it buy drink, he says. I tell him a beer would be fine. Budweiser. He raises his hand, catches the bartender's attention and shouts, Bud! Joy looks for a man needing company. Kris sits with me. Boris is standing at the door checking IDs. My beer arrives. Joy is sitting with some flyboy in a booth. She laughs at something he says. She pats his forearm. A bottle of champagne arrives for them. Kris tells me that some nights she makes a hundred dollars in tips. He says he knows it sounds crazy, but it happens. He says that some guys offer her their paychecks for a piece of ass. He adds that he's never had to pay for a piece of ass in his life. Women throw themselves at him. I remember Pappas saying something similar a certain Christmas Eve and having the mom split his head open for it.

Kris buys me another beer and says his break is over. So the hour passes as I drink beer, watch sexy girls, see that they dance mostly to the same tunes and make the same moves up there, no enthusiasm. Saving their energy. They all look good on stage. Look like movie stars. Up close some of them, like Angie, don't look the same, fabulous faces and bodies turning out to be illusions caused by the way the Sourdough is lit, the way the lights change colors, their beams shooting slantwise from the ceiling. But the more I drink, the more fantastic the girls appear. Not a dog in there by the time midnight arrives and I'm six sheets to the wind.

Joy and some guy have gotten close. They are whispering in each other's ears. The bottle of champagne is upside down in the bucket. He keeps buying her drinks. She keeps knocking them back as if she's drinking nothing but tea. (I find out later that's exactly what it is.) Angie has taken her guy behind the door at the back of the bar. The loud music is making my bad ear bubble.

Leaving the Sourdough, I hit the next bar down the street. Where I'm asked for my ID number. The guy looks me up and down. His eyes saying he doesn't believe I'm twenty-one and a soldier. My long hair is a dead give-away. He lets me in anyway. Standing at the bar with the crowd, I order scotch and waterback because I heard someone else ordering it. Voices buzzing inside my head. My bad ear sounding like a siren. After a few minutes I can't make out a single thing anyone is saying. The scotch tastes more like medicine than vodka does. I polish it off and leave. Try the next bar. Lots of bars in Anchorage. But this time when the doorman asks my number I've forgotten it. Quote the first four numbers and forget the rest. The guy stares at me hard and says: Last chance, Peter P. I try again and end up mumbling nonsense. Get outta here, he says. Go home to Mommy. Ain't got no mommy, I tell him.

As I stroll the street, there is a feeling in me of not happiness exactly but a fine contentment and no fear. My feet flop a little, like I'm wearing clown shoes. But I can walk well enough and light my cigarettes with a steady hand and smile at people passing. Do not bother anyone and they will not bother you. I'm in Alaska. I'm fifteen. I'm having adventures to write about. Pretty much free to do as I want. What more could a curious kid ask? Only thing missing is Joy on my arm. I love her so! But it was Angie who wanted to plank me. Never heard that expression before. See myself planking her. I'd have to tie a board to my ass. My thoughts go to Lori, the one night with her, the 69, the number of guys that have pulled a train on her. I know for a fact she took on four at the same time. Also thinking: I bet there's nothing Angie wouldn't do either.

And then I see her. Not Angie. But sure enough Eskimo Mary. She is with some white guy. I follow them to the Victory Lounge and stand outside memorizing my number again, saying it over and over, until in spite of my pickled brain and my ear buzzing I won't mess up again. Going inside I rattle the number to the bouncer as fast as I can. Mary is sitting at a table alone when I get there. Mary, hey, it's you! She looks at me. Squints as if she's nearsighted. Who you? she says. I'm Duffy, remember? You came to my house and we danced. Remember Nick and Norman and Carl? Shee, she says, what you doin here, doll? Checking things out, you know. I was at the Sourdough with some friends. You alone, Mary? She says her friend is in the head and will be right back. Can I buy you a drink, Mary? She ponders the offer. Her eyes reflecting the neon lights blinking behind the bar. Mary's eyes remind me of Sherrye's eyes, same hair too, same brown skin. Its color: walnut shell. Same strong cheekbones. Some other time, she says. I got a car, I tell her. Shee, you got a car? Yeah. She looks toward the GENTS and says, Hoah, let's go. This guy's been goin all night like he's got a dose or somethin.

Walking back to the Sourdough, we see two men arguing outside another bar. Both are staggering, both having their fists up. Circling each other unsteadily. A crowd has gathered. Lots of yelling. A guy in the crowd says: One don't wanna fight and the other's damn glad of it! The crowd laughs. A punch is thrown, misses, and the man falls flat on his face. He tries to get up but can't. The other guy kicks him in the ribs and says: Fuck with me I kill you! Kill him! Kill him! people are chanting. Some are laughing. Mary is laughing. She's got her arm around my neck and is laughing and saying Kill him! I steer her around the crowd to the Chrysler.

We stop at a liquor store and she buys a bottle of Old Crow. We drive around aimlessly, passing the bottle back and forth. She makes fun of how I have to stop the car by easing on the emergency brake. Shee, you gotta be crazy drive a car like this, she says. I reply, Gotta be crazy to ride with a driver who is crazy enough to drive a car like this. She come-hithers me. Hoah, I like you, you cute, she says. I want to know if she's full blood Eskimo. She says part Inuit. Other half French-Canadian. She lives with her mother in an apartment at the end of Tudor Road. She is twenty-three years old. Never married and never wants to be. She adds, Men! Hoah, to hell with em. Yes, to hell with men Grandma Inez would agree. So would the mom on her man-bash days.

Mary tells me she lived with a guy for a while, but he would get drunk and beat her. The night I saw her crying he had slugged her in the stomach so hard he had knocked the wind out of her. He still comes around, but when he does she hides behind the clothes in the closet and her mother tells him she is still living in Fairbanks with her aunt. So far Mary has been able to avoid him. It is nearly one-thirty in the morning when I take her home and make a date to drive out to the bay for a picnic.

Back at the Sourdough I see Pappas with Angie. You're here? I say. What you fuckin doin here? he says. Why ain't you in bed? He is loose-lipped sloppy bleary-eyed suspicious. Angie tells me to take him home. He tells me to give him his money. Sorry, sir, I say. I only got a couple of bucks. The rest is at the house. Fuck you, he says. He pulls a twenty out of his wallet, gives it to Angie. Yanks her into his lap, one hand cupping her breast.

Later, I drive him back to the cabin. Guide him to his room. Take off his shoes and socks. Cover him with a blanket. He's asleep before I close the door. I make up the couch bed and lie there feeling everything spinning and wondering if I'm going to be sick again. Am I an alcoholic now? Not a day passes without booze. Feels to me like booze is saving my psyche. The peace it brings. The calm nerves I have now. I definitely dig why Pappas drinks so much. Only he generally gets nasty mean, wants to fight somebody, whereas I get mellow and happy and fearless. Even when I throw up and have hangovers, getting drunk is worth it.

Kris and Joy come home around 3:00. Not long after they go inside their room I'm listening to them sucking and screwing. And I'm wondering how many times she has already done it tonight. Did she go behind the door like Angie did? And what kind of money did she make? And how does a girl open herself to total strangers like that? Lots of them. Lots of strange cock night after night. Lips, hands, arms. I tell myself what the hell, sex is just a deeper kind of kissing. Sex is just sex. Nothing special. There are billions of people in the world, plenty of them banging each other every second. It's an orgy out there. Sex has been an intimate part of my life for as far back as I can remember. My sister my mother myself, the world around us, the walls of our house, the cars we traveled in, the hiding places where we indulged ourselves, all of it oozing memoirs of broken commandments. Thou shalt not ... Yes we will. I was ten and I know children who were even younger when they first got started. Carol Marie was what, five or six? And it never lets up. It's nature, it's natural, it's no big deal unless you make it a big deal.

~~

Next morning Pappas gets up, showers, gets me up and says he wants to have breakfast with Angie at her place. He says she promised to whip something up. He wants me to drive him over and then go for groceries and come back in a couple hours. Not a damn thing to eat in this house, he says. Your job, Duffy. Why you think I let you handle the money? Am I asking too much? Gimmee a hundred bucks.

So over to Angie's we go. When he knocks on the door, she opens it wearing a sheer nightie. I see monster knockers. Nipples. Shaded pubic hair. Think about how Pappas has said he still loves the mom and he wants me to tell her how much he's changed, how good he is, how he wishes she would quit her job and move to Anchorage. I've only written her two letters and nearly every word in them is what he told me to say. She hasn't written back. Glad to be rid of me, out of sight out of mind. I remember her coming home one day and saying there was this young man working for her who had stolen her mothering heart. Long tall drink of water, she called him. Honest as the day is long, she said. Handsome and sweet, she said. He's just like a son to me, she said. And I knew she was wishing she could replace me with him. No contest.

I get groceries and tick off two hours before I pull to the curb in front of Angie's place and wait. The Chrysler reeks of stale smoke and brake fluid and seven years of Anchorage mud and dust. Pappas comes out. Slides onto the seat. Tells me to take him to the Sourdough parking lot to pick up the Pontiac. Driving along he says he couldn't do it. Nope, he started thinking about how much he loves my mom and he couldn't screw Angie. I want to say: But hahnee, I luff you! Of course I don't say a word.

~~

Saturday, Eskimo Mary and I go on our picnic. Stop and buy beer and chips, cheese and crackers. We spread a blanket on the sand. In front of us is the sparkling bay. All around are bunches of long stemmed grasses poking out of the sand. We drink beer and pick at the munchies and talk. The wind is blowing, peppering us with grains of sand, so we get back inside the car. Turn the radio on. The song playing is Little Darlin. We sing it to each other. Smiling and singing Little Darlin ... *a-hoopa a-hoopa.*

At some point Mary kisses me. I taste beer. I taste cheese. I taste crackers. All of it soaked in booze breath. She feels me up and I feel her up too. Small breasts. Sherrye's are small the same way. Nice little handfuls. It's not fair to Mary, but I close my eyes and picture Sherrye. Sherrye in the Oldsmobile stuck in the snow in Nevada. Sherrye and the two times screwing her. Sherrye who finally went all the way, but it took stealing a car and stealing gas and running from the cops and nearly spinning off the face of the earth to get inside her at last. Whacky way to get a piece of ass. I'd like to try it in more hospitable surroundings. Do it better. Have a memory of titanic sex to fantasize about whenever I'm horny.

Also thinking: Mary is hot to trot! I start sliding my hand inside her pants, but she pushes back and says: Shee, I can't do it to you, Duffy. What's up, Mary? She hesitates. Then she says: Shee, Duffy, I got the dose. If we fuck, you get it too. Listen, I take care of you. She puts her hand on my cock and lowers her mouth. I feel her breath as she says: When I get well we do lot more. But the heat runs out of me like a lit candle dipped in water, the picture of Sherrye lying under me evaporating: poof. Also thinking of that cocksucking Paul seducing me with vodka and those pictures of naked whores fingering themselves and giving blow jobs. No, no, I whisper, pulling on Mary. She looks at me with puzzled eyes. Shee, I don't mind, she says. I'm looking out the window, the sun dragging hard light behind darkened clouds.

Limp in her hand. I'm shaking my head and putting my pitiful prick away. The two of us end up lying there holding each other, while she tells me it was her boyfriend, the one who beat her. Filthy bastard gimme the dose, she says. She didn't know she had it for a long time. She thought it was a bladder infection. But finally she went to the doctor and he gave her penicillin. She's getting better now, but not all well yet. And by the way, Carl probably has it too. Hoah, maybe you should warn him, ey? She wants to kiss and grope. Her hand down there coaxing, but I'm really turned off by the fact that her pussy is sick and it is like all of her is sick and maybe I can catch it from the spit in her mouth. All her manipulations don't do any good and I find myself saying, I'm sorry, Mary. Also thinking: I just want to hurry time and get away. Shudder to think I might have planked her and have VD. What does that feel like? It's a burning when you pee, I've heard. I take Mary home. Drop her off and tell her I'll see her around. She smiles bitterly and says: No you won't.

~~

When I get to the house, Joy and Kris are sitting side by side on the sofa.

Hanging from Joy's hand is a letter from her mother in Los Angeles. Joy is weeping. What's up? I ask. Bluntly, Kris says: Her son he dead. She has a son? She had son. Hearing this, Joy cries harder, lowers her head onto her knees and sobs. The sound is the sound of a broken heart, the sound the mom made the night she ran Pappas out of the house and got drunk in her bedroom. I feel real bad for Joy but don't know what to do to help her. I'm real sorry, Joy, I say. She lifts her head, wipes her eyes with the heel of her hand. My poor baby, she whispers. I failed him. We should have taken him with us. No, says Kris. Was good for to stay with you mother was good. She shakes her head. I should have kept him and taken care of him! Her mouth nose eyes leaking all over. For a second she stares at Kris as if she hates him. Her eyes saying it's your fault, you bastard!

He looks at me and says they were going to send for the kid one of these days. I'll never see him again, says Joy, her voice squeaking. Never ever ever. Everything's too late. My baby's dead! And her head goes down and the sobs begin again, her body shaking the way Michele Renee shakes when she is all-out bawling over no one loving her enough. Kris leans his elbows on his knees, his head in his hands. He looks sad. He looks beaten. He listens to Joy for a few more seconds. Then he stands up. Grabs her. Lifts her into his arms. Carries her into the bedroom. Seconds later I hear him plowing her for all he's worth. It's pretty much the last thing I would have thought to do. How do you fuck someone who is grieving so hard for her dead son? But then again what do I know?

They stay in the bedroom almost an hour. When they come out, he says they're going to move to a furnished apartment downtown within walking distance of the Sourdough. He's already talked to the manager about it. He asks me to lend him 100 bucks to pay the deposit. I tell him the money belongs to my father. If I give you that much money, he'll kick my ass. Kris insists that Pappas will never know. He says he'll give it back to me next week for sure. For Joy you do it, he says. Joy comes out of the bathroom looking ethereal in a wispy white dress, her orange hair falling to her shoulders, her blue eyes fragile. She doesn't smile, but she doesn't look so destroyed anymore either. Not serene but enduring. So maybe the best thing you can do for a grieving woman is fuck her? Get her mind off the other world and back into this one?

She and Kris pack their clothes—the clothes Pappas bought them with his bar tab. They ask for a ride to Cordova Street. I take them there and Kris talks the landlord into letting them move in early. I give Kris the 100 bucks. He gives it to the landlord. I take them to Ship Creek Market. I buy their food for the week. Leave them at their new apartment getting ready for work. They have asked me to come by tonight. I tell them I will. But really I don't want to.

I spend the night with Pappas and Carl and Norman sitting around the table drinking and talking about fishing, hunting, air force officers who are bastards, women who like it in the ass. Pappas slips his ancestry into the conversation, reminding everyone of the superiority of the Greeks who started civilization and think how far advanced we'd be if their ideas had taken over the world! Pappas wants me to tell them about Grandpa Mike. Tell em about your grandpa, Duffy. Tell em how smart he is. He's just a coalminer, but he speaks seven languages. Reads Socrates cover to cover. He knows Crete history from the Minoans to the First World War. Tell them, Duffy, tell them how he was a hero in the First World War. Decorated twice for valor. Tell em about your grandpa, Duffy. Yeah, I say. Yeah, he owns a farm. He was a coalminer until he hurt his back. He speaks Spanish. Lots of languages.

I don't know what more to tell them about Grandpa Mike. Is Pappas saying a bunch of lies? Seven languages? Better make that three. Four if you want to count his heavily accented English. He's read Socrates? Maybe so. And maybe he is a Minoan historian. What do I know? I know he was in the First World War. I've seen a picture of him in his uniform. He has a saber, the same one he gave me to hang on my bedroom wall. When he opens his trunk and picks through all his mementos, I've seen an album full of war photos. Decorated twice? I've never seen his medals. Nor did he ever mention them. But who knows where the truth ends and where the wish list takes over?

I get so drunk I can barely stagger to bed at midnight. The men stay up drinking beer and laying down the rules for how the world should be run. Hear Pappas saying, First thing you do is drop the bomb on Russia and China. Get rid of them fuckers and no one will fuck with us. I close the door, get in bed, pull my Peter Pan cover up to my chin and think about Mary and how I almost got burned by her. I neglect to tell Carl that he should get himself checked out because he might have VD. If he has it he'll know soon enough.

~~

In the morning I wake to loud voices, an enraged man shouting so angrily it creates a rerun terror of the times Pappas came for me. I'm panting as I sit up in bed, my heart throbbing. I'm fifteen, he won't beat me anymore. Will he? The voices are coming from the kitchen, so maybe Carl and Norman are still there and they are arguing? But the voice I hear clearest is Jimmy the Greek. Hear him bellowing: You no fucking with me, Pappy! You fucker, you owe it me my fucking money!

I slip my jeans on and take Pappas's rifle out of the closet and the K-Bar out of the drawer, slip the knife into my waistband. Tiptoe into the living room to the kitchen entrance. Peeking round the corner, I see Jim and a heavyset man in a suit sitting at the table with Pappas at the far end looking pale and frightened. I make a decision to put the rifle away and come back and see if I can talk to Jim. Talk nice. Calm him down. As I turn toward the bedroom, I see a man sitting in the chair next to the sofa, a ghastly smile on his face. In his hand is a revolver. I hurry past him and get rid of the rifle. I put a shirt on. The knife hides behind it.

As I enter the kitchen, I say: What's going on, guys? What's the matter, Jim? What matter? You fucking father fucking Jim, says Jim. He owe it me my money and now he no come round? He no return it my calls to office. This way to treat you friend? Sure I say it Pappy make payments. But I see payment? Fuck no, he spend it my money for Sourdough bitchees. Jim slams the table with his hand. Pappas jumps. His eyes rivet on me as he says: Pay him, Duffy. Give him the money. How much, sir? I ask. The amount on his tab is $358.

So I go to my room. Take from the drawer $125 of the $150 left. When I return I hand the money to Jim, who says: What fuck this? You still wanting cheating me? Give him all of it, Duffy! says Pappas. I tell him I paid the rent and groceries and utilities. This is all I got left, sir, honest. Pappas looks flabbergasted. That can't be all, he says. Where's the rest of it? That's when I have to fess up that I loaned a hundred bucks to Kris to get the new apartment. He's going to pay me back next week, I say. And I gave you a hundred last Sunday. For Angie. Jesus Christ, moans Pappas.

I sit close to Jim and say: Look, Jim, I promise to God we'll give you the rest on the first of the month. I will personally bring it to you, Jim. Okay? He thinks awhile, his handlebar mustache twitching like fleas are crawling through it. You bring it me my money? he says. I nod firmly. You can trust me, Jim. First thing I do payday is bring you the money in cash. He looks at Pappas. Pappas raises a hand and says, Swear to God, Jim. Smiling weakly, his teeth looking like they belong in the mouth of a toddler. A few seconds tick by before Jim stands up. He stares at me, points his finger but doesn't say anything. Then he and the other two men leave.

Pappas wipes his hand through his hair and says: Jesus Christ that was close. That fucker was gonna shoot me. A moment later he looks at me and says: You let me down, you little bastard. He shakes his head, says: See what I get for trusting that fuckin whore? She goes out and buys all them clothes and I get stuck with the fuckin bill. And how does she pay me back? Gives me not a goddamn thing. Nothin! Rotten bitch almost gets me shot. Jesus, what a fuckin world I'm livin in.

I nod agreement, but I could say that a lot of his tab at D & D is his own doing, always buying drinks for others. Put it on my tab, he's always saying, being the nice guy he is, wanting everyone to love him. Put it on my tab. And face it, he thought he'd get in Joy's pants by buying her those clothes, but she fooled him. The only thing I ever saw her do was kiss his cheek and say thank you. He was putty in her hands, but she didn't want him in her hands. Or anywhere else.

While I'm putting on my socks and boots, I hear his big feet booming towards me. This is a man who never walks softly. When I look up, Pappas is standing in the doorway, a burning hatred in his eyes. A look that says murder. My heart sinks and I tell myself: Duffy, pull the Ka-Bar and stab him. Stab him. Then run the fuck out of here. Jump in the car and get away from Alaska! But I know I won't do that. Or maybe I will. Maybe now is the time. Is it? If he comes for me I will. I put my hand near the knife, ready to pull it.

You give my fuckin money to Kris, he says, a harsh statement, not a question. I answer that the money was a loan. And say: He's our friend, sir. Pappas shouts: Not my fuckin friend! I hold up my hand and say, C'mon, Daddy, don't be like that. His voice drowns mine: Don't Daddy me, you stupid bastard! I trust you with my money and you don't even have enough respect to ask me if you can loan it to that fucker? You know goddamn well you should've asked me, you dumb sonofabitch! He's right I should have asked him. You're right, I should have asked you. I'm sorry. But look, we get it back next week, soon as Kris gets paid. If Jim hadn't showed up, we'd be fine till payday.

Pappas's eyes look like flamethrowers as he roars, That fucking bastard! I ought to shoot that fucking bastard! Who does he think he is coming in here threatening me? I'm Nick Pappas, goddammit! And that fuckin Joy, that two-faced bitch! You think she's even offered to pay me back? Hell no! And, shit, goddammit to hell, I have to pay that motherfucker who fixed the Chrysler. That sonofabitch wrote my commanding officer. He chewed my ass! Another motherfucker that needs to get shot. I'm a veteran. I'm decorated, goddammit! I got war wounds and they treat me like this? And then YOU come along fucking me in the ass too. I thought I could trust you, but you're as much a moron as you always was. You're not takin care of the money no more, that's fuckin sure. You see how you're looking at me? You mad, Duffy? You fuckin mad enough to take a swing at this old man? Come on, go ahead, give it a try, you bony little bastard, I'll break you in half. When I'm eighty I'll still be able to kick your ass! He stands there beer-bellied and half blind, his bad eye leaking, his thick lips curling, a wandering vein throbbing in his forehead, hands itching to get at me. He needs to kill me. I believe he would if he could get away with it. Bury me in the woods. No one in Anchorage would miss me. I hang my head in sorrow. I really feel like crying. Everything hopeless. Everything so goddamn sad. This life. Everything.

The moment passes and Pappas is shaking his head. You still do it, he says, you still push my buttons and make me say things I don't mean. When are you going to grow up, Duffy? When you gonna start acting responsible? When you gonna act like a man? When I was your age I—

Don't listen to him: heard it so often I could repeat it like a dummy sitting on the lap of a ventriloquist. All I know for sure is that I don't want this anymore. While he's glorifying himself, my mind is elsewhere, to ways out of town. To driving the wounded Chrysler over the Alcan through Alaska, the Yukon, British Columbia, into Washington, south to Colorado and my suffering mother. I think about the Canadian border. How will I get across the border? They might just wave me through. If Pappas hasn't called ahead and told them to stop me. But the real rub is that Alaska is still a territory: I'll have to go through customs. I have no I.D. to show except Private Peter P. Pearson's.

No, driving isn't the answer, driving won't cut it.

Kids these days, Pappas is saying, his tone full of contempt, they don't know shit about how fuckin tough life can be. It's lucky we're not in a war and have to depend on your generation. He pokes my shoulder over and over while saying, I want you to find a job. You understand me? Go see that fuckin Greek and ask him if you can wash dishes or somethin. Put your application in. There's lots of places you could work. I got to do flight time. I'll be gone to goddamn Guam three days. When I come back you better have a job. You listening? He pauses a moment. Then says, You know that cocksucker isn't going to pay you back. You know that, don't you? I know his kind. You don't know him. You don't know nothin about people, Duffy. You can't trust nobody. When you gonna learn? How old are you, fifteen? For fifteen you're really stupid. If you had a brain you'd take it out and play with it.

Yeah, I agree with him. It really bothers me to be as dumb as I am, but I don't know what to do to fix me. You ought to go into the service, he says. The service is where guys like you can make a living. If you stay long enough and do your job, you could get rank and live good. Look how well I've done. I'm a master sergeant. I've nearly reached the top grade for non-commissioned officers. I've worked hard to get where I am. His voice has gentled, the hatred bleeding out of his bleeding eyes, which seem to be crying real tears, tiny trickles. I'm not going to get my ass kicked or have to stab him, not right now, anyway. Talking about how he came up in life has made him melancholy. All my hard work for what? A cabin in Anchorage, Alaska and you? Why doesn't your mother understand she was the only chance I had? Why won't she take me back? I love her. I never loved no woman but her. He takes out a hanky, wipes his eyes, blows his nose, coughs, clears his throat, says: Fuck it, we should get breakfast and then you stay in town and put your application in, and get a job and pay me back. Yeah, if you think Kris is coming through, you're full of shit as a Christmas goose.

~~

When Pappas flies to Guam the next day, I go to a phone booth and call the mom collect and tell her my letters to her about good Pappas are full of lies. I tell her he dictated what I wrote. And truth is he still drinks like a fish, him and his alcoholic cronies. And I'm drinking heavily too, hanging out in bars and driving around in a car that only has a handbrake. In my mind I can see her thumb and forefinger rubbing her temples, a migraine knocking. What is she to do with this boy? So much trouble! She would be way better off if he would just disappear. Vanish. Kids! Nothing but heartache. Leeches. Parasites. I can hear her hearthounded breath whistling. She needs to make another decision about her no good son.

    She tells me she sold the house in Aurora and is renting one in Denver. Uncle Dean and Aunt Marge are living in the basement, helping her make ends meet. Carol Marie has her hands full taking care of baby Janis. It's a full house and a full life. If she lets me come home I have to swear to God on the Bible I'll be a help, not a hindrance. I promise not to make trouble. Let me tell you something, she says, I've cried over you like I've never cried over anyone, not even when your father died. I've cried so much over you that I'm all cried out inside. I've shed my last tears for you, buster. You better believe it. She pauses. Then says: God, I'm probably going to regret this. But I suppose you could come live here. But don't you dare get in touch with Lee or Sherrye. And you stay out of Aurora! Surely by now you've learned your lesson, haven't you? Yes, ma'am for sure, I answer. She says she'll arrange a plane ticket and get back to me.

*Love, let us be true to one another*

*- Matthew Arnold*

I go to the airport and abandon the Chrysler. I don't take anything with me, not the clothes in the closet or the drawers, not the Ka-Bar. Nothing but the clothes on my back and the twenty-five bucks I kept hidden. So when Pappas comes home he won't be alerted to my running away from him.

That night, after the plane lands in Seattle, customs phones the mom and verifies my American citizenship. After a six hour layover and a four hour flight, it is morning and I'm standing at the curb of Stapleton Airfield in Colorado waiting to be picked up. A cop car cruises by with two cops inside. And I'm thinking, Fuck you, you bastards, I'm back!

The mom arrives in her clunky maroon Desoto and takes me to the new house. It's a brick house, looks sturdy. Has a nice lawn. A fenced back yard. Middle-class house. Nothing trashy about the neighborhood. You'll have to sleep on the sofa for now, she says. I tell her, I'm glad to be back, glad to be anywhere where Pappas isn't. Just don't screw it up, she says. You'll get us both in big trouble if you do.

We go inside and Michele Renee screams Duffy! She runs into my arms. I whirl her around. I kiss Carol Marie and the baby. My aunt and uncle look at me like I'm an alien. In some ways I am. They get up and without a word go down to their basement bedroom. Michele Renee and Carol Marie want to know about Alaska. So I tell them Alaska is Colorado magnified. Alaska is larger-than-life. Larger mountains. Larger trees. Larger rivers and lakes. Larger animals like moose and grizzlies. I tell them about the moose I saw when my plane was landing in Anchorage. I tell them I saw a thirteen foot Kodiak slapping salmon out of the Kenai River. I tell them that some of the salmon I caught were as tall as me. I tell them Alaska is the place for guys whose dreams are big, guys who are pioneers and tough as the old mountain men who explored the Rockies. On and on I embroider Alaska and find myself missing it, find myself saying that one of these days I'll live in Alaska, be a bush pilot, a trapper, a writer writing tales of adventure. Michele Renee says she wants to go too. I promise to take her as soon as she's old enough.

Carol Marie says: You've never held my baby. Here, take her. I hold the little thing and she's looking better than when I saw her from behind bars in Brighton. I sway with her, whirl her around and do a little dance, telling her I'm giving her rhythm, putting rhythm into her bones. It's an excuse for my sisters to dance, so a record goes on. It's Gogi Grant singing about the wayward wind again. My favorite, the mom says, can't get enough of her voice, listen to her. We waltz, we sing along, sing the wayward wind is a restless wind.

~~

The next day when only Carol Marie and Janis are home, I get on the phone and call you. Your mother answers. I should hang up, but stupidly I say, Is Sherrye there? There's a gasp and a pause and then you come on the line. It's me, I say. Again a gasp and a pause. And then you say: You calling from Alaska? Naw, I've come back, Sherrye. I'm in Denver at my mom's new house. And you say: Judge Jacobucci let you come back? Course not, I say, I'm here in secret. Don't tell anyone or it's my neck. Next thing I know you're yelling, saying you've had it with me. I've had it with you, Duffy Pappas! And you slam the phone in my ear. I'm stunned. Can't figure out what your problem is. What did I do? I thought you were going to be thrilled and want to see me. But no, you obviously hate me now. Well, fuck you, you little bitch! You're no longer the love of my life.

Not more than three hours later there's a knock on the door. I look outside and see a squad car. I tell Carol Marie to tell the cops she hasn't seen me. I run down to the basement and hide. Hear voices above. Then Carol Marie is at the top of the stairs saying, It's no use, he knows you're here. I'm thinking about you, Sherrye. I'm thinking you turned me in. Unbelievable! Why? How could you do it? I go upstairs and hold my wrists out for the cop to cuff me. But he waves me off. He's a sad-eyed guy looking like he doesn't really want this job. To Carol Marie he says, Sorry, miss. Hanging my head in defeat I go with him to the car. He opens the door on the passenger side, sits me on the front seat, pulls out a pack of Camels and offers me one. I take it and we both light up.

The ride to the county jail in Brighton is done in silence.

~~

And once again here I am: same cell, same scene outside except now it is late spring and the trees have leaves. The apple tree across the street is drowning in blossoms, people strolling in short sleeves and Bermudas, children running on the courthouse lawn, cars going somewhere. Everyone free. I lie down on a bunk and curl fetal.

Feel fatal.

Late in the afternoon the mom shows. She looks through the bars and says: There's nothing I can do, Duffy. If only you hadn't broken probation so many times. If only you hadn't gone looking for trouble in the first place. She shakes her head and tells me we're out of options, time to pay the piper. I don't say anything. What is there to say?

~~

Days go by. Weeks in isolation. Is it the end of June? Maybe it's early July.

I don't really know how many days have passed. A month? Without seeing anyone. It's lonely in a cell all by yourself. You try to stay on your feet, do exercises, pushups, sit-ups, squats, running in place, pacing wall to wall, stand on your hands, try to tire yourself out. But no naps, no sleeping. If you sleep during the day, you'll end up not sleeping at night, which will make time really crawl. Your mind will go over every second of every single fuck up. You'll hate yourself for being so goddamn stupid, just like Pappas has always said you are. It's gotta be true. Look where you are again! If that's not stupid, what is?

If I could only have some books I'd be able to handle the solitude better, but no books allowed, no cigarettes. Nothing. Just those two meals a day to look forward to and they're as tasteless as TV dinners. I need clean socks and underwear, but I don't get any. My socks are so smelly I can't stand them, so I start washing my socks and underwear at the sink and hanging them on the bars. Which keeps me busy for a little while at least. And the days come. And the days go and I keep wondering why they don't just transport my sorry ass to Golden. Get it over with. What's taking so long? Are they keeping me in solitary to teach me a lesson? Okay, lesson learned.

~~

Finally the door opens and I'm thinking this is it. Next stop the Industrial School. I steel myself. Tell myself: make the other boys think you're crazy. Walk wild, talk wild, pick fights, threaten, intimidate, let them believe you're insane and they'll leave you alone, Duffy. I stand up and take a deep breath. My eyes on the open doorway.

Nothing ever happens the way you think it will. You plan and plan. You imagine scenarios. It's all worked out in your head. But it never happens the way it happens in your head. No officers enter to cuff me, haul me away, drive me to Golden and hand me over to a sadist who beats me, just so I'll know who's boss. None of that occurs. In its place is Jean Jacobucci wearing a suit and a tie. He looks around the cell as if he's imagining how it would feel to be locked up in it. I'm dumbfounded, madly amazed to see him. A judge coming to see a jackass like me locked in a jail cell? Unheard of. Impossible. Are you dreaming, Duffy? He looks at me with those worried Italian eyes and says, Sit down, son. I want to talk to you. We sit at the steel table in the center of the floor facing each other.

Sherrye, listen to this: The judge tells me *your* father insists I be sent to the Industrial School. He's threatening to sue the court and the county and Jean Jacobucci personally. The judge shakes his head and says he believes putting me away would wreck me permanently. What you'll learn may be a useful trade, but more likely you'll just learn more ways to break more laws. More ways to live up to your incorrigible label. He tells me that some boys are so hopeless there isn't anything to do but send them to a reformatory, get them off the streets until they're eighteen, even though when they come out most of them will be right back into trouble and probably worse trouble, armed robbery, assault with a deadly weapon. Maybe murder. Many of them will end up in the penitentiary doing ten to twenty, maybe in Canon City, or a prison in some other state. Some of them will be in prison for life. Do you want that? he asks.

No sir, I sure don't, I tell him. I know I've gotten more chances than I deserve. I know Mom should wash her hands of me. You and the courts have bent over backwards and I haven't been very grateful. Well, actually I was grateful that you sent me to Alaska, and maybe I should have stayed there, stuck it out. But I was headed the wrong way again. I had to take the chance of coming back. I had to get away from him.

The judge wants to know why. What's so bad about him? he says. I think about that, I think about why. I think about bad. I don't know how to answer the judge. I mean, what is so bad about Pappas? He's scary, but lots of kids have scary fathers and they survive. I know for sure that Pappas was scared of his father. He was mean and Pappas turned mean too. Yeah, so he's mean, but I've seen meanness all my life. What kid hasn't? So how to put it into words. Why? What's so bad? I hear Carol Marie's voice saying, He's a man who, even if he doesn't actually kill you, kills you. So that's what I tell the judge. Adding: If that makes any sense. And I tell him about all the alcohol, how the only way I could stand living with Pappas was to drink myself into a stupor every night. I tell him about hanging out with B-girls at the Sourdough. I tell him about driving all over Anchorage without a license. I tell him about the Chrysler having only a handbrake to stop it. I tell him about Jimmy the Greek coming over and threatening to kill Pappas for money owed. I tell him about the guy with the gun sitting behind me smiling when I came out of the bedroom with the rifle thinking I might have to shoot somebody. I tell him about Kris borrowing money and Pappas wanting to murder me for it. I tell him about the K-Bar. I tell him that if Pappas had come for me, I would have stabbed him.

The judge looks pretty upset. And sad. Sadder and sadder. I know he's really troubled about what I've told him, and he's probably thinking: What the hell am I to do with this boy? His eyes looking mystified when he finally says, But ... but your mother wanted you to go to him. Why do you suppose that is? Why send you to a man like that? I tell the judge it was desperation. I tell him she didn't know what else to do. Nick Pappas was the last resort, the last chance to keep me out of reform school. Which she also believes will ruin me forever.

Jacobucci is nodding. And yet, he says, I find out now that you have relatives in Minnesota. You have a grandmother there and uncles and aunts related to your father. You have cousins. Do you remember them? I tell him I don't remember them at all, didn't know they existed until a couple of years ago when

Carol Marie told me. Well, he says, lucky for you your mother got in touch with them and they want you. You have an Uncle George and an Aunt Katie who say they have room for you and you're welcome to live with them. The judge puts his hand on my shoulder. The touch of his hand makes me choke up. You broke probation by coming back, he says, but you didn't commit another felony. You had good reasons to return, I understand that, son. In your shoes I might have done it too. You can quit worrying about Golden. I'm not sending you there. As soon as arrangements can be made, you'll be on your way. I'm sure we're both grateful that we have one last option. You will leave Colorado again and you will not return, at least not before you're eighteen. This is your final chance for sure. Understand?

~~

A day later I'm released into the custody of the mom, who will take me to the train station and send me to Minnesota. Carol Marie and Janis are going with me, so they can visit the relatives for a few weeks before returning to Colorado. Carol Marie and I talk about it, about the mom contacting Uncle George and Aunt Katie. Carol Marie saying the mom should have contacted them long ago, but her pride kept her from doing it. Also, she's hated by our father's people, says Carol Marie. They blame her for his death. Mom told me this herself, she says. We had a long heart-to-heart. She said she left him because he was tied to his mother's apron strings. His mother the matriarch, the queen bee. She rules. She rules everybody, but she couldn't rule our mom. Our father left Minnesota after she took us to California. He took the job in New Orleans to show her that he was independent. He wanted her to join him there and patch things up. He told her his mother wouldn't have anything to say about how they lived their lives. Maybe it would have happened that way if he hadn't died. Or maybe she would have just stayed in California and lived the life she lived with us. Who knows?

The phone rings. Carol Marie answers it. She hands it to me and says, It's Sherrye. I take the phone and you say you heard from your father that I was out and being sent to Minnesota. You ask me if I'm all right. I answer: What the fuck do you care? You say you care a lot. You say you love me, you'll always love me. You say your mother told your father that Duffy Pappas had come back. My mom didn't want to do it, Duffy. My dad is the one that insisted you be arrested. I argued with him. I tried to stop him, but you can't stop him once he gets his mind set. He hates you so much! While you're telling your tale I'm thinking of your tobacco-drooling daddy spurting nasty brown spit into a Folgers coffee can. I'm standing there in your living room pretending not to notice, but it looks like diarrhea coming from his mouth and I'm wondering who could kiss such a man? I'm still holding the phone and listening to you rattling on, blah, blah, blah, so I stop you by saying, Look, Sherrye, what do you want from me?

Silence. I can almost hear the gears whirring in your head: what do I want from him? Then you say: Don't hate me, Duffy. I would never have turned you in. I swear to God I wouldn't. It wasn't me, it was Dad. You're crying, you're sniffing. I'm listening to all that heartbroken blubbering into the phone and the sound of it starts me blubbering too. We cry together. In between sobs we are saying we love each other. We'll always love each other. Always keep in touch. I'll write you. You'll write me. We'll talk on the phone. C'mon, shit, it's not over! Fuck no! When I'm eighteen I'll come back to Colorado and marry you. Together we'll finish what we started. We'll go to California, where your father won't find us. To hell with your fuckin father! Ah yes, love will conquer, love will find a way. But not now. Not right this minute or next week or next month. Years. It may take years, Sherrye. Colorado fading. A new world. A new way of behaving. A lost life rewinding—Minnesota dreaming. Goodbye, my Sherrye. I love you. Goodbye, Duffy. I love you too.

I hang up knowing I never will erase you, Sherrye. You're etched inside me. Forever fourteen. Unforgettable.

> *We're bound together like sailors, swaying across*
> *a dark ocean, resigned to each other's odd humors*
>
> *- Joseph Millar*

    You have to ask yourself what will be the course of your life from this point forward? Will Pappas always be your excuse? Look at it this way: what he did to tear you down, actually resulted in building you up. And look at it this way too. Without his nearly fatal influence, would you have had the rage to fuel the energy driving you, driving your body and your brain, to create a rationale for the ruin you became? Take him out of the picture and most likely what you have is a pretty dull past. Maybe that would be good, but you wouldn't be you still tied to the boy you were, the boy with the words following you, the shadow that will never leave you, not in this life.

    Yes, but what if he had never been a factor? How would we have turned out, my sisters and I? (Actually, Michele Renee wouldn't even be alive.) These Greeks: they know *agon*, They know that the struggle is ultimately all there is. Fate is fate. Make the commitment. Or maybe you shouldn't. Who decides? Would I have been a better person, kinder, more trustworthy, more reliable, more courageous, if I had not had Pappas in my life? I might have remained a contemptible sissy without him around. Perhaps my nose would be more symmetrical, rather than the squashed knob that it is. Perhaps my right ear wouldn't ring and bubble and buzz. But some other stepfather might have been even worse. Or better. Who can say?

~~

Stick to it.
Be stoic.
No regrets.
Say thank you to Pappas.
Thank you, Daddy.
You're welcome. I told you I'd make you a man, didn't I?
Yes, you did, sir. But I'm not the man you were making. Or am I?
What do I know? What do you know?
    I know Grandma Inez died in 1978: throat cancer. She was 82. Greetings (*Booz-hoo ahnee*), Grandma. No one knows exactly when Grandpa Mike died. He ended in a nursing home trying to speak English to the caregivers, but no one could understand him. Someone there traced the mom to Prescott and called

her. The nurses didn't know what he was trying to tell them. They put him on the phone and he said, Jinny, Jinny co-down, co-down, Crampa! She didn't go get him. She couldn't.

Carol Marie has survived well enough despite the traumas in her life. Just because a child is sexually and/ or mentally abused doesn't mean she will be forever spoiled, forever broken, forever moaning about her fucked up past. Carol Marie is not a moaner. She never complains about anything. She lives in southern California. She's very religious, goes to mass every morning, takes Communion and prays. She is an office manager for the doctor to whom she's married. Her daughter Janis, the tiny tyke I first saw when I was behind bars, has grown into a beautiful woman who, unfortunately, is now battling multiple sclerosis. And so it goes. Yes. Michele Renee is a nurse practitioner smart as they come, one of those born to give orders. She lives in Arizona, has married twice. She was wild in her youth. Aren't we all, at least to some degree? If our hearts had been pure, we might have spent our lives grieving our lost innocence. It pays to be capable of sin now and then. With dots of wickedness peppering your heart, the world quickly ceases to shock or surprise you.

Looking back on it, exhuming it from the burial site of unreliable memories, it seems to me my own life has been a succession of sporadic, pointless, illogical zigzags, reflexive reactions to the environment surrounding me. Reactions full of innate errors brought on by crosswired DNA and kismet.

~~

In 1996, I went back to Colorado to re-trace the route we took when we ran away in 1957. I wanted to write a fictional version of what happened. When I went to Brighton to find Judge Jean Jacobucci, I learned that he had died. I tried to see his wife, but she was ailing and unable to talk to me. I wanted to tell her what her husband had done for me, how hugely influential he was in my life. I regret that I waited so long to see him. Regrets: wasted energy. Best to let regrets go. But to tell you the truth I'm not very good at taking my own advice.

For years I dreamed of meeting Nick Pappas and punching his lights out. But who knows how that would have gone? Maybe he was right. Maybe even if he lived to be 80 he would still be able to kick my ass. It's pointless speculation now. Pappas died January 10, 1967. He was forty-three years old. He had been at a New Year's Eve party when his ulcers burst and they rushed him to a hospital. Over the next ten days his condition worsened into uncontrollable bleeding caused by varices in both his esophagus and stomach. This time the doctors couldn't save him. Before he died he called the mom. Told her she was the great love of his life and he was sorry for everything he had done to her.

When she told me the news of his death I felt nothing at first. Like a lot of things in this life, his death was another anticlimax. As the years went by I lost all thirst for revenge and instead began a quest to understand him. The mom said he was sorry, and so I wonder if he would now be anything like the reminiscing narrator in Pushkin's "Tis time, my friend" regretting the terrible things he had done. I mean, if he could come back and read his life, would Pappas be horrified? Would he shudder? Would he curse? Would he bitterly regret and pour forth bitter tears knowing he was unable to wash those grievous lines away? Probably not. Seriously, I doubt it. But I do know that he blew it. He blew his life. For me his bleeding ulcers symbolize his ultimate self-destruction, his wretchedness. But then again, maybe that's not true. Or maybe in some fundamental way Nick Pappas is part of the collective unconscious in all of us. Perhaps we all blow our lives. I came perilously close to blowing mine and may yet accomplish that act before I die.

So what do I know?

I know that when I think of him long gone after all the years he drank and brawled, fucked and farted, his body bloating, his operations and accidents, scars all over his belly, the frowning mouth of a scar the mom gave him on the back of his head, the mustard eye weeping for more than a decade, the hard hatred in me weakens and I know I wouldn't hurt him if he were miraculously resurrected and came to see me. I'm still curious. I'd like to know the story from his side, the story of his life unfolding as he saw it. What drove him? Would knowing make anything better? I can't imagine it would. It doesn't matter. Nothing matters. Except getting on with this inexplicable existence, not wasting it, living it as various as possible, the sound and fury that ends in silence, the peace that passes understanding. We all become Pappas in the end: full of dead winters freezing the flesh from our bones, our eyes shrinking from our eye sockets, our lips thinning, sinking (voluptuous or not), our teeth grinning wider and wider, until at last we're clichéd versions—no meat on our bones, slumbering ever skeletons that know not the kiss, the desire, the feel of a cunt or a cock. The feeling of dying for it.

His life crackled for an instant then vanished—the kissable, the fuckable, the booze worthy, the war worthy, the rage and the hatred, the love forever *nothing* in his empty head now. I see him, hear him, his feet pounding towards me down the hall, the fierce face contorted with fury, the great anvils of his hands. My image of him is the only life he has now, and soon enough even that will be nothing but dust.

> ***Forgive these ghost hands bringing you nothing,***
> ***this heart filled with cobwebs and rain.***
>
> *- Joseph Millar*

    Jittery. Very tired. Eyes bloodshot, vision mildly blurry, deep furrows etching my brow. Temples rapidly graying. I don't want to make this trip. But I'm making it anyway. It's my *duty*. Next to me on the passenger seat is a 4 X 7 cedar wood box containing what's left of the mom's little dog. A brass label on the lid announces in capital letters HO TEP.

    I've been drinking too much lately and at Michele Renee's house I know I'll be drinking more. But I promise to stop after this visit—this *special* visit to bury a handful of ashes next to the mom's ashes in the Rose Garden at Prescott's Mountain View Cemetery. After I return home, I'll settle down, concentrate, write better, be my old disciplined self, no alcohol draining my brain, no guilty conscience about ... about everything. Maybe with this last obligation out of the way, I'll be calmer, my hand won't shake when I pick up a pen or sit at a keyboard. Is it the tremor of too much liquor? Or stress? Or age? Or the nerve damage I suffered years ago in a motorcycle mishap? Or the combination of all four? Common tremor the doctor calls it. Says it will slowly get worse. I've seen the same affliction in other men battling the morbidities of aging. Another dirty trick life springs on us. A way of adding to the sum of our knowledge. Though we'd rather not.

    I hate the pounding traffic. The countless vehicles flying by burning up Earth's limited resources. Every thought in my head reveals how old I'm getting. Call me a curmudgeon. No longer at all the youth who would do anything to get behind the wheel of a car and recklessly tear up the streets of Aurora. Who was that kid? I haven't a clue. Certainly not the late-springtime version of a 57-year-old senior citizen losing his hair, eyesight dimming, unable to sleep for more than four or five hours a night without getting up to go pee-pee. It's the prostate. That cursed walnut choking my urethra, making it impossible to empty my bladder. My colon is irritable about the whole thing. Who designed such flaws of the flesh, anyway? God can't be male. No male would create a prostate.

    Where's everyone going? Why in such a furious hurry? How did the world get so crowded with people and lethal machines? What in the world are they after? They're after movement. Keep moving. When I was a teenager, the thing to do was *just keep moving*. Now I'm an old man and nothing much has changed in that regard. Moving, moving. And don't think about how pointless it is. Take it from me, life is a cock-up from cradle to grave, you'll never be happy. The best thing you can do is *distract* yourself! Distraction is the key. Work and booze and sex ... work and booze and sex. Movement distracting you from remembering that death has no end, no period put in the right place. Good to be amused by your musings. Good to be sidetracked. Good to be absorbed in the belief that what you're doing is not marginal. In the long run futile.

~~

Decadence plagues the outskirts of El Centro. Slants of dusty light. Tufts of shrubbery, broken down shacks, geometric junkers in yards dysfunctional. An antique tractor framed by fractal sage and cacti, flashes of glittering eclecticism. Pyramidal sand dunes sifting the Colorado narrowing through Yuma, a fanning trickle gasping its way to the Sea of Cortez. I'm headed in the opposite direction, north by northeast. Prescott, the younger sister, the cemetery. Bury the dog and you're discharged, Duffy.

Why aren't there more signs to guide me? I need signs telling me where to go. Signs pointing the way, saying *do this and you'll be safe: life will be fine if you follow the signs*. It's Arizona's fault. Arizona doesn't believe in spending money on signs for nerve-frayed travelers such as yours truly.

In Yuma I leave the 8, go north on 95, a two lane rollercoaster flicking past assortments of cacti, desert brush, volcanic rock. Skeletons of failed buildings, a shuttered café, the remains of a gas station with its rusty pumps: tombstones marking the death of God knows how many dreams. American lives chasing the future. Entrepreneurs lost in the bowels of illusion, the state of grace prompting us to rise in the morning and venture forth believing we'll be home with our loved ones for dinner when the day is over.

~~

To *distract* myself I put on a taped lecture—some professor pontificating, saying that Philip Roth writes absurdist comedy influenced by Freud and Beckett, all three men writing what amounts to existential jokes. Woody Allen. Mel Brooks. Richard Pryor. Absurdists, all of them reminding us not to take life seriously. Everything so goddamn goofy, you gotta laugh. Or bawl your eyes out. Fantasize suicide, perhaps.

An hour later, settling into the rhythm of 10 east, the car eating miles of miles, I listen to more lectures. I'm doing sixty-five. Cars flaming by me. All of them rushing to destruction. Chaos in the making. Days like this, I'm consumed by outrage, indignation, ire. The model is Dante's *Inferno*: Comedy, says the professor, is a mixing of otherwise separate conventions, certain kinds of people, words, events, or situations and submitting them to criticism and/or ridicule, mainly satire. Illicit love is full of comic possibilities. The phrase echoes—*illicit love, illicit love*. I once asked the mom if she had ever been unfaithful to Nick

Pappas. We had been talking about his insane jealousy.

Did you ever give him any reason to mistrust you?

Never! she answered. Sick bastard.

Did I believe her? I believed her. Why not? What does it matter now?

The professor is talking about Sheridan's *The Rivals*, whose center is built on linguistic pretense—especially Mrs. Malaprop, who uses words *mal a propos*, out of place:

*As headstrong as an allegory on the banks of the Nile.*

*Illiterate him, I say, quite from your memory.*

Illiterate her, Duff. Or if you must remember her, remember her qualities.

*Use every man* [woman] *after his* [her] *deserts and who would escape whipping?*

*Be not angry that you cannot make others as you wish them to be, since you cannot make yourself as you wish to be.*

The professor's voice is reassuring. *Let comedy be your Utopia*, he says.

No longer anxious, I find myself not listening, but rather wondering what those little trees are, their flowers spreading out like butterflies, yellow clouds that seem to be levitating. Yellow bed of blossoms for Vishnu to sit upon. Palo Verde in bloom. Palo Verde. Poetic Palo Verde.

I pass a sign that claims:

+ A LIBRARY IS A TREE OF DIABOLICAL KNOWLEDGE +

+ TRUST IN THE WORD OF THE LORD ONLY +

Burn the libraries, burn the books, especially the works of the heretics, myself included.

A few miles from Prescott, I watch the sun dissolving as slowly as a wafer in the mouth of a penitent.

Sunsets always remind me that I'm only a guest here, a faulty contraption designed to continually break down, this body dribbling molecules, a particle here, microbe there, and one day you're back where you started, the land of non, just like the mom and her many husbands and Ho Tep. All of us cognizant that there is nothing to be done about it. It's a scandal handed on to other guests who will watch sunsets after we're gone.

~~

Pulling into Michele Renee's driveway, I see lights on. She's at the top of the steps sitting on the porch, a cigarette in hand, a glass of white wine beside her. She smiles, she waves.

It's about time! she hollers. I been waitin all day!

I park in front of the garage, ease my weary limbs out of the car. Hell of a boring drive, I tell her. Ugly till you get to your mountains.

Rushing down the stairs, she throws herself at me, hugs me as if she wants to stuff me inside her, take up residence in that chamber she set aside long ago, the one marked for the Duffer.

So glad you're here, bro, she says. A catch in her voice. Eyes damp. She's still the crier she always was.

Me too. You got any vodka? You got ice?

Let me make you a martini, she says.

I follow her up the steps. She's thin, she's tall, she's round shouldered from trying to look smaller. She has her father's imposing nose and oversized feet. I sit at the table on the porch. In minutes a chilled martini appears. Two swallows and it's gone. She brings the pitcher out and says, Have at it, bro.

I'm feeling better already, I tell her. Vodka narcotics flushing through me, soothing away the tension. How does anyone handle life without liquor, I wonder?

You didn't forget Ho Tep? she says.

Jerking my thumb towards the car I tell her, Little fella gots the passenger seat to himself. He's always loved traveling.

She says, He was the last connection to when she still had her wits.

This burying him next to her, you're sure it's all right with whoever runs the joint?

Michele Renee shrugs. She says, Hey, I won't tell if you don't. For all they'll know we're bringing her flowers and tidying up her site.

~~

What do we talk about this night? We talk about the mom, of course, and Carol Marie and my many shortcomings as the mom's caretaker.

Carol Marie has confessed that her behavior puzzles her. She doesn't understand how she could have treated the mom the way she did during the final months of her illness, staying away, refusing to take her in, refusing to give her the guest room. My own observation is that no one knows who they are or what they're capable of when it comes to dealing with the nasty process of watching someone dying. Some people turn their backs. Some stand fast and do what needs doing. I did a little of both and can't blame anyone for anything.

This poor excuse of a son let her down, I tell Michele Renee. Hard to forgive myself for what I let happen. What a selfish stinker I've been.

I forgive you, bro, she says.

You forgive me?

I forgive you.

And what about you, sis? How do you rate your performance?

She pulls long on her cigarette. Jets of smoke stream from her mouth and sizeable nostrils. I did the best I could, she says simply. No one knows how much I suffered, Duffy. It was plenty, it was a lot. When you came and got her, you saved me from a nervous breakdown. I was going to pieces, bro. When it comes to shit like this, there's a point where your mind tells you it's either you or it's her. If you hadn't taken Mom away, she would have killed me. It's self-preservation, bro. That's why you put her in that place, instead of taking her home. That's why Carol Marie wouldn't take her in either. How can you deal with a woman who has lost her mind and is no longer the person you knew all your life? Her body might have been here, but the rest of her wasn't. Christ, Duffy, half the time she didn't even know my name! Her own daughter!

True enough. True enough. In the final days, she didn't know anyone's name. All she knew was that she was frightened and bewildered. What she needed was her home and someone to comfort her, someone to take care of her and tell her everything was all right. I should have done that better, but I didn't. You might forgive me, but I doubt I'll ever forgive myself.

It's time to move on, bro. If you keep wallowing in guilt, it'll drown you. Time to be strong.

Yeah, but truth to tell, the mom is a ghost haunting me constantly. In my dreams, in my daylight thoughts, can't get her out of my mind, even though it's been four years since she died. How stupid am I?

I close my mouth. Look past my sister's shoulder, staring at lives far faraway now. Flanking us are cottonwoods and pointed firs absorbing our voices and the noise of traffic. Straight above us are stars in infinite numbers. Billions of billions of suns on fire. Is Heaven there? The mind boggles.

What did you think of the memoir I sent you? I ask my sister. Could you stand to read it?

Several awkward seconds pass while Michele Renee gathers her thoughts. Finally she says, Parts of it are kind of funny in a dark way. I didn't expect anything funny. Nothing funny really about the way we grew up. I expected more sad parts. But on the other hand, I learned a lot about my dad that I didn't know. I'm sorry he beat you so much, bro. No wonder you're so fucked up. Hah, hah!

I laugh too. I tell her, Hey, don't be sorry. None of it is your fault.

I know it's not, but I still feel guilty. Guilty by blood, you know? Guilty and sad and depressed. She raises her glass and says, To the future. Fuck the past.

I pour the past down my throat and say, It could have been worse.

Michele Renee nods. And continues: Carol Marie and I talked about your book. We like it and we hate it. Carol Marie doesn't remember some of the stuff you wrote about her, like that guy Rodney. She doesn't remember him. Or Mike the Knife. But most of the scenes with her in them she says probably happened. Lots of stuff she's just not totally sure of. She says she's blocked a lot of it out. Turned the switch off. Oh, and she said she thought she knew you, but your memoir proves she didn't know you very well at all.

Memory is a tricky thing, sis.

Michele Renee agrees, Yeah, it is. But when it comes to the mom's story, at the very least, you're loose with the truth, wouldn't you agree?

No, I wouldn't, I tell her. It's my side of the story. I wish Carol Marie would write her own memoir. I'd like to see our lives from her perspective. Or yours. Or the mom's if she was alive. Every memoir is written by an unreliable narrator. It goes with the territory, same as historians writing history, differing versions of it if you know what I mean.

Carol Marie thinks you're too hard on the mom. She says the mom was basically a good person and a hell of a fighter. Once she got something into her head, she went for it. Nothing stopped her. For a woman alone, you have to admit she had lots of guts. She made her own way in this bitch of a world, which in her day was ten times harder to do than it is now.

She needed a keeper, I answer.

No, she didn't.

Yes, she did. Look at how she changed after she married George Miles. She calmed down, didn't drink much. Became more of a homebody.

Well, okay, maybe she did need a keeper a little.

Again, there is a long pause. The stars are brighter, no moon rising yet. Cicadas continue their desperate calling. Is she up there? Is she listening?

Michele Renee says, Yeah, she did go nuts after he died. Who wouldn't? He was the love of her life. She didn't know what to do with herself, so she went back to what she did know. The bar life, dancing, drinking, and plenty of men willing to keep her company. She was raised that way if Grandma is any example. You know ... Minnesota stuff, I'm sayin.

He who is without sin, throw the first stone, I answer.

You need another martini?

She rises. Goes forth. Brings back another shaker of dry martinis. The night deepens. We talk of other things. Her two grown children making their way in the world now. Her divorce. The fair percentage of her ex's fortune the judge awarded her. She seems to need to justify it. She worked as hard as he did from the time they first married, she says, all through the establishment of their trucking business and the property they bought in Prescott, the rentals. She worked, she raised the kids, she supported him, loved him, gave him twenty years of her life. But ultimately couldn't stand his coldness, his lack of emotion. The emotional disconnect left an unbearable vacuum in their marriage. Her whole life had been emotion and drama. To go from that to her husband's laidback stoicism was suffocating. In the end, she just couldn't take it anymore.

When she leans forward looking at me for a reply, an opinion, a verdict, all I can say is, No stones here either, sis. You're the most emotional woman I know. Bad chemistry, you and that guy. Some couples just shouldn't get married. Maybe most shouldn't. Given the rate of divorce, I mean.

Men! she says gritting her teeth, reminding me of Grandma Inez. Then she adds, Yeah, but without him I wouldn't have those two kids I love more than my life.

It's a fair tradeoff, I tell her.

~~

Spending a restless night in a basement smelling of old cement and stale bedding, I continue listening to the mating call of sleepless cicadas, their whirr a version of nature's white noise. Staring upward through the window, I whisper to the dark, I am an absurd man, an absurdist comedy. What am I doing here? This is stupid.

After awhile, I pull out my journal and write it all down, the day driving, the evening with my sister.

Then I go to bed, tossing turning, playing the trip over in my head. Except instead of Ho Tep silent on the seat beside me, the mom materializes, the mom's head, her thinning hair quivering as she opines that her no good son is a lousy driver. She tells me that I drive like an old fart, a retard, and I'm hard on the brakes, and she is tired of explaining my faults to me. For Christ's sake you're not a child anymore! Haven't you learned that the roads are full of imbeciles who will run you over if you give them a chance? I tell her I have the gun, my .25 caliber semi-automatic. And will use it if I'm forced to. So all them road rage motherfuckers better keep outta my face, Ma!

*Éirinn go Brágh!* she whispers fiercely.

Out of bed again, I turn on the lamp, open my journal and write it down, knowing I'll use it later. Leafing through the journal I find an entry dated—

Wednesday, January 25, 1995

You dropped by her apartment at Gateway to drive her to a doctor's appointment and found her wearing a checkered blouse (orange and white stripes), purple polka dot pants and galoshes, the old-fashioned black buckle-ups she used to wear in Prescott when the weather was bad. A delicate gold chain around her neck, along with an Indian bead choker, black beads saying in Navajo **TSEGI** (sacred ground), and the key to her apartment hanging from a safety pin pushed through the hole in her earlobe. Thick red lipstick zigzagging over and under her sunken lips. On her cheeks were swipes of rouge. Her teeth were on the kitchen counter grinning. The smell of old skin, humid rug, something exhumed, something not quite dead beginning to rot. The bed hadn't been made and the sheets were as gritty as the Billy and Bruce sheets the night you slept over with them and told them their mother was too lazy to do the laundry. The mom's place was déjà vu. Dirty clothes strewn across the furniture. Dirty dishes and half-eaten TV dinners piled in the sink. As she stood in front of a full-length mirror admiring herself, the mom was muttering something that sounded like, Unk, unk, unky unk.

What are you doing, Mom? you asked her. I met this *man*. I got a date. How do I look? You told her she had a doctor's appointment. She loves going to doctors, so she gave you no trouble. She was out and down the hall before you could lock the front door.

The doctor examined her and told you she was definitely in the mid-to-late stages of Alzheimer's. He gave you a prescription to fill and told you to get her on vitamins and make sure she ate well and exercised and drank coffee every morning or at least something with caffeine in it. Gatorade during the day to keep her electrolytes in balance would be helpful. Give her plenty of liquids, she's mildly dehydrated. She'll need lots of care now, he said. Someone to watch over her. He looked at you out of the sides of his eyes, a look that said he didn't believe you were up to the job.

Is anyone?

I like that man, the mom said as the two of you were leaving the office. Make him my doctor for everything.

He *is* your doctor for everything, Mom.

Goodie!

Except he doesn't do facelifts. That's Dr. Cox.

Dr. Cox? Who's Dr. Cox?

The doctor who did your facelift when you were sixty-two.

She looked at you with puzzlement. I had a facelift? she said.

Cost you ten thousand dollars, you told her.

You took her back to her apartment. Hired one of the Gateway's available caregivers who will come in everyday to bathe and dress her and make sure she gets her meds and eats well.

With the caregiver added in, the monthly expenses are now over four thousand a month, of which you pay a thousand, while your sisters pay five hundred each. The mom's social security and retirement handles the rest. The thirty thousand left over from the sale of her house in Prescott was put in a savings account at Union Bank.

The next entry was—

Friday, February 10, 1995

Maybe the medication is actually doing its job. You went to visit her today and found her bouncy and chatty and giving orders. She had a notion she had been hired as an employee to work with the elderly. She took her job seriously. She was teaching ballroom dancing lessons in the rec room. She was a joy to have around, the staff told you.

What would you like me to bring you next time, Mom? you asked her, hoping to keep her animated and smiling.

What do I care? she grumbled.

How about a new ball gown? For dancing?

What for?

For your ballroom dancing.

Ballroom dancing! Listen to him. Square dancing is about the best my crew can do. If the caller uses a bullhorn. Half deaf, these old duffers. The other half so arthritic it's snap, crackle, pop. Ballroom dancing, where'd you get that one?

I'll look for a nice square dance dress then, you said. Would you like that?

She gave you a are-you-out-of-your-mind look. Quit trying to buy me off, Duffy. You lock me away in here and then you try to buy me off. Some son you turned out to be.

Got to go, Mom. Got to hit the road.

Abandon me. Go ahead. All you want me to do is die.

That's not true, Mom. [Well, sort of true.]

It's true. I'm a anchor round your neck, an albadross.

Albatross.

You and that sister of yours. What's her name?

Carol Marie.

That's the one. She never comes sees me. I spose to live with her in my old age. She promised it. She and that husband of hers. A pair of goddamn liars.

She glared as if you had told her something outrageous, contemptible. And then she said, Just remember this from the mom who knows everything there is to know about it. Wagging her chipped nail in your face she said, You can't control what you love or what loves you. Don't even try. It ain't possible. I tried four times. Or was it five? She started counting husbands on her fingers. Hud one, George one, Nick the bastard who broke my eye. George two, loved him, but he was another no-goodnik. Up and died on me. Left me to fend for myself. What happened to him?

Liver failure.

Too much booze killed that bastard. He bled to death internally. No, that was Nick. Dumb bastard. And there was another and another. Wasn't there?

Tony and Dewayne, you said.

How many is that?

Six.

She counted them on her fingers. I haven't been married that many times, have I?

To change the subject you said, You're wasting away to nothing, Mom. I want you to eat more.

You should talk! she told you. Nothing but skin and bones. You look like death warmed over. What kind of man you turned into? She leaned in nose to nose, You need a WIFE, she said. And then she said, How come your sister never comes see me? I should have stayed with whats-her-name, your other sister—

Michele Renee.

She's my real friend. You talked me into coming to this godforsaken ... You kidnapped me. I didn't wanna go. You made me. Pausing, she looked around. Her voice full of loss as she asked. Where am I?

California, you told her.

You mark my words, she said, she'll end up in here before long in a wheelchair.

Who?

You know who!

Don't be mad at her. She suffers a lot over what's happened to you, Mom.

So do I! You ever think about that?

You patted her shoulder. Got to get moving, you said. You kissed your mother's brittle hair and left her room. Left her standing there with foggy eyes, a vacant look on her face.

Seconds later, she was beside you, catching your elbow and saying she would walk you to the door. This job is wearing me out, she said. So exhausted I can't think straight. I fall in bed and sleep like the dead.

You told her the place would fall to pieces without her.

That's what everyone tells me, she said. It's always Janice, Janice. Everywhere I turn they want something from me.

It's good to be useful, I told her.

She smiled brightly. And repeated her mantra: I want to drop dead on the dance floor. I want to drop dead in harness just like the old gray mare.

The hallway light shining on her profile revealed silver strands running through her henna hair. The braid pinned to the back of her head was coming loose, sagging.

At the top of the stairs you hugged her and said, I hope you get your wish, Mom. You better get back in there now. Your girls need you.

See you next week, she said.

Yes, next week.

Take me out for chocolate covered cherries and Pepsi!

You got it, baby. You be good now.

Be good? That's all I ever am, kid. Whatever the hand finds to do, do it for there is no work ... unk! ... what's the rest of it?

Nor device nor knowledge nor wisdom in the grave whither thou goest.

Are you sure? That doesn't sound right, Duffer. Are you sure? Do you know? What do you know, Duffer?

Not a damn thing, Mom.
She threw her head back laughing hysterically.

~~

Mountains. They blow them up, make them into open mine pits. Nothing safe these days, nothing permanent. Especially not love. Is there such a thing as love? Beyond the word itself is there anything other than wishing it were so? A word used to describe something incoherent, something illogical, something that comes in a rush of inarticulate feeling that always catches us unaware. Something that can be lost as fast as it's found. Or is it just me? Do other people know love the same way the mom knew God? She didn't need logic. She didn't need to be rational. She didn't need to think deeply about it. I know God exists because I know God exists, she said. I feel God in my soul. I feel God in my heart. I feel God in every organ of my body. I know because I just know!

Why hasn't that way of knowing ever worked for me? For how many millennia has the human engine run on such specious logic? None of it makes sense, none of it reasonable. God and Santa are one.

But then again if God exists, there's also Heaven, a place of many mansions where Janice still dances. Eternal bliss. Not ashes in the urn. Dusty discards. She shuffled off her mortal coil. The essence is elsewhere. It knows nothing of pain or fear. It knows nothing of senility, loss of dignity. It knows nothing of no longer being here. Nothing of children turning away and saying, That's not the mom. That's a shell of the person we call Janice.

You'll carry that with you the rest of your days, Duff. And if you live long enough, it will be you they're talking about. Let him go. Let him die. He's making us suffer. He's making us sad beyond words.

I wonder if I'll know if I'm going senile. I wonder if memorizing the first page of *Finnegans Wake* will be enough to keep Alzheimer's at bay. I wonder if I'll have it in me to take my own life, rather than subject myself to the slow disintegration of my brain cells and what my changing personality is doing to others. Is there some point at which you flip and no longer see that it's time?

*Dying is an art, like everything else.* Stick your head in an oven, turn on the gas. Blow your brains out with a shotgun. Open a vein. Cut your throat. The pills, the hanging, the leap into space. The water beckoning below the bridge. In one of her honest moods the mom told me she would have committed suicide long ago if she had had the guts. I didn't have the guts, she said.

It occurs to me at this point that I'm musing on an abstraction, my own death. It's easy to talk about dying when it's an event you believe is far in the future. Maybe twenty or thirty years. Making plans for tomorrow: homage to optimism. Mother oh mother.

~~

June 13, 1999 we go to Mountain View Cemetery. To the Rose Garden lush with rainbow roses. The mom's grave is behind a long, low cement wall painted white with brick trim on the top. On the wall are bronze tablets commemorating the dead. Hers says:

Janice E. Miles

May 27 1920 – May 25 1995

Next to her is the love of her life:

George L. Miles

June 10 1925 – April 7 1975

In between them is a bronze vase affixed to the wall. We fill the vase with a bouquet of carnations, all red.

Using a garden trowel, I dig a hole next to the mom's urn. Ho Tep as usual is no trouble. I lower his coffin into the void, cover it, stick a red carnation in the dirt as a grave marker. Michele Renee and I clean the site of a few weeds, a Juicy Fruit gum wrapper, a yellowed receipt from Walgreen's. We rake the location with our fingers. Michele Renee folds her hands, bows her head and prays, Be careful with our mom, Jesus. She's precious. And that's the end of it—over ... through.

# Acknowledgements

Without the courage and openness of my sister Carol Marie, *Murdering the Mom* might never have been written. Her willingness to share so many intimate stories about those early years of her life were vital to the enrichment and authenticity I was searching for when I started this memoir. I thank her and love her with all my heart. I also wish to thank my loving sister Michele Renee for sending me almost all of the photos I used. The only picture of the mom that I personally own is a copy of the one adorning the cover of this book. How very beautiful she was.

I owe a huge THANK YOU to David Memmott at Wordcraft of Oregon who offered to publish *Murdering the Mom*. Thanks also to Thomas E. Kennedy, Chauncey Mabe, DeWitt Henry, and James Brown for their willingness to set aside time from their busy lives to read the manuscript and comment on it. Thanks also to Kristin Summer for the cover design and Robert Mast for the digital conversion and enhancement of the photos used within the book.

My gratitude to the following authors for permission to quote from their works:

Jack Marshall, *The Steel Veil* (Coffee House Press, 2008).
Yahia Lababidi, *Signposts to Elsewhere* (Jane Street Press, 2008)
Dorianne Laux, *The Book of Men* (Norton, 2011).
Joseph Millar, *Overtime* (Eastern Washington University Press, 2007).
Steve Davenport, *Uncontainable Noise* (Pavement Saw Press, 2006).

Special acknowledgements to William Shakespeare (1564-1616) for the famous quote from *King Lear: How sharper than a serpent's tooth it is/ to have a thankless child!*; John Keats (1795-1821) "Lamia"; Matthew Arnold (1822-1888) "Dover Beach"; Franz Kafka (1883-1924) diary entry: *. . . follow your most intense obsessions mercilessly:* and Philip Larkin (1922-1985) for the well-known quote from "This Be the Verse"—*They fuck you up your mum and dad . . .*

Duff Brenna shouldering *Mamie*. (2006)
Photo by David Memmott

DUFF BRENNA is the author of six novels, including *The Book of Mamie*, which won the AWP Award for Best Novel; *The Holy Book of the Beard*, named "an underground classic" by *The New York Times*; *Too Cool*, a *New York Times* Noteworthy Book; *The Altar of the Body*, given the Editors Prize Favorite Book of the Year Award, *South Florida Sun-Sentinel*, and also received a San Diego Writers Association Award for Best Novel in 2002. He is the recipient of a National Endowment for the Arts award, *Milwaukee Magazine's* Best Short Story of the Year Award, and a Pushcart Prize Honorable Mention. His work has been translated into six languages. His collection of short stories, *Minnesota Memoirs*, was published by Serving House Books in February, 2012.

For more information on titles published
by Wordcraft of Oregon, LLC,
please visit our website at:
http://www.wordcraftoforegon.com

or contact editor at: editor@wordcraftoforegon.com